THE EUROPEAN TRAVEL DIARIES
OF ALBERT BRISBANE 1830-1832

THE EUROPEAN TRAVEL DIARIES OF ALBERT BRISBANE 1830-1832

Discovering Fourierism for America

Edited by

Abigail Mellen

and

Allaire Brisbane Stallsmith

The Edwin Mellen Press
Lewiston•Queenston•Lampeter

Library of Congress Cataloging-in-Publication Data

Brisbane, Albert, 1809-1890.
  [Diaries. Selections]
  The European travel diaries of Albert Brisbane, 1830-1832 : discovering Fourierism for
America / edited by Abigail Mellen and Allaire Brisbane Stallsmith.
    p. cm.
  Includes bibliographical references and index.
  ISBN 0-7734-6070-5
    1. Brisbane, Albert, 1809-1890--Diaries. 2. Brisbane, Albert,
1809-1890--Travel--Europe. 3. Utopian socialism--United States--History--19th century.
4. Fourier, Charles, 1772-1837--Influence. 5. Europe--Description and travel. I. Mellen,
Abigail. II. Stallsmith, Allaire Brisbane. III. Title.

HX84.B74A3 2005
914.04'283--dc22

                                                                        2005049238

A CIP catalog record for this book is available from the British Library.

Front cover: Brisbane, painted by his wife Adèle, done between ages 25-29
              In private collection; used by permission of the family; photographed by the authors

        The Edwin Mellen Press   The Edwin Mellen Press
             Box 450   Box 67
        Lewiston, New York   Queenston, Ontario
        USA 14092-0450   CANADA L0S 1L0

                    The Edwin Mellen Press, Ltd.
                    Lampeter, Ceredigion, Wales
                    UNITED KINGDOM SA48 8LT

                Printed in the United States of America

Clarissimo proavo nostro
in memoriam

This excellent edition–obviously an enterprise of dedication–is an important contribution to American intellectual and political history, for the following reasons:

1) It clarifies Brisbane's controversial and largely neglected role in transmitting mid 19th century European utopian socialist doctrines–so vital for future reform movements–to antebellum America.

2) It places the formative influences on Brisbane's socialist conversion in a richer and deeper context than is to be found in his unreliable "Mental Biography," thus far the only available printed source on the topic. This alone makes the Diaries worth publishing.

3) The Diaries offer a fascinating mirror of major 19th century philosophical, historical, and political movements: French, German, English, as well as Italian. As such, they are a compelling entrée into a highly creative phase of European civilization, the aftereffects of which are still experienced today.

Dr. Karl W. Schweizer
Department of Social Science
New Jersey Institute of Technology

CONTENTS

❧

LIST OF ILLUSTRATIONS
(*following page 140*)

FOREWORD

The eminent literary historian F. O. Matthiessen once labeled the two decades before the Civil War "the Age of Fourier" in American social thought. In the 1840s and 1850s the theories of the eccentric French utopian Charles Fourier seemed to be on everyone's must-read list. Ralph Waldo Emerson planned to write a chapter on Fourier as one of history's "Representative Men," but decided instead to promote the concept of self-reliance as a riposte to Fourier's socialistic doctrine. Feminists and free-love advocates adopted Fourier's critique of bourgeois marriage and the "isolated household." Abolitionists debated Fourierist labor organizers over the comparative evils of chattel slavery and "wage slavery." Southern proslavery apologists used Fourierist concepts to indict Northern capitalism. Most dramatically, nearly thirty miniature communal experiments sprang up from the outskirts of New York City to frontier Iowa, all calling themselves "phalanxes" and pledging allegiance to Fourier's "doctrine of Association."

These first flowerings of socialistic agitation resulted from new seeds of European thought which were taking root in American soil. Obviously, conditions in the young nation had to be favorable for these seeds to sprout: abolitionism and other reform movements were spreading an ethic of social improvement, American commercialism had spawned its first dissenters, and a severe depression had put artisans and farmers out of work. Many Americans were ready to test theories of social reconstruction that had been bred in the older and more developed society of Europe. But someone had to introduce those theories to them. That crucial role was played by an idealistic wanderer and persistent propagandist from New York named Albert

Brisbane. It was Brisbane who returned from Europe in 1834 with first-hand knowledge of Fourier's doctrines and who marshaled under the banner of "Association" the varied forces of social discontent and social longing that were emerging in antebellum America.

How Brisbane came to be a disciple of Fourier has never been entirely clear. Until recently, little was known about Brisbane's early development outside of a series of autobiographical musings that Brisbane dictated to his wife when in his seventies. In this "Mental Biography" the aging utopian socialist portrayed his development as a schematic object-lesson in which the young student of life discovers one by one the leading ideas of Fourierism. Reality is rarely so neat. More than half a century ago Arthur Bestor, the pioneering scholar of American utopianism, warned that Brisbane's autobiography mixed fact with fiction and told far too tidy a tale.

Now, thanks to the careful editorial work of Abigail Mellen and Allaire Stallsmith, we have a fascinating glimpse of the real story, which is less tidy but much more interesting. This published version of Brisbane's two surviving European travel diaries follows him from October 1830 to January 1831, and again from September 1831 to January 1832. These diary entries – fragments from a larger whole but still rich in description and insight – chart the young Brisbane's course of intellectual meandering, document his convictions and hesitations, and preview his eventual embrace of socialism as a doctrine and lifestyle.

On the surface, Brisbane's story was unique and improbable: the son of a western New York merchant and landowner, the young Brisbane studied French and philosophy in New York City, then left in 1828 for six years of study and travel in Europe. Toward the end of his sojourn Brisbane encountered Fourier and decided to devote his life to understanding and publicizing the Frenchman's "social science." To enroll at the University of Berlin and to travel through Greece, Malta, and southern Italy were rare occurrences for Jacksonian Americans, and Brisbane's diary is full of interesting impressions and incidents. Yet his journey has a representative, even archetypal quality as well. Looking at its larger patterns, we find a coming-of-age story blended with the drama of social and ideological discovery. In the diary's pages the cocky but innocent American confronts the weight of tradition and history; the callow youth experiments with sexual freedom;

the curious student skims his way through several schools of philosophy; and the determined nonconformist feels the attraction of losing himself in socialist doctrine.

The range of acquaintances Brisbane made during his tour was impressive. It included Felix Mendelssohn, Franz Liszt, Heinrich Heine, the eminent German philosophers Edouard Gans and Karl Michelet, and the famous salon hostess Rahel Varnhagen von Ense as well as fellow Americans James Fenimore Cooper and Horatio Greenough. But what gave Brisbane's sojourn coherence – and unifies his diary entries – was his obsessive search for an intellectual system to engage his energies. In his ready though superficial absorption of ideas, Brisbane whirled through several of the major trends in nineteenth-century social philosophy, from the eclecticism of Victor Cousin to Hegel's metaphysics to the socialist Christianity of Saint-Simon.

Interestingly, the diaries show that despite his militantly rationalist upbringing Brisbane came to utopian socialism through the essentially emotional lure of the Saint-Simonian religion. Here, too, Brisbane's story is emblematic: broadly speaking, his travels from philosophical idealism through French "social romanticism" to the doctrines of utopian "social science" encapsulated the evolution of a generation of young radicals on both sides of the Atlantic. Similar journeys would soon be taken by the Transcendentalists in New England, by French utopian socialists such as Etienne Cabet and Victor Considérant, and by Fyodor Dostoyevsky and his circle of young Russian dissidents.

Energetic and intellectually ambitious, but not a deep or original thinker, Brisbane was cut out to be a disciple. A few months after the second travel diary ends he discovered the works of Fourier, whose theories, to his mind, combined his previous enthusiasms into a grand and inspiring synthesis. Once Brisbane returned to his homeland, his great achievement was to streamline Fourier's vast and eccentric theory for Americans, stripping its frank hedonism and futuristic fantasies and whittling the remainder down to a simple blueprint for cooperative communal experiments. Thoroughly impractical himself, he nevertheless helped to entice northern farmers, workers, and reformers into over two dozen short-lived "phalanxes."

Even the Transcendentalists at Brook Farm outside Boston were mesmerized. As Marianne Dwight reported, Brisbane was "so full of feeling and entire devotion to the cause of God and humanity, that he has won our hearts." Under Brisbane's tutelage Brook Farm became a Fourierist phalanx in 1845 and the busy propaganda headquarters of the American movement.

It all unraveled very quickly as the poorly financed communities collapsed through inefficiency and internal conflicts. By the late 1840s the Fourierist movement was in disarray and Brisbane retreated to more limited and practical workers' reforms such as producer and consumer cooperatives. But he continued to draw inspiration from European socialists, returning to take part in the Revolution of 1848, and when it failed, to entice the French Fourierist Victor Considérant to establish a communal experiment in Texas. After the Civil War Brisbane remained active as an advocate of Fourierism, latching onto newer reform crusades such as currency reform and the Knights of Labor and hoping to inject Fourierist influence into them. Introduced to Edward Bellamy, he tutored the young journalist in details of Fourier's system that would later surface in Bellamy's best-selling utopian novel, *Looking Backward* (1888).

By then, however, most radicals had abandoned the Fourierist idea of model communities in favor of programs of economic redistribution and government ownership. Faced with the unprecedented scale of social problems created by modern urbanism and industrialism, many American intellectuals in the half-century after Brisbane's death made their own Atlantic crossings to study European developments. Returning armed with new social-democratic ideas and practices to promote, they helped to build the Progressive movement, the New Deal, and the American welfare state.

While Brisbane traveled through Europe, Alexis de Tocqueville and other Old World liberals were touring the young United States to learn what they could expect for a democratized Europe of the future. Tocqueville's *Democracy in America* remains the most brilliant in a long series of foreign meditations on the American experiment. Brisbane was no Tocqueville, to be sure. But the travel diaries of his student years document the birth moment of an important counter-tradition to Tocqueville's, one whereby New World idealists returned to the Old World in search of plans that might hasten America's "social destiny." It is good to have them finally available in print.

Carl Guarneri
History Department
Saint Mary's College of California

PREFACE

We began this enterprise some ten years ago as a result of a curious conjunction of our research interests and our personal connection to the diarist, Albert Brisbane, our great-grandfather. Family table talk had frequently referred to the interesting life and radical theories of our forebear, who was usually presented as a dreamer who had frittered away a vast fortune on mad Socialist schemes. A close examination of the documentary sources demonstrates that this was a gross exaggeration.

Our curiosity about this quaint relative's adventures faded as we grew up, each pursuing academic interests: Allaire Brisbane Stallsmith as a historian of Greece, and Abigail Mellen as a modern European historian. In researching her Ph.D. dissertation on the French politician Adolphe Thiers, (1797–1872)[1] Mellen found several references to Albert Brisbane among American visitors to Paris early in the nineteenth century. Mellen's mother, Sarah Brisbane Mellen, had been at one time in possession of Brisbane's travel diaries and other family papers, which she had deposited in the George Arendts Research Library for Special Collections at Syracuse University, Syracuse, New York.[2]

Meanwhile Stallsmith's studies of ancient Greek agronomy had led her to readings in modern Greek landscape history, and she came to appreci-

---

[1] Mellen, A.: "Adolphe Thiers, The Making of a Conservative Liberal," Ph.D. dissertation, New York University, New York, 1990.

[2] Brisbane papers are also in the A. Bestor collection, the Illinois Historical Survey, University of Illinois, Champaign-Urbana.

[3] Brumfield, A. (Stallsmith): "Agriculture and Rural Settlement in Ottoman Crete, 1669–1898: A Modern Site Survey" in Baram, U. and Carroll, L., eds., *A Historical*

ate the value of travelers' diaries as primary sources;[3] she was interested in Albert Brisbane's observations of the nineteenth century Mediterranean. The existence of *Albert Brisbane: a Mental Biography* (1893), the collected notes made at Brisbane's dictation by his adoring last wife, Redelia Brisbane, and of Brisbane's published writings, notably the *Social Destiny of Man* (1840), made an edition of the diaries a realistic possibility. Thus our project was born.

Of particular interest to us were the two manuscript diaries which make up this volume. Written between 1830 and 1832, and internally numbered as volumes four and seven, they indicate the possible existence of at least five other volumes, whose location is unknown. It is our hope that the publication of these two diaries may reveal the location of the other, lost volumes. Albert Brisbane was one of the earliest Americans to travel in Greece and the Ottoman Empire and write about the experience; his diaries are of historical value.[4]

A word on transcribing the holograph diaries

In transcribing the diaries we have used the following editorial notations: Original pagination is indicated by square "[ ]" brackets. Foreign words are in italics, and translations of words in the text are in "( )" parentheses. Illegible or unknown words, and words inserted to clarify the text are in curly "{ }" brackets. Modern punctuation and paragraph spacing are used.

For readability, we have rearranged some sections of the diaries. Scribbled notations overleaf in the front of each diary preceding Brisbane's entries have been moved to the end, just after his index.

In transcribing a manuscript from an earlier century, it is a matter of judgement as to how much clarification and general background to supply and where to insert it. The introduction provides general historical context for the non-specialist reader. Certain issues are more profitably addressed at the point where they arise, hence the numerous and sometimes lengthy footnotes in the text of the diary.

Archaeology of the Ottoman Empire; Breaking New Ground, New York, New York, 2000: 37–78.

[4] At least one American preceded him to Greece. See McNeal, R. A.: *Nicholas Biddle in Greece; the Journals and Letters of 1806*, University Park, Pennsylvania, 1993.

Three relatively long documents pertaining to important moments in Brisbane's life have been included in an appendix: the obituary of his father, James Brisbane, published in 1851; a letter by Brisbane about his first wife Adèle, of unknown date; and finally a speech Brisbane delivered to a socialist gathering in Paris, published in 1849.

ACKNOWLEDGMENTS

W̶e would like to thank Michael McCrary for research and documentary assistance, Arthur Brisbane for bibliographical help, and Gary Cohn for access to unpublished Brisbane family documents. The librarians of the Illinois Historical Survey and the George Arendts Special Collections library at Syracuse University were extremely generous with their time and assistance. We are grateful to Professor Carl Guarneri for reviewing the manuscript and for contributing the foreword.

We thank Rachel Abram for editing, Roy Murphy for book design and indexing, and our research assistant Betsy Brumfield for library help. Professor Martin Burke, of Lehman College, and Professor Armin Mruck, of Towson University, kindly agreed to read the text.

Mellen would like to thank Darline Levy for encouragement on the initial project, Roger Whitney for bottomless patience and the CUNY Lehman history faculty for their continued enthusiasm.

Stallsmith is grateful to Harry Piotrowski for help with German sources, William Stallsmith for musicological expertise, and Iris Carulli for Italian translation.

We are grateful to the staff of Mellen press for their commitment to this project, though similarity in name with one of the authors is coincidental.

INTRODUCTION

"What is the work of man on this earth? What was he put here for and what has he to do?"[1] Pondering this weighty question, the 19-year-old American, Albert Brisbane (1809–1890) sailed from New York City in 1828 in search of an answer. Brisbane traveled for six years and became acquainted with many of the great thinkers of Europe; he kept a diary for much of this time, of which two volumes remain: the fourth volume, dated 14 October 1830 to 5 January 1831 (Diary I), and the seventh (or eighth) volume, dated 26 September 1831 to 29 January 1832 (Diary II).[2] These volumes are the focus of this study.

Attending lectures, visiting the salons of Paris and Berlin, and traveling through the European countryside, Brisbane was impressed by the wretched economic and political condition of the population. He found himself drawn to ideas of social reform, initially those of the French utopian, Claude-Henri Rouvroy de Saint-Simon (1760–1825). Saint-Simon had been reared at the courts of Louis XV and Louis XVI and educated in the enlightenment tradition. Sensitive to the extravagance of the court and the misery of the poor, Saint-Simon argued that society would collapse if the condition of the peasantry were not improved. He focused on technology, engineering, and mechanics as the means of reform, and he argued in lengthy, but ill-organized, writings[3] that the new leaders of society would

---

[1] Brisbane, R. 1893: *Albert Brisbane, A Mental Biography* (hereafter *MB*), Boston, 1893, 56. Albert Brisbane dictated much of the text of this biography to his third wife, Redelia Bates Brisbane (1842–1943).

[2] These two holograph diaries are kept in the Department of Special Collections, George Arendts Research Library, Syracuse University, Syracuse, New York.

[3] *Oeuvres de Saint-Simon et d'Enfantin, Publiées par les membres du conseil institué par*

come from these fields. In the late years of the Napoleonic Empire, he began attracting followers, young men drawn for the most part from the Grandes Ecoles, the new technical universities created by Napoleon.[4]

The Bourbon restoration of 1815 had limited the opportunities available to the merchant and manufacturing families from which many of these young men came. The followers of Saint-Simon therefore saw him as a visionary who had comprehended their circumstances. In 1829, following his death, the Saint-Simonians established a "religion" to propagate his theory, led by the two Pères Suprèmes, the "supreme fathers," Saint-Armand Bazard and Barthelèmy-Prosper Enfantin. A large headquarters that provided communal dining and assembly rooms was established on the Rue Taitbout in Paris. Lectures and Sunday sermons were offered, while lecturers toured the countryside, expounding Saint-Simonian theory. In addition, the word was spread through the pages of the movement's widely-circulated daily newspaper, *Le Globe*, edited by Pierre Leroux.

In October of 1831, however, a schism developed between the two "supreme fathers" concerning issues of dogma and the status of women, a schism only made worse by the revelation that Bazard's wife was having an affair with Enfantin. As the dispute intensified, a number of people left the Saint-Simonians: particularly their two principal publicists, Abel Transon and Jules Lechevalier, who both subsequently joined the followers of Charles Fourier[5] and brought their organizational and editorial skills to that movement.

Enfantin pour l'exécution de ses dernières volontés, 47 vols. Paris, 1865–1878.

[4] Most important of this group were Saint-Armand Bazard (1791–1832), Hippolyte Carnot (1801–1888), Michel Chevalier (1806–1879), Auguste Comte (1798–1874), Charles Duveyrier (1803–1866), Barthelèmy-Prosper Enfantin (1796–1864), Pierre Leroux (1791–1871), Jules Lechevalier (1800–1850), Jules Michelet (1798–1874), Isaac Pereire (1806–1880), Emile Pereire (1800–1875) and Abel Transon (1805–1876). The best account of the Saint-Simonian movement in English is Carlisle, R.: *The Proffered Crown*, Ithaca, New York, 1987.

[5] Charles Fourier (1772–1837), a French social theorist, was almost unknown in the English-speaking world until Brisbane popularized his theories. See Bestor, A.: "Albert Brisbane, Propagandist for Socialism in the 1840's," *New York History*, 1947, 28: 128-58. On Fourier, see Beecher, J.: *Charles Fourier: The Visionary and his World*, Berkeley, California, 1986; Pellarin, C.: *Life of Charles Fourier*, 2nd ed., (tr. F. G. Shaw), New York, 1948; and Guarneri, C.: *The Utopian Alternative: Fourierism in Nineteenth-Century America*, Ithaca, New York, 1991.

Brisbane had first become acquainted with Saint-Simonian writings while traveling in Holland, probably in early 1831.[6] The previous winter (1829–1830) Brisbane had met Lechevalier in Berlin where they were studying at the university. On returning to Paris in the spring of 1831 Brisbane contacted his Berlin friend (now an active member of the Saint-Simonians) who encouraged Brisbane to attend the Saint-Simonian assemblies and sermons that summer and fall. However, the developing rupture in the movement distressed Brisbane. In November 1831 he left Paris, again to study in Berlin, although he stayed in contact with the Saint-Simonians. When Lechevalier (now involved with the Fourierists) sent Fourier's writings to Brisbane in the spring of 1832, Brisbane was so impressed with Fourier's ideas of "attractive industry," he returned to Paris to study with Fourier. (*MB*: 171) [7]

In contrast to the Saint-Simonian cult of technology, Fourier focused his attention on human nature. Born into a moderately wealthy merchant family that saw much of its prosperity destroyed in the revolution, Fourier, like Saint-Simon, was deeply affected by the miserable condition of the poor. In a series of notebooks written between 1799 and his death in 1837[8] he argued that humankind's woes could all be solved by organizing people according to their inclinations and passions. These, he calculated at great length and complexity, combined into 810 personalities. Fourier theorized that if people were organized into communities (called phalanxes)[9] in which these passional personalities were well balanced, then each of the phalanx' necessary activities would appeal to the passions of some of its members. Thus all industry would be attractive, all would perform their duties willingly and well, and each phalanx could produce goods for trade and its own consumption and successfully compete with producers in other systems.

Because he despised competitive capitalism, Fourier based the phalanx entirely on a vision of a pre-industrial economy that emphasized cottage

---

[6] Diary I: 317, December 25, 1830; Diary II: 194, January 4, 1832.

[7] Diary II: 195-97, January 4, 1832.

[8] *Fonds Fourier et Considérant* (Victor), Archives Sociétaires, 10AS, inventoried by E. Thomas, Archives Nationales, Paris. Fourier, C.: *Oeuvres Complètes de Charles Fourier*, 12 vols., Paris, 1966-1968.

[9] Whether or not Fourier derived the phalanx from the ancient Macedonian military formation is unclear; however, the term had a long afterlife in European revolutionary politics (e.g., the Phalangists of the Spanish Civil War).

industry and artisan production. Brisbane, on the other hand, in his efforts to translate Fourier's theories for the American experience, offered a more flexible vision that was willing to accommodate factory methods as long as they benefited the group and matched individual inclination (following Fourier's principles of "passional attraction"). Brisbane's promotional efforts enabled the "attractive industry" movement to gain wide support in the American intellectual community. Between 1843 and 1857 twenty-eight Fourierist phalanxes were established in the United States, including Brook Farm, in Massachusetts, which was championed by such important American thinkers as Ralph Waldo Emerson (1803–1882), Charles Dana (1819–1897), Nathaniel Hawthorne (1804–1864), Margaret Fuller (1810–1850) and William H. Channing (1810–1884).

In the end, Brook Farm failed to support itself, as did all the other phalanxes from Kansas to New Jersey. As Brisbane explained at the end of his life: "When I saw all these little associations disbanding, one after another, I was deeply impressed with the evil of a too hasty propaganda, and with the entire want of preparation in the men who undertook to realize the ideas thus rapidly." (*MB*: 218) The onset of the Civil War moved the focus of popular concern from schemes for the betterment of humanity to the more immediate problem of national unity. Yet utopian topics re-emerged with the cessation of hostilities and Fourierist ideas of work association and co-operation ultimately made their way into labor union ideology.

Today Brisbane is of interest to intellectual historians because his efforts contributed substantially to the development of American associationist and co-operative movements. Despite their brevity, it is fortunate that these two volumes (out of eight or more) of his travel diaries remain. They provide insight into Brisbane's thinking at a critical time when he was beginning to question the effectiveness of political or economic reforms of traditional society. This was also the moment when he first encountered the utopian approach, which called for social reform through the creation of an entirely new system outside the traditional order.

Later in life, dictating material for the *Mental Biography* to his wife Redelia, he summed up his mental state in 1834, after six years of foreign travel and study:

I had now completed the first cycle in my mental development, which I may sum up finally. The first fact in this cycle was the intuition of the boy of fifteen that the individual formed one with his race; that humanity was a collective whole, which whole had some great work to do, in which the individual should participate, and that his highest duty was to fill his place in the ranks of the great hierarchy. The second fact was the conviction of the emptiness of the highest philosophical speculation of the age. The third was the importance of woman in the social world, her immense influence on the development of man, and through him on the development of the entire social system. Combined with this was the conception of the real character of wealth and the means of its production, which two conceptions came to me through impressions made by my travels in Turkey and Greece. The fourth was the idea of a classification of human societies: an analysis of the civilizations of Europe and America, with the simple system of the Indian and the barbaric system of the Turks, led me to distinguish between the great social organism as a whole and one of its branches – the political – and to see how little the political organization, alone, could effect the practical and general life of a people living in these different civilizations; to see that the political system was, so to speak, a dress over the body social, and that the dress could not affect the health or disease of this body. . . . The fifth was my discovery of the great creation of Fourier: his conception of a new social order, in which the practical interests and relations of men should be organized on principles of justice and equity. (*MB:* 196–97)

Beyond his role as propagator of Fourierism, Brisbane's intellectual contacts and enthusiasms are of interest because they illustrate the development of an early nineteenth century American intellect and the means by which European ideas were translated into the American idiom. As such, these diaries have relevance for a broad spectrum of contemporary scholarship on nineteenth-century political philosophy.

Current scholarship

Since before its founding, the United States has accommodated the settlement of widely varied utopian communities. This has included religious communities such as the Puritans, the Amish, the Mormons, the celibate Shakers and John Humphry Noyes' Perfectionists with their system of complex marriages. There have also been secular communitarian experiments such as the Fourierist phalanx and Robert Owen's New Harmony. One need only read through the annotated list of utopian communities compiled by Okugawa in Fogarty's *Dictionary of American Communal and Utopian History* or review the communities described in Stockwell's *Encyclopedia of American Communities* to get a sense of the scope of this tradition.[10]

The publication of Bestor's *Backwoods Utopias* in 1950 stimulated a revival of scholarly interest in these organizations. Several hundred studies of utopias in the United States have been written in English as well as other languages discussing their origins, theories, practices, and impact on the development of American society. Particularly useful to understanding the long history of utopianism in the United States and elsewhere is the Manuels' 1979 classic, *Utopian Thought in the Western World*, which traces the diverse development of utopian ideas from Judeo-Christian Milennarianism and accompanying visions of Paradise.[11]

Specific to the United States are such works as Fellman's *The Unbounded Frame: Freedom and Community in Nineteenth Century American Utopianism*, Kephart's *Extraordinary Groups: An Examination of Unconventional Life-Styles*, in its third edition because of its wide use in college classrooms, Pitzer's *America's Communal Utopias*, and Berry's *Americans' Utopian Experiments: Communal Havens from Long-Wave Crises*, which examines American utopian projects as a response to long-range economic cycles.[12]

---

[10] Fogarty, R.: *Dictionary of American Communal and Utopian History*, Westport, Connecticut, 1980; Stockwell, F.: *Encyclopedia of American Communities*, Jefferson, North Carolina, 1998.

[11] Bestor, A.: *Backwoods Utopias*, Philadelphia, Pennsylvania, 1950; Manuel, F. and F.: *Utopian Thought in the Western World*, Cambridge, Massachusetts, 1979.

[12] Fellman, M.: *The Unbounded Frame: Freedom and Community in Nineteenth Century American Utopianism*, Westport, Connecticut, 1973; Kephart, W.: *Extraordinary Groups: An Examination of Unconventional Life-Styles*, 3rd ed., New York, New York, 1987;

In addition to these comparative studies, scholars have studied and published the records of thousands of individual communities.[13] The growth in research has also encouraged the establishment of learned societies (with affiliated journals), among them The Communal Studies Association, The Society for Utopian Studies and The International Communal Studies Association.[14]

In the context of this utopian literature Guarneri's study of Fourierism and the Associationist movement in America has focused on Brisbane's role in its advancement.[15] The diaries transcribed and annotated here complement his analysis by providing a sense of how Brisbane's personal engagement with utopian ideas developed.[16] Recently recovered family papers have provided further insight into Brisbane's thinking.[17]

Brisbane's early life and contemporary society

In 1798 the Holland Land Company's principal agent, Joseph Ellicott,[18] hired Brisbane's father, James Brisbane, and several other young men to survey and begin settling the company's four hundred million acre site in the Genesee Valley on the shores of Lakes Erie and Ontario. In 1801 Ellicott

Pitzer, D. ed.: *America's Communal Utopias*, Chapel Hill, North Carolina, 1997; Berry, B.: *Americans' Utopian Experiments: Communal Havens from Long-Wave Crises*, Hanover, New Hampshire, 1992.

[13] Representative of this literature (relevant to this study) is Delano, S.F.: *The Harbinger and New England Transcendentalism*, Rutherford, New Jersey, 1983, which includes descriptions of Brisbane's involvement with Brook Farm and the Associationist Movement.

[14] Reflecting this current interest, in 2000 the New York Public Library, in conjunction with the Bibliothéque National, mounted "Utopia," a major exhibition on the last 500 years of Utopianism in western civilization.

[15] Introduction: 2 n. 5.

[16] It was characteristic of Brisbane that he regarded his personal life as of no interest and only reluctantly agreed, in later life, to dictate his memoirs to his wife Redelia. He saw the history of the individual as insignificant, compared to the great work which humanity had to perform, an insight which came to him, he recalled, at the age of fifteen. (*MB*: 196)

[17] We are indebted to Gary Cohn, who has made available to us Brisbane papers and transcriptions of interviews with Brisbane's widow Redelia, his surviving children, Arthur and Alice, and his grand-daughter Sarah Brisbane. These materials, hereafter referred to as "Brisbane papers, private collection," are in the process of being entered into the Brisbane Archive in the department of Special Collections, in the George Arendts Library, Syracuse University.

[18] See Chazanof, W.: *Joseph Ellicott and the Holland Land Company: The Opening of Western New York*, Syracuse, New York, 1970, and Williams, C. L. T.: *Joseph Ellicott and Stories of the Holland Purchase*, Batavia, New York, 1936.

established the company's first settlement, Batavia, about 25 miles east of Buffalo. In 1802 James Brisbane became the first postmaster of Batavia, and opened the town's first general store. As postmaster and storekeeper, he was able to make a considerable fortune in land speculation.[19] In 1803 he bought the first frame house built in Batavia, for seven hundred dollars. Shortly thereafter James married an Englishwoman, Mary Stevens, sister of one of the earliest settlers; his fellow surveyor, Trumbull Cary, married James' sister Margaret Eleanor. Here Albert was born in 1809, followed by his brother George three years later.

Brisbane's frontier upbringing gave him little exposure to, or sympathy with, religious orthodoxy,[20] a sensibility which would later color his response to Saint-Simonian ideological demands.[21] Until its seventh year, there was no church in the Batavia settlement, probably a reflection of its first residents' views. "The founders of this little village were – what was then extremely rare – men of liberal views, I might almost say freethinkers." (*MB*: 49) James Brisbane had revolted against his natal Presbyterian faith in early youth:

> A story in point is related of him in connection with the great Mil-
> lerite movement in 1843.[22] On the eve of the day on which the
> prophecy was to be fulfilled, one of the Advent enthusiasts, accost-
> ing him on the street, said: "Mr. Brisbane, do you know the world
> is coming to an end to-morrow?" My father replied: "Damned glad
> of it, sir! Damned glad of it. This experiment of the human race is
> a total failure!" (*MB*: 50)

Young Brisbane's distrust of religion and religious fervor may have been further strengthened by indirect experience of the revivalist movement that,

---

[19] At his death in 1851 James Brisbane left an estate valued at half a million dollars, divided equally between his two sons. See his obituary in "Spirit of the Times" June 3, 1851, Batavia, New York (Appendix 1).

[20] Brisbane's widow Redelia described James as ". . . what they call an infidel . . .," and stated that Albert ". . . had no religious education, he used to wander around the churches during service and listen." (Brisbane papers, private collection)

[21] Diary II: 138-46, November 30 to December 7, 1831 and 213-16, January 8-15, 1832.

[22] William Miller, a Baptist minister in New York State, announced in 1831 that he had calculated the date of the second coming of Christ, which would be in 1843. Many of his followers sold all their possessions and purchased white robes, to be ready for the heavenly ascent. The remnants of this sect would eventually become the Seventh-Day-Adventists.

in the excitement after the war of 1812, was beginning to pass through the Genesee Valley and on to the shores of Lake Erie with such intensity that the area was known as the "burned-over district." Batavia residents would probably have traveled to meetings, even if the village was too small to attract revivalist speakers. Although Brisbane does not mention it, he may have heard something of these exciting events.[23]

Brisbane grew up in a highly literate household. His father, the son of a Scottish physician, was a trained surveyor, and his English mother ". . . was a student, interested in all the sciences within her reach, especially astronomy. It was thus at my mother's knee that I began my synthetic education." (*MB*: 51–52) Attendance at the community school held little interest for him, compared to the charms of the natural world. Eventually Brisbane gained his liberty, and from the age of ten pursued "the feathery and the finny tribe" in the woods around Batavia. At this age he already possessed three guns and had free use of the horses in his father's stable. Needing help with traps and tackle, he soon discovered that ". . . the carpenter, the saddler, and even the blacksmith were important personages." The Batavia of Brisbane's childhood was a community of artisans and farmers. Self-sufficient and egalitarian in their daily affairs, Batavia residents reflected the Jeffersonian ideal of republican virtue.[24] Here Brisbane would early absorb a view of the world as offering boundless opportunities for anyone sufficiently energetic to explore it. He later spoke of the "immense restless enterprise characteristic of the American people." (*MB*: 53–54)

Eventually James Brisbane decided that his son's arboreal program of independent study was not providing sufficient training, so, in 1824, at the age of fifteen, Brisbane began a progress through a succession of schools in New York City, where he met with limited success. After two years of this, he was put in the care of a tutor, Jean Manesca, a French-Haitian planter and a refugee from the Santo Domingo revolution. Manesca had been educated in the French Enlightenment tradition. As Brisbane explained

---

[23] See Cross, W. R.: *The Burned-Over District: The Social and Intellectual History of Enthusiastic Religion in Western New York, 1800-1850*, Ithaca, New York, 1950.

[24] On the impact of Jeffersonian thought in this period, see Appleby, J. O.: *Capitalism and the New Social Order: Republicanism of the 1790's*, New York, 1984, and *Inheriting the Revolution*, Cambridge, Massachusetts, 2000; also Matthews, J.: *Toward a New Society: American Thought and Culture 1800–1830*, Boston, Massachusetts, 1991.

it: "Manesca based his views on the popular philosophy of the eighteenth century, and one of his favorite authorities was Helvétius.[25] Through his influence, I inclined to accept the same doctrine." (*MB*: 63)

Already an enthusiast, and impressed by what he learned of European scholarship in two years of study with Manesca, Brisbane came to the conclusion that European thinkers, America's intellectual forefathers, offered humanity its best prospects for realizing its potential. So, in 1828 he asked his father to allow him to study in Europe ". . . in order to solve the mystery of man's destiny, to penetrate the why and the wherefore of his advent on this planet." (*MB*: 63) After a few months of consideration James Brisbane decided to allow his son to go, and Brisbane set sail for Europe, shaped by the values of his childhood community. He was convinced that he was capable of learning and doing whatever he wanted, in a world in which the possibilities for individuals, as for society as a whole, were limitless.

Brisbane's travels

The European intellectual and political world to which Brisbane was traveling was in considerable upheaval. Prince Clemens von Metternich's[26] plans to restore traditional order had begun to break down almost immediately after the Congress of Vienna in 1815, since the signers of that agreement were unwilling to agree to common action in the face of upheavals in Greece, Spain and Italy. In France, the ancient Bourbon family had been restored to the throne in the person of Louis XVIII (r. 1815–1824), who granted a very restricted Constitutional Charter.[27] His successor, the reactionary Charles X (r. 1824–1830),[28] attempted to suspend the Charter in 1830,

---

[25] Claude Adrien Helvétius (1715–1771), a French enlightenment thinker, considered that all human effort was driven by a concern to seek pleasure, the ultimate source of all good, and to avoid pain, the source of all evil. From this premise Helvétius developed a theory of social engineering, arguing that governments, by encouraging pleasant human endeavors and discouraging painful ones, could improve society. See Levy, P.: *The Enlightenment, an Interpretation*, New York, 1966.

[26] Prince Clemens Wenzel Lothar von Metternich (1773–1859), was Austrian foreign minister and architect of the Congress of Vienna, which attempted to reverse the political and territorial changes created by the wars of Napoleon.

[27] The terms of the 1815 charter created an elected Chamber of Deputies from which a government ministry was chosen which shared power with the monarchy. However, representation was extremely narrow, since eligibility to vote and hold office was limited to owners of substantial property.

which provoked revolution in France, placing Louis Philippe d'Orleans (a cousin of the Bourbons) on the throne.[29]

Revolutions subsequently broke out in Belgium, Saxony and Poland, and there were rumblings about the granting of a constitution in Prussia, all of which Brisbane noted as hopeful auguries of the dawning of a new age. The aftershocks of the Greek Revolution against the Ottoman Empire, 1821–1827, were still reverberating when he visited Greece in 1830; in the Kingdom of the Two Sicilies, Brisbane witnessed the repressive monarchy's constant surveillance of the population. He recorded these impressions in his travel diaries, from which his later ideas about ideal government would develop.

Brisbane arrived at le Havre in the fall of 1828, as France was enduring the final years of the repressive rule of Charles X. His first year in France was spent at the Sorbonne, following the lectures of François Guizot, Victor Cousin, and François Villemain.[30] Initially, Brisbane had been hopeful that the French political process would result ". . . in the later realization of a Republic. I thought it would take place and I had confidence in its success." However, he soon became interested in the eclectic philosophy of Cousin, ". . . his idea being to take up the various systems of the past, to select

---

[28] Charles, Comte d'Artoise, Louis XVI's youngest brother, had led the flight of noble *emigrés* from France in August 1789, when noble privileges had ended. Vowing to uphold the principles of the *Ancien Régime*, he was known as "the king who never forgot and never forgave."

[29] Charles X's actions offered an opportunity for a narrow liberal opposition, led by François Guizot (1787–1874), Prince Charles Périgord de Talleyrand (1754–1838), and Achille Charles Léonce Victor de Broglie (1785–1879), to encourage upheaval. While these men opposed the monarch's efforts to concentrate his authority, they did not want to extend power much beyond the wealthy elite stipulated in the constitutional charter of 1815. Therefore, the revisions of the charter introduced in 1830 limited the monarch's authority but only slightly extended the franchise.

[30] Called the "three greats of liberal arts" (by B. de Sauvigny, G.: *The Bourbon Restoration*, Philadelphia, Pennsylvania, 1966: 341–42), François Guizot, Victor Cousin (1792–1867) and Abel François Villemain (1790–1870) were liberals who had supported the restoration of a limited monarchy in 1815. However, the autocratic actions of Charles X prompted them to protest. Guizot's lectures on the monarchy incurred the displeasure of the King and in 1826 he was removed from his chair at the Sorbonne, only returning to the podium in 1828, the year Brisbane began attending lectures. Guizot and his followers would become the leaders of the opposition in the Chamber of Deputies and would convince Charles X's cousin, Louis-Philippe d'Orleans, to claim the throne in 1830 (by which time Brisbane had left Paris).

from them what might be considered truths, and putting these together, form a new and perfect system." (*MB*: 72) Brisbane's studies with Cousin represented his first contact with the utopian assumption that among the infinity of possible systems there might be one which perfectly explained everything, and which could identify the best way for organizing society. Brisbane's American optimism attracted him to such a concept, and this, in turn, strengthened his own positive thinking.

Gradually concluding that no great truths were in fact emerging from his French studies, but impressed with Cousin's frequent references to German philosophy and especially to Friedrich Hegel,[31] Brisbane speculated that ". . . possibly he [Cousin] had not properly interpreted these men and that if I could study them personally I might arrive at some satisfactory result". (*MB*: 75) Brisbane therefore began studying German, and in the spring of 1829 traveled eastward to attend courses at the University of Berlin. It was on the way to Berlin that Brisbane met Lechevalier, a French fellow student, who would later introduce Brisbane to the Saint-Simonian religion and to the works of Fourier.

Berlin in 1829 was the capital of Prussia, a member of the German Confederation created at the Congress of Vienna out of the remnants of Napoleon's German conquests. Prussia was an independent kingdom ruled by Frederick William III, though still heavily under the thumb of the Austrians and Metternich. As an American student and traveler in Berlin, Brisbane found himself to be the ". . . subject of some social curiosity."[32] (*MB*: 80) He quickly became established in the most renowned Jewish intellectual salon in Berlin at the time, that of Rahel Levin Varnhagen von Ense and her husband, Karl.[33] Rahel's salon included the Mendelssohn family and several

---

[31] George Wilhelm Friedrich Hegel (1770–1831) was a German philosopher of history who developed the dialectical model of social change later employed by Karl Marx.

[32] The first American had enrolled at the University of Berlin only four years before. See Bestor, 1947: 132.

[33] The salon of Rahel Levin Varnhagen von Ense (1771–1833) brought together leading Berlin intellectuals and businessmen. Rahel's circle is discussed by her husband in Varnhagen von Ense, K. A.: *Denwürdigkeiten des Lebens*, Karlsruhe, 1845. A recent study is Tewarson, H.: *Rahel Levin Varnhagen: the Life and Work of a German Jewish Intellectual*, Lincoln, Nebraska, 1998. Brisbane's correspondence with Karl Varnhagen (1785–1858) has been published in Pickett, T., and F. de Rocher: *Letters of the American Socialist Albert Brisbane to K. A. Varnhagen von Ense*, Heidelberg, 1986.

university professors associated with Hegel, among them Edouard Gans and Karl Ludwig Michelet.[34] Brisbane was probably introduced to Rahel's circle by another Berlin *salonière*, Henrietta Solmar, who took a particular interest in foreigners.[35] Brisbane was very impressed with the friendliness and the lively conversations of the Berlin salons he attended, and he seems to have felt much more at home in that city than he had in Paris. However, he found following Hegel's courses in German quite taxing. He offers an interesting description of Hegel's lecturing style:

> At the sound of the gong which brought to a close preceding lectures, the students rushed pell-mell into this hall and took their seats. Presently Hegel walked in, in a business-like manner, and without salutation or preliminary of any sort, took his place at the desk, opened a roll of manuscript and began to read. His eyes were constantly fixed on the manuscript, while his head moved slowly from side to side of the page. His delivery was uniform and monotonous – his whole manner expressing a simple desire to present the subject matter without the slightest vanity of mannerism or any attempt at elocution. When the moment came to close the lecture, again indicated by the sound of the gong, it mattered not if it came in the midst of a phrase, all was stopped and snapped off with mechanical abruptness. The lecturer arose, and in the same unconcerned manner passed out of the hall. (*MB*: 88–89)

Brisbane's rigorous study of Hegel did not apparently provide him with ". . . some conclusion, some synthesis of a high and positive value." (*MB*: 94) In this unsatisfied and melancholy frame of mind he decided to travel, and in the spring of 1830 began an extended trip through Austria, Turkey, Greece and Italy.

---

[34] Gans (1798–1839) was a Hegelian and a professor of law; Michelet (1801–1893) was a descendant of French exiles and a professor of philosophy. Together they tutored Brisbane through a course of Hegel's lectures.

[35] Henrietta Solmar (1794–1886) was a friend of the Varnhagens mentioned in Rahel's writings. Inspired by Rahel, Henrietta had established her own salon in the late 1820s to which she often invited foreign visitors. Although almost 15 years his senior, she seems to have established a romantic relationship with the young American. See Diary II: 34-38, October 11, 1831; 107-09, November 17, 1831; 179-82, December 25-31, 1831.

From Berlin, Brisbane first traveled to Vienna, where he had occasion to mingle with the Viennese aristocracy. In his *Mental Biography*, he quotes from his diary of April 20, 1830:

> I saw this morning the young Napoleon.[36] He was just returning from the parade ground with the Kronprinz and other officers; and as his horse walked, I had a good chance to observe him carefully. The Bourbons [the French monarchy] may rest in peace as far as he is concerned, if there is any truth in physiognomy.[37] He has light hair and light blue eyes, overhung by heavy, uneven eyebrows. There is quite a deep line under the eyes, and the lids seem thick. The mouth appears bad, the large under-lip droops as he speaks. I could not see much of the forehead, but I should judge it to be his best feature. In short, I am greatly disappointed in this face! It does not indicate vigor of mind. The flesh looks coarse, without compactness or smoothness on this long, pale, face with its restless eyes glancing slowly from side to side in vague expression. This is the son of Napoleon only in the flesh. The great military genius did not give him his mind – I even think he has but little mind. He has much more of the Austrian in him than the French. (*MB*: 98)

Brisbane then went to Trieste, and from there by ship to Istanbul, the capital of the Ottoman Empire. Here he spent almost two months, and was

---

[36] Napoleon II (1811–1832), the Duke of Reichstadt, called *Roi du Rome*, the son of Napoleon Bonaparte by Marie-Louise.

[37] Brisbane's use of the term "physiognomy" reflected an ancient theory expressed as early as the Greek medical writer Hippocrates, that character and ability could be discerned from the features of the face and head. By the nineteenth century, scholars were attempting to establish scientific links between physiognomy, emotions and character. See, for example, Darwin, C., *Expression of Emotion in Man and Animals*, London, 1872; Lavater, G., *L'art de connaître les hommes par la physionomie*, Paris, 1820; O'Leary, A., *Delineation of Character as Determined by the Teachings of Phrenology, Physiology and Physiognomy*, Boston, 1860. In this observation, dictated in later life, Brisbane suggested personal reservations about the theory of physiognomy. Nevertheless as a young man he used the concept quite extensively in his diaries to try to extract the essence or racial character of a people, as did other contemporary European travelers. See Diary I: 6–8, October 14, 1830; 35–44, October 21; 93, November 6; 134, 138, November 21; 204, December 1; 268–71, December 13; 273, December 15; 284, December 17; 304, December 20; 327, December 28.

deeply impressed by what he learned. It was in Turkey that Brisbane made what he considered to be his most important discovery: that the political order was of less importance for the progress of a nation than its social order. As he wrote, years later, in reflecting on his months in Istanbul and environs:

> I had left my own country imbued with a sentiment of democracy; republican institutions and political liberty were ideas which had grown with my growth and become a part of my being. On observing the political condition of France, for instance, I imagined that the sole thing requisite to remedy all imperfection was the substitution of a republic for a monarchy; and this exalted idea of republican and democratic institutions continued through my sojourn in France and Germany. I had not yet analyzed deeply enough to discover the real unity underlying the civilizations of the New and the Old World; but when I came to see Turkey, fresh ideas began to dawn upon my mind. Here was an entirely new world, the most salient feature of which to me was the degradation of woman. (*MB*: 113–14) The second important conception which came to me in Turkey was that a particular form or system of government did not affect the fundamental constitution of society. I discovered that the American Republic was simply a new dress on old institutions. It retained the same system of social relations, the same system of commerce, the same rights of property and capital; and I began to ponder on the problem of an entirely new order of society. (*MB*: 118, cf. *MB*: 196–97)[38]

From Istanbul, Brisbane and his Romanian interpreter went to Smyrna, whence they sailed to Nauplion, then the capital of Greece. They explored the Peloponnesus on horseback, visiting Mycenae, Sparta, Navarino and finally Athens, where they stayed with Gropius, the Austrian consul. Brisbane explored the Acropolis and the countryside around Athens:

---

[38] See also Diary I: 59–73, October 29, 1830. It is interesting that a nineteen-year-old perceived the relative insignificance of governmental systems for the basic functioning of society. This undoubtedly fueled his interest in Saint-Simonianism. See Diary II, 194–97, January 1–8, 1832.

Another incident during my sojourn in Athens came very near costing me my life. I had been warned against excursions in the surrounding country, as there were known to be roving bands of Albanians in the neighborhood; in other words, the robbing desperadoes of Greece and the regions around. I was rather heedless of what had been said to me regarding the Albanians. Mounted on a young and spirited horse, I started off on my trip one day just at noon. Fortunate hour! For at a few miles from Athens I came upon an Albanian camp, through which lay my route. It was their hour of repose, and the men were asleep under the shade of some trees. The sound of my horse awakened them, and springing to their feet, they saw me pass rapidly by. In an instant their large shaggy greyhounds were speeding after me, and my horse, sniffing the danger, rushed on with frantic fleetness . . . [at last] I distanced them. Had they caught me, I should unquestionably have been sacrificed. (*MB*: 180–81)

From Athens, Brisbane returned to Nauplion, where Diary I begins, in October 1830. From Nauplion he sailed to Malta and Sicily, and then traveled up the Italian peninsula by land to Naples, where the diary ends.[39] From there he traveled to Rome, where he spent some months. Here he met Felix Mendelssohn again, whom he had known in Berlin,[40] and made the acquaintance of his fellow Americans Horatio Greenough and Samuel Morse,[41] with whom he traveled to Florence. Also during his Italian sojourn he met Adèle LeBrun, whom he would marry in 1833 and bring home to Batavia in 1834. After a month in Florence, he traveled through Switzerland, to England and Holland, returning to Paris in late August of 1831.

---

[39] Illustration 10 provides a map of Brisbane's travel route in Italy.

[40] During the previous winter in Berlin, Brisbane had become friendly with the composer Felix Mendelssohn (1809–1847). They met again in Rome in February, 1831, on the night of the election of Pope Gregory XVI. See Mendelssohn-Bartholdy, F.: *Letters from Italy and Switzerland*, tr. A. Wallace, London, 1862: 234.

[41] Both were studying painting at the time. Morse (1791–1872) remained committed to painting and only reluctantly returned to his family's business (creating the telegraph code that bears his name) when he realized he could not make a living as an artist. Greenough (1805–1852) became a sculptor and produced the famous colossal statue of George Washington in a toga, now in the Smithsonian in Washington, D.C.

These travels of Brisbane through the British Isles and Holland were particularly important because of the impression he formed there of rural Irish and industrial English poverty and because somewhere on these expeditions he first encountered Saint-Simonian writings. Yet his diaries and later accounts do not provide a definitive chronology of his European travels. We can construct something of his English travels from several diary entries. In an early November, 1831 entry (Diary II: 100–01, November 10–11, 1831) discussing his second trip from Paris to Berlin, Brisbane described getting along much better with an English fellow traveler than he had gotten on with any Englishman before. From this comment we can assume Brisbane had spent some time in England before November 1831, and possibly had found Saint-Simonian writings somewhere on the way. In a later entry in Diary II (195–98, January 4, 1832) Brisbane described first encountering Saint-Simonian writings in Holland and then meeting the group on his return to Paris. Later in the same entry he described leaving Paris and traveling to England in a fit of frustration with his friend Lechevalier and the Saint-Simonians. This second trip to England would have occurred sometime in the late summer or early fall of 1831, probably before he went to Berlin in November of that year. From these entries it appears that Brisbane must have traveled from Paris several times.

In his autobiography, dictated almost fifty years later, Brisbane described traveling through Holland and the British Isles and encountering Saint-Simonianism on his way to Berlin in 1829, before the first diary begins in October, 1830 – a recollection that does not coincide with his diaries. Further, it does not seem likely that he encountered Saint-Simonian materials so early for there is no mention of Saint-Simon or his ideas in the first diary – an omission that seems odd in light of the powerful impression these ideas made on him (Diary II: 2, September 26, 1831 and 194–95, January 4, 1832). In a Diary I entry (317, December 25, 1830) Brisbane states that his father wanted him to go to Amsterdam. This suggests a trip to Holland sometime in 1831. We conclude from these materials that Brisbane possibly traveled in Holland and perhaps England not only on his way to Berlin in 1829 but also on his way back to Paris in the late spring of 1831. It was most probably on this second trip that he first came across Saint-Simon's writings because it was after his return to Paris in the summer of 1831 that Brisbane contacted Lechevalier, his friend and fellow student from Berlin, and asked Lechevalier to introduce him to the Saint-Simonian society and lectures being offered in their hall in the Rue Taitbout.

Diary II, beginning in October, 1831 after Brisbane had returned to Paris, probably in late August, details his activities there, at the theater, visiting acquaintances, and above all attending the Saint-Simonian gatherings. Brisbane showed a growing enthusiasm for the movement, both for its intellectual aspects and the greater social and possibly sexual opportunities it offered. From Brisbane's description of the attractiveness of the Saint-Simonian ladies and the openness of their association (see especially Diary II: 74, October 22, 1831), the reader may infer that Brisbane at some level hoped for opportunities of greater intimacy as well as intellectual stimulation in that context. In Diary I Brisbane had described varied sexual activities with prostitutes as well as with respectable ladies, so clearly he had interests and aspirations in this area.[42] He also had discussed the philosophical basis (or rationalization) for his sexual behavior. (Diary I: 44–50, October 21, 22, 1830; 131–32, November 21, 1830; 175–79, November 27, 1830; 191–93, November 29, 1830; 328–29, December 28, 1830) As a great thinker and reformer, he had to avoid entanglements, and thus concluded in a *billet-doux* to Henrietta Solmar recorded toward the end of Diary I:

> When at the end of my life I have produced nothing, I am without result, then it shall be indifferent to me whether the name of Albert Brisbane be coupled with villain, scoundrel or devil. . . . It is, however, true that I am too indifferent with regard to such things. I cannot apply to myself a virtuous code of morals. It seems to have no value in my eyes, inasmuch as it exerts no influence upon what I wish to attain. . . . One of my general rules is, "Act as you think, and think nobly." This is with regard to the mind, but with regard to that part of man which is animal, there are various indifferent particularities without rules and method. (Diary I: 311–12, December 23, 1830)

---

[42] At one point Brisbane describes himself as enslaved by his sexual feelings. Diary I: 111, November 16, 1830.

His conviction that the reformer cannot afford to entangle himself emotionally is also expressed later in Diary II with regard to his future wife, Adèle LeBrun: ". . . her letters are beautifully written and with the greatest depth and purity of sentiment. However, was (sic) she still far superior to what she is, I could not think of any nearer connection. I must remain alone, independent, without feeling or care of a personal nature." (Diary II: 230–33, January 22–29, 1832)

At the same time that Brisbane was considering his growing interests and concerns about personal and sexual commitments, he revealed new apprehensions about the depth of commitment required by the religion of the Saint-Simonians. (Diary II: 50–56, October 14–16, 1831) In his correspondence with his former tutor Manesca, Brisbane also reflected a new sense of purpose. While he may have initially come to Europe to study out of a general intellectual curiosity, that curiosity had been transformed into a mission to rebuild society and solve the world's problems. In the process he had begun to see himself as a guide and leader, no longer as a student and follower. The youthful, egalitarian woodland hunter chattering away with the carpenter and blacksmith had long since disappeared.

Anxious about the divisions among the Saint-Simonians, and having quarreled with Lechevalier, Brisbane determined to return to Berlin in November 1831 for a second winter of study at the university. Once in Berlin, he was at first pleased to be back among friends and to discuss Saint-Simonian theory with them.[43] However, he soon began to complain of the shallowness of Berlin society and to agonize over the Saint-Simonian schism he left behind in Paris.

This second diary leaves Brisbane hanging; disillusioned with his friends and studies in Berlin, unable to commit to the Saint-Simonian movement, yet still convinced that the answer he sought would provide the key to the

---

[43] Pickett suggests (Pickett, T. and F. de Pocher, *Letters of the American Socialist Albert Brisbane to K. A. Varnhagen von Ense*, Heidelberg, 1986: 9) that Brisbane may have introduced the Varnhagens to Saint-Simonian writings and in doing so, may have been the first person to bring Saint-Simon's works to Germany. Certainly Brisbane was one of the earliest to do so, and his distribution of *Le Globe* in Berlin and elsewhere was important in spreading the philosophy. See Albert Brisbane, letter to Michel Chevalier, April 24, 1832, MS 7601; *Fonds Enfantin, Bibliothèque de l'Arsenal*, Michel Chevalier; letter to Albert Brisbane, May 24, 1832, MS 7646; Archives IV, *Fonds Enfantin, Bibliothèque Nationale*; and *MB*: 173–74.

reform of society. We can see that his social consciousness had been sharply raised by his journeys in many diverse lands.

Brisbane's youthful intensity was noted by his fellow American, Greenough, who humorously referred to him as ". . . the windmill, Brisbang."[44] A letter written from Paris by James Fenimore Cooper to Greenough in December 1831, just after Brisbane's departure for Berlin, described the young Brisbane: "Do not be alarmed, however, for as yet we steer clear of St. Simonism. We owe this grace to the absence of Mr. Brisbane, who, it would appear, has quite driven the cholera from Berlin. Brisbane is a clever fellow, in his way, though a little of the development of a crotchet."[45]

A little later, Cooper wrote: "Brisbane is here still, and with a famous new crotchet. He has got a glass eye,[46] and thinks he can see into a mill-stone. Animal magnetism is his hobby now . . . I was much amused with Brisbane. . . . Still, he is a good fellow, with upright views and benevolent feelings."[47]

While in his second winter in Berlin, in 1831–1832, Brisbane received a copy of Fourier's *L'Association Domestique-Agricole* from Lechevalier, with whom he had continued to correspond requesting that he send "all that was published on social ideas in Paris." (*MB*: 170) Reading through the introduction, Brisbane was so struck by Fourier's idea of "attractive industry" that he ". . . sprang to [his] feet, threw down the book and began pacing the floor in a tumult of emotion." (*MB*: 170–71) Returning to Paris in November 1832, Brisbane made his way to the offices of Fourier where he managed to convince the haughty but impoverished gentleman to "tutor" him in his doctrine.

The picture of Brisbane that emerges from these early writings is of an earnest young man who, while unsure of his commitments, felt confident of his abilities and his sensibilities. For a youth in his early twenties (21 in

---

[44] Wright, N., ed.: *Letters of Horatio Greenough to Samuel Morse*, Madison, Wisconsin, 1972: 131.

[45] Beard, J. F., ed.: *Letters and Journals of James Fenimore Cooper*, Cambridge, Massachusetts, 1960, vol. II: 163. Cooper declined to attend a Saint-Simonian meeting and explained his reasons (p. 168): "*Un dieu que je pourrais comprendre deviendrait un égal, et les égaux ne s'adorent pas.*" (A god whom I could understand would become an equal, and equals do not adore one another.)

[46] Apparently Brisbane had lost an eye sometime in his youth. See Diary 1: 87, November 3, 1830. However, from this reference in 1833, it would seem he had only begun to use a glass eye after coming to Europe.

[47] Beard: *Letters*, volume II: 371.

1830), he displayed a naive arrogance about the impact he would exercise on the future of society; yet for all his self-assurance, it was channeled in a very thoughtful direction.

Brisbane's role as a propagandist

Brisbane returned from Europe in 1834 with a blueprint for the Fourier-ist model community, the phalanx. He also brought his new wife, Adèle LeBrun, whom his parents refused to meet in New York because she was a Catholic. However, his aunt, Eleanor Brisbane Cary, (James Brisbane's sister) drove her coach down to the city and brought the couple back to her house in Batavia.[48] Albert and Adèle were eventually reconciled with his parents and lived in Batavia for some years, during which time Adèle bore a son and a daughter. During this period it seems Brisbane was engaged in repairing his health and the family resources, probably through land speculation. By 1838, his relations with Adèle had deteriorated, in part over an impetuous religious vow she had made,[49] and she returned to Italy with their surviving son Charles. The name and fate of their daughter is unknown. She may not have survived to adulthood. Adèle's departure did not extinguish Brisbane's interest in the fair sex. By 1839 he had begun a liaison with Lodoisca Man-esca Durand which continued intermittently until 1872.[50]

---

[48] From the recollections of Brisbane's daughter Alice Brisbane Thursby (1859–1953) and his granddaughter Sarah Brisbane Mellen (Brisbane papers, private collection).

[49] The story of this vow was told by Brisbane's daughter Alice Brisbane Thursby: "One night he [Albert] went out after dinner, and during that time there was a fire in Buffalo – in Batavia – where she was living . . . his Italian wife vowed if he came back safely she'd give away all her silver. And she presented all her silver to the church, as Catholics do." (Brisbane papers, private collection) Albert was evidently enraged when she went through with her commitment. Albert's negative opinion of Catholic custom is clearly expressed in Diary I, during his travels in southern Italy.

[50] Lodoisca was the daughter of Brisbane's former tutor Jean Manesca. It is not impossible that their relationship began when Brisbane was a teenager living in his tutor's household. "Lodi" later married an engraver, A. G. Durand, on whose behalf Brisbane solicited a con-tract for engraving currency from William Seward, Governor of New York, in 1838. (Albert Brisbane, letter to William Seward, July 19, 1838, Seward Archives, Princeton University) When Durand and his father, both engravers, relocated to Europe in 1840, Brisbane recom-mended their currency engraving skills to Karl Varnhagen von Ense. (Pickett, *Letters*: 47) The evidence for this liaison emerges in the documents of Lodoisca's 1883 bigamy action against Brisbane, a lawsuit largely orchestrated by Brisbane's younger brother, George Bris-bane. According to Lodoisca, Brisbane had married her in 1847, and they had cohabited until

At this point Brisbane turned wholeheartedly to the business of Fourierism. In 1840 he published *The Social Destiny of Man*, a detailed explanation of Fourier's program. He enlisted the aid of Horace Greeley, a convert to Fourierism, publishing a series of editorials in Greeley's *New York Tribune*,[51] and embarked on a series of lecture tours to promote the establishment of Fourierist phalanxes. Soon there were many phalanxes scattered across New York, Pennsylvania, Ohio and extending into Iowa. Of these, the largest and most long-lived was the North American phalanx in New Jersey.[52] Although Brisbane promoted and encouraged Fourierism, he never actually lived in any of the phalanxes and invested little of his own funds.

In 1843 Brisbane sailed to Europe for the second time, to try to persuade the French Fourierists to give him access to the manuscripts of Fourier, who had died six years earlier. He returned to the United States in December 1844, with Fourier's notebooks, to study and try to make a coherent statement of them.

The Fourierist phalanxes were controversial, as was so often the case with utopian communities. Fourier's theories about the sexual dimensions of "passional attraction" were guaranteed to offend nineteenth century

---

1872. He had introduced her to his friends as his wife, and she had been known as Lodoisca M. Brisbane. The basis of her bigamy charges was that Brisbane had never legally divorced his first wife, Adèle LeBrun. Therefore, his subsequent marriages, and particularly his existing marriage to Redelia Bates, were bigamous. Brisbane's testimony differed in some significant details: after Adèle returned to Europe in 1839, he moved into the Manesca boarding house, where his liaison with Lodoisca began. When her husband Albert Durand returned from Europe and learned the situation, he divorced her. Albert left her in 1842, but lived with her again from 1848 to 1857. During this period their three children were born: a son in 1848, who died, a daughter, name unknown (1851–1869), and in 1856, Flora M. Richards, who died in 1884, at age 28. In 1858 Brisbane married Sarah White of Batavia, who bore him five children. Brisbane's only offspring to survive him were from this marriage: Alice Brisbane Thursby (1859–1953), Arthur Brisbane (1864–1936) and Fowell Brisbane (1866–1911). Hugo (1862–1871) – named for Victor Hugo – died at age nine, Albert (1861?) in infancy. His oldest son, by Adèle, Charles (1836–1867?) married and left a son, Howard Brisbane. See letters from Albert to his son Charles in *Fonds Fourier et Considérant (Victor)*, 10 As 28 dossier 9. After Sarah's death of childbed fever in 1866, Brisbane asked Lodoisca to move in with him to take care of the children. This arrangement lasted until 1872, when Brisbane married Redelia Bates. This material is discussed by Pettitt, R.: "Albert Brisbane, Apostle of Fourierism in The United States 1834-1890," Ph.D. Thesis, Oxford, Ohio, 1982.

[51] Horace Greeley (1811–1872), a liberal Whig newspaperman, founded the *New York Tribune* in 1841.

[52] Guarneri, 1991: Appendix table 1, 407–08.

mores, despite Brisbane's judicious editing in his American texts.[53] Insufficient funding in the establishment of the phalanxes caused financial problems; as a result, the communities were not able to sustain themselves, let alone become thriving examples of harmonious productivity.

Inspired by the turbulence erupting in the winter of 1848, first in Paris and then in the rest of Europe, Brisbane hurried to cross the Atlantic and witness the insurrection. Arriving in Paris on June 23 in the midst of the "June days" of violence,[54] Brisbane witnessed street battles between workers and police. (*MB*: 267–69) After Paris he visited Germany, where he met Karl Marx, whom he described years later as ". . . the man whose writings on Labor and Capital have had more influence on the socialistic movement of Europe than any other. . . ." (*MB*: 273) Traveling to Rome and Naples to observe revolutionary movements, Brisbane visited his first wife Adèle, who, having obtained an annulment of her first marriage, was now remarried to Count Agosto della Rocca.[55]

Brisbane returned to Paris at the end of the year to find that his old friends had organized themselves in support of revolution, despite the conservative trend that had followed the revolt of 1848. On February 24, 1849, Brisbane gave a rousing speech to his fellow revolutionaries and workers at

---

[53] See Brock, W. H.: "Phalanx on a Hill: Responses to Fourierism in the Transcendentalist Circle," Ph.D. Thesis, Loyola University, Chicago, Illinois, 1996, for a discussion of responses to sexual aspects of Fourier's theory.

[54] The national workshops established by the provisional government to provide some relief to the unemployed were being shut down, and the efforts of the middle-class national guard to clear the now desperate urban workers out of the city provoked class war in the streets of Paris.

[55] Brisbane described this visit to his friend Henry Clay McDougal, who wrote: "When first I met [Brisbane], he was far past the allotted time of man; but was strong and vigorous in body and mind. He had then been the lawful husband of three wives and in various countries had accumulated nearly as many concubines as the Book credits to the account of the sweet singer of Israel. His first wife was Countess Adèle, with whom he lived for a time in Italy. Their affection for each other was so great as to be oppressive to both, and largely on that account they separated. She became the wife of an Italian nobleman later; but their friendly visits were kept up and they each wrote to the other until her death only a few years before his. He once made a visit to her at her chateau, during which her Italian husband had the extreme courtesy to go off to the city. As they were sipping their wine alone one evening, in a most pathetic way, he told me of the accidental meeting of their hands upon the table. No word was spoken, until in Italian, she finally asked: 'O my friend, can any woman ever forget the father of her first-born?'" (McDougal, 1910: 296) See Appendix 2, "Letter on Adèle" for Brisbane's impressions of this visit.

a meeting of the Icarian Society in Paris.[56] His incendiary language caused the French government to deport him in 1849 as a dangerous radical.[57] He returned to France in 1851 and was once again deported in the following year, this time bringing his and Adèle's son Charles Brisbane back to the United States with him.[58]

Back in America, Brisbane continued his efforts to champion idealistic Fourierist principles. However, as the internecine tensions that would build into the Civil War began to mount, the intellectual community became less inclined to focus on the subtleties of ideal social and economic organizations. Fourierist phalanxes, like other utopian communities characteristic of the 1840s and 1850s, faded from the American landscape. Brisbane continued to promote his ideas and the works of Fourier, despite declining public interest, publishing his two-volume *Theory of the Human Passions* in 1856–57. By now the father of numerous children and concerned to support his family, in the 1860s and 1870s Brisbane was heavily involved in real estate investment, and other capital speculation.[59] However, he continued active

---

[56] *MB*: 296–99. See also Appendix 3, "Extracts from the *Démocratie Pacifique*." This was the journal of the *Ecole Sociétaire*, the Fourierist movement, which included such Republican notables as Alexandre-Auguste Ledru-Rollin (1807–1874), Pierre-Joseph Proudhon (1809–1865), and Victor Considérant (1808–1893).

[57] Cooper writes to his wife from London in April, 1849: "Do you see that that rantipole Brisbane has got himself ordered out of France, and says he will not go, without force. He must be in a delightful agitation in the affair . . ." Beard, *Letters*, II: 25.

[58] According to Brisbane's daughter Alice Brisbane Thursby: "Charles . . . went to the war [?] and got killed or something. . . . He was Italian and not much good, I imagine . . . soft kind of a person. . . . He'd been in Italy all that time . . . must have been an awful bore to my father." It is not clear to which war Alice Thursby was referring. Charles was certainly still alive in 1867 after the end of the American civil war because correspondence existed between Charles and Abert into that year. See Introduction: 21, n. 50. Albert's grand-daughter Sarah Brisbane Mellen added: ". . . when [Charles] was about fifteen, my grandfather decided he ought to come home. He wasn't on very good terms with Adèle then. He met him in Paris and decided to leave him in Paris . . . went to Italy to see Adèle . . . went to Rome . . . stayed a few days and came back to Paris and found that this fifteen year old had been wildly riding over Paris and spent every cent of his credit . . . very wild and furious. Aunt Alice [Thursby] wouldn't bear to think of it, so he took Charles home. . . . My grandfather didn't like him, his grandson [?] at all. You see, Charles was a gay dog and I don't think my grandfather approved of him one bit." (Brisbane papers, private collection) Albert's son Arthur refers to this incident in a letter to his son Seward: "My half-brother caused my Father great expense and difficulty by signing [promissory] notes out of good nature." Arthur Brisbane, letter to Seward Brisbane, May 14, 1936. (Brisbane papers, private collection)

[59] In the 1880s Brisbane promoted various business ventures with his oldest surviving son,

in promoting Fourierist communities in the West, even though his kind of socialist communitarianism had become increasingly marginalized.

He maintained his contacts with France and French ideas. In 1873, after their marriage, he and Redelia traveled to Paris, taking his surviving three children, who were placed in schools there. It was in Paris that Redelia began her notes for the *Mental Biography*, a document that is generally deemed to offer an impressionistic rather than a rigorously accurate accounting, especially of Brisbane's later life. By the 1880s Brisbane was living in Kansas City escaping the lawsuit brought against him by his brother and his common-law wife, Lodoisca.

Conclusion

When Brisbane died in 1890 at the age of eighty-one (on May 1, the workingman's holiday), he left no established movement. His promotional efforts, over a span of some fifty years, had produced numerous newspaper articles in *The New York Daily Tribune*, and in Fourierist papers such as *The Harbinger*, (Brook Farm), *The Phalanx* (Buffalo, New York) *The Future*, (New York) *The Present* (New York), and *The Crayon* (New York). He wrote six books which attempted to make Fourier's theory attractive and comprehensible, a formidable task given the state in which Fourier's writings were preserved.[60]

How far he had journeyed from the youth of 19 who had set out to learn, "What is the work of man on this earth? What was he put here for and what has he to do?" (*MB*: 56) Posterity saw him as a dreamer whose communitarian goals had not been realized, and whose utopian socialism was overtaken by more revolutionary political forms of socialism. Did his influence flow into the great stream of associationist ideas and the labor union movement? Should we view Brisbane as a forerunner of Marxism?

Arthur Brisbane, such as a plan to aerate and fertilize the soil by means of underground pipes, and to import Spanish port.

[60] Brisbane, A.: *The Social Destiny of Man; or Association and Reorganization of Industry,* Philadelphia, 1840; *Association; or, A Concise Exposition of the Practical Part of Fourier's Social Science,* New York, 1843; *A Concise Exposition of the Doctrine of Association,* New York, 1844; *Theory of the Function of the Human Passions, Followed by an Outline View of the Fundamental Principles of Fourier's Theories of Social Science,* vol. 1, New York, 1856; *Treatise on the Function of the Human Passions; An Outline of Fourier's System,* vol 2, New York, 1857; *General Introduction to Social Science,* New York, 1876.

Can we recognize his work, though youthful and subjective, as prefiguring the sexual revolution, the feminist movement, and the human potential movement? At the age of twenty-one, confronted with the squalor of southern Europe, he burst out with the following heartfelt soliloquy:

> What material misery, and what mental degradation coupled with it! I have almost got into a fever with having the image of the thing in my mind. What fatality is it, or what principles in a people may it be that create such a social state? Was it possible to better the thing? Could not some change of government amend the present state of the people? How much to be desired, how godlike to be longed for! Could but the head of power see and comprehend it, should he sacrifice all his power were he a man, he would find, in the thought of having raised the condition of so many individuals, a thousand times repayment of his sacrifice. He could exist in the thought of the world of improvement he had created. (Diary I: 184, November 11–28, 1830)

Brisbane was seeking a system of reform, a principle of organization to better society, behind which he could throw all his considerable enthusiasm and energy. By the time he sailed home to the United States with his new wife Adèle in 1834, he had finally found in Fourier's doctrine a movement that could give his life meaning, a system he could believe in and devote his life to. The task he now set for himself was to begin the work of propaganda and interpretation, which he achieved by reshaping Fourier's somewhat confused set of pronunciamentos into a form more suitable for American consumption.

It is not our task to offer here an assessment of Brisbane's legacy. But what can we suggest? How far had he come on his search to learn ". . . the work of man on this earth"?

The Albert Brisbane of 1832 was an intelligent, sensitive young man, concerned about his fellow beings in the abstract and in the specific. Human distress tormented him, and he yearned to solve the world's ills; his youthful naivety convinced him that a solution existed or could be found. His enthusiasm easily aroused, he was quick to take up all opportunities – intellectual and physical – that presented themselves.

From his earliest childhood he must have experienced himself as something of an odd creature beside his fellow Batavians. His flight to Europe may have in part been driven by a craving to find a community of minds with whom he felt more comfortable. His sudden intense enthusiasms and disillusionments may reflect his ups and downs in trying to determine who he was and what he wanted.

Brisbane's youthful but easily scattered intensity would stay with him throughout his mental and physical pilgrimage. He would continue to be seduced by ideas; in his later commitment to Fourier's system he would expend much energy on the idea, arguing it in discussion and in writing. While he was attracted to and impressed by those who actually rolled up their sleeves and attempted to build these systems, in reality Brisbane never engaged in the process of organizing phalanxes or any other communities.

By the end of the second diary, Brisbane was anxious to make these radical ideas about social organization his own, but was not yet able to offer to any one system the complete submission and acceptance its prophets called for. In 1832 we leave him as an enigma: burning with eager enthusiasm, but for an ideal that was not yet clear.

DIARY I

October 1830 to January 1831

*I*n May 1828, at the age of eighteen, Albert Brisbane sailed for Europe. After two years of study in Paris and Berlin, he took ship from Trieste, at the head of the Adriatic, for Istanbul, capital of the Ottoman empire. From there he sailed to Smyrna, and across the Aegean to Nauplion, capital of Greece. The first three volumes of his diary, covering his travels from Paris to Istanbul and Greece, have not been found. The fourth volume of his diary begins after an extensive tour of the Peloponnesus, as he is preparing to sail to Italy.

Nauplia:[1] *Thursday 14th October* (continued from volume 3rd)

After seeing the secretary, Mr Bignani, I saw the President himself.[2] I had a conversation with him of some length. He spoke of Greece, and the difficulties to vanquish to establish a regular government here. He said "The Greeks have no idea of rights of property; under the Turks there were but few proprietors, and who held their property by no regular titles. When the revolution broke out, every one took as he could. Some pretended that

---

[1] The capital of the new Greek Republic was called Nauplia or Nauplion. (*Napoli di Romania* was its full title, to distinguish it from *Napoli d'Italia*, or Naples). Nauplion was the port of Argos in antiquity, and a Venetian capital from the fourteenth century. The city fell to the Ottoman Turks in 1715.

[2] The President of Greece in 1830 was Count John Capodistrias, formerly the foreign minister of Czar Alexander I. The Greek rebellion against the Ottoman empire had begun in the Peloponnesus in 1821. In 1827, at the battle of Navarino, off the coast of Messenia, the combined British, French and Russian fleets defeated the Ottoman armada and created an independent Greece. In 1828 Capodistrias moved the provisional government of the Greek Republic from the island of Aegina to Nauplion. (Athens was still in Ottoman hands.)

houses and land belonged to them, because they had taken possession of them; thus there were [2] few valid and regular titles. What I am to work at, and which is a very intricate affair, is to examine all the titles of possessions, and to accord new ones to the same persons, by which means there may be something valid."[3]

He wished to impress the people with the idea of the necessity of the rights of property. He said, he wished to have each person possess a piece of land, if it were but small. "When I came here," says he, "I examined the manner in which the elections were done. I found that when a person wished to be elected, he would get out of the province, and search all his friends, and when the day came, they arrived [3] there, cried that they would make this man so and so, and that he must receive the office, etc. Thus," said he, "were the elections carried on. Seeing this abuse, I took the elections out of their hands, and the government created all the officers. Now," said he, "what I wish is this: I wish each person to have a piece of land, to have them divided into provinces, that these provinces elect their officers; but then it will be arranged so that no one can vote out of his province. The persons inhabiting the province will have their names inscribed, so that only those who live there can vote."

He said all the people were at present pell mell; that there [4] was no arrangement among them, that they must be classed: *qu'il fallait les encadrier.* When he could do this, that would be a great step gained; then he could go farther. With the present generation he thought there was but little to be done. They were still used to the Turkish system, and could not get out of it. He said he could find no men fit to make public officers. He could not find a judge that would be impartial. If he got a customs house officer he would embezzle the money for his own use, so that he could find no men to make officers; these men are to make. Consequently, before he could [5] create a regular and stable government, he had to educate his men.

If time was given him, he could do it in five years, he said.[4] For this reason he wished to have strangers' aid, but there were but few persons of

---

[3] The Ottoman system of land ownership regarded all land as technically the property of the Sultan; military or administrative personnel could obtain its use, or the taxes due from it, but only for life. Hence there would have been no legal titles of ownership.

[4] Unfortunately, time would not be given him. The very next year (1831) Capodistrias, probably the most capable man in Greek political life at the time, would be assassinated by two

merit who would care to devote their time to Greece, and then their not knowing the language is a great hindrance. He destroyed piracy, he said, by offering the pirates the power of becoming soldiers, (many of which had been so before, but by retiring to the islands with their families for one reason and another they had equipped these pirate boats) and, as he knew some persons must furnish them with money to commence, and buy the cargoes they robbed, he [6] hindered this. A number of their boats being burnt at the same time, numbers of the pirates came and joined the camp he had established at Poros.

Capodistrias sent me in the afternoon a letter for Admiral Ricord,[5] who in his turn was to request Malcolm[6] to give me a passage on board the vessel he was to send to Malta. Ricord is a man rather aged. He may be fifty-five, but he has still all the activity of a middle-aged man. He has a good face. There is something agreeable in his physiognomy; his manner of talking is open and frank; rather bald on top of his head. He received me very politely and the first thing, almost, was to ask me to dinner for tomorrow. He has an intelligent look, and [7] has not so much of the Russian physiognomy.[7] He introduced me to his wife, who is much younger than he. She has not an intelligent countenance, but her conversation is not bad; face broad, and the Russian physiognomy in it. The Admiral's vessel is fitted up in very fine style. He has large handsomely furnished rooms, and is as well lodged as in a palace.

It appears a revolution has also taken place in Saxony. They are coming in fashion, but I don't understand this Revolution, because the Saxons appeared to me to have but little political education and showed but few signs of a political spirit among them.[8] I don't know whether they have demanded a constitution, [8] liberty of the press, and if they have done it, and get it, they will do honor to themselves; I know nothing about the facts, but here is what I would think. I suspect it has more been the work of the

---

sons of the old Petrobey Mavromichalis, a bandit chieftain and guerrilla fighter disappointed at the elimination of the spoils system.

[5] Admiral Ricord was the commander of the Russian fleet.

[6] Admiral Malcolm was the commander of the British fleet.

[7] By the term physiognomy, Brisbane refers to the nineteenth century theory that facial characteristics indicate racial character and capacity. See Introduction: 14, n. 37.

[8] Brisbane uses the word "spirit" to denote intellectual character or sensibility, rather than mood. It is closer in meaning to the French *esprit*: mind, mental capacity.

poorer classes than the upper ones; the spirit that guides it has been more that of redressing material than spiritual needs. I don't think it has been done for the liberty of the press, and freedom of opinion. Hatred against Jesuitism has been one principle; odiousness of the King another;[9] redress of the wants of some of the manufacturing, and labouring classes, etc.

The political spirit in Prussia and the desire of the liberty of the press and a constitution are strong, but there is a great military spirit which [9] counterbalances it, and the King is liked. He is not against the spirit of the people. He protects the arts, and sciences etc., but should a revolution there take place, it would be more violent than in any other part of Germany. Under the present King it will not take place, but when his son comes to the throne, it may be otherwise.[10] He does not favor the military spirit so much, more the aristocracy. If he undertakes to repress the spirit of science, etc. to give less freedom to scientific opinions, and their discussion, etc. he will probably kindle into action the – already in a measure prepared – spirit.

[10] *Friday 15th October*

Vasilaki. Hotel des Trois Puissances. 92 piastres of Turkey.[11]

The weather today is cloudy, damp, and very disagreeable. It began yesterday, and has rained a good deal. An idea came in my head today, which I may execute, when I have time before me. I will here mention it, that it may recur to me. I would describe, as well as I can recollect, my early years: what activities most pleased my mind, at what studies, and at what things I was engaged with the most pleasure, and the gradual interior progress the boy makes. I recollect some epochs, some favorite occupations, but the time, and a great many particularities escape me.

[11] At two o'clock I went on board of Admiral Ricord's vessel to dine with him. He had requested Admiral Malcolm to give me a passage, which

---

9 The odious Saxon king in question was Antony (r. 1827–1836), brother of Frederic Augustus I (r. 1768–1827). The July revolution in France in 1830 had stimulated a number of revolts in Belgium, Poland, and the German states.

10 The King of Prussia in 1830 was Frederick William III (r. 1797–1840) who was reluctant to grant a constitution. His son, Frederick William IV (r. 1840–1858) would become hopelessly mad. See below: Diary I: 349, January 3, 1831, n. 135.

11 92 Turkish piasters were equal to about $4.00. The "three powers" were Russia, France and England, who in the treaty of London, in 1827, had guaranteed the autonomy of Greece, under Ottoman suzerainty.

he did. After dinner I bid him adieu, promising when I came to Petersburg to find him out. From there I went on board of Admiral Malcolm's huge vessel, who gave me a note to the Captain of the Brig "Rifleman", who is to sail for Malta this evening. I returned on shore, and took leave {of} Gropius, Mavrocordatos, and Capodistrias.[12] With Mavrocordatos I had a considerable [12] long conversation. He appears very much against the present system, and the President, but he expects too much from Greece. He said they might send a foreign Prince if they chose, but that they must let the Greeks make their own constitution, and the Prince must govern according to it.[13]

After bidding these persons adieu I returned home, arranged my things, did not pay the keeper of the Hotel as I had not money enough, but I told him I would send it from Malta, so he believed me and was contented.[14] As I left the shore in the boat, it seemed as [13] if I had done with this part of the world, and that this voyage was finished. A new year seemed to begin, or rather a new set of travels. I had finished my summer work; it was done with, and this moment I commenced the winter one. As I left the shore, I said, "It is done." "*Entschieden*" (decided) came into my mouth. The great result pressed on my mind at this moment with regard to my late journey. I said to myself, one idea this seeing of these countries has given me, is to be better able to appreciate my own civilization. [14] Soon after 8 o'clock we set sail; the night is very dark, but a light breeze blows down the gulf.

Saturday 16th October

The breeze fell off towards morning, and there is now scarcely any wind. We are about twenty miles from Nauplia, but the Palimidia and the Fortress of Argos are very plainly to be seen.[15] Where we are, it is cloudy, but there,

---

[12] George Gropius was the Austrian consul in Athens; Brisbane had stayed in his house, which was one of the few left standing after the Turkish destruction of the city. Alexander Mavrocordatos was a Greek from Constantinople who fought in the War of Independence and served in the Capodistrias government.

[13] "They," the three powers, put Prince Otto of Bavaria on the Greek throne in 1833. He ruled absolutely until a revolution in 1843 forced him to accept a constitution.

[14] Travelers in this period paid for their needs through notes of credit arranged through acquaintances, or letters of introduction from home to the local consul, usually a native who had agreed to look after the needs of travelers.

[15] The Palamidi was the Venetian fortress of Nauplion. The Larissa, stronghold of Argos, about seven miles to the northwest, was a medieval fortress built by Byzantines and Franks on ancient foundations.

it appears fine weather, and the sun gilds the mountains in that part, which produces a very pretty appearance. Today we have made but very little headway.

In the morning a sailor was whipped upon deck. The sailors were all collected to see it. The officers had on their uniforms. They gave the poor fellow twenty-four cuts. It is a severe chastisement, and he begged for [15] mercy most piteously. The Captain let him off one dozen, and pardoned another fellow who also was to be whipped.[16]

Today my eye has troubled me a little, so I have not done much. In the evening we played a few games of whist, but without betting. The officers appear in general economical.

An idea struck me today with regard to the influence different parts of society might have upon the whole. For example, England has had a great navy for some time; it has formed a spirit of its own. The officers, as they enter young, are impregnated with it, and they form themselves upon it. Consequently, there are a large class of men [16] who, being the expression of this spirit, carry it into society, where it must realize itself more or less, because it is so considerable. With regard to the English Navy, a decided spirit characterizes it; it has been so long in existence that it has formed, as it were, a world distinct of itself, or at least it has taken a decided form, and has become a separate class or side of society in itself. The sailor does not carry the spirit of the land on board of the vessel; on the contrary, he is the expression of the sea spirit, and carries it into general society. Consequently this spirit of this class must work upon general society.

With regard to the Russians, for example, it is [17] different. They are new at sea, and have not yet formed a Navy spirit. You see the land spirit, and that of general society there, governing the individuals; they are still in it, except the mechanical part of the thing. Thus, we see the principle of the navy does not act upon the land principle. General society is not influenced by this class.

With regard to the American Navy, it strikes me that it is again different. You neither find the land spirit in the Navy nor does the Navy spirit carry itself into general society. There is a spirit there which is higher than either, and from which they both draw their force. These classes have their char-

---

[16] This episode also appears in Brisbane's autobiography. (*MB*: 135)

acteristics, [18] but this higher spirit, which soars above them, gives them its essence and impregnates them with its spirit. I know not what name to give this spirit unless you would call it the American spirit. You might give it some attributes, the first would be interior force and life; it also is active, enterprising, improving, full of encouragement, and advancing; this spirit modulates all the different classes and sides of society, it gives them their life, and when they are out of the mere sphere, which characterizes them, they fall into it, and become its expression. This is the American spirit which gives a harmony to all classes and [19] sides of general society.[17]

With regard to England, for example, I should like to know what effect the continual carrying of the Navy spirit into general society has produced there; how it has acted upon the general spirit. In society we find different sides, and inasmuch as they are sides or classes they have characteristics. A characteristic is the effect of the object, which one of these sides may have in view. A side has a determination, and the more this determination is realized, the more developed is its spirit, consequently the more force it has, and consequently the more it acts upon the spirit of the other classes.

Thus each class throws its influence in the general scale, and the [20] sum of all these spirits, acting and working upon each other, produce that general spirit which is the characteristic of a country. This general spirit in its turn acts upon the individual sides and gives them the coloring of harmony. When some of these sides get predominant, which have a resemblance among themselves, then they may give a marked direction to the general spirit. The general spirit is the feeling, (the principles and the thought) of a country, which determines the individual's aim.

But there is something original which was before and which is above the spirit, resulting from the minor spirits of the different sides, or classes of general society; that is, the [21] principles of a civilization. The principles of a civilization are the profoundest truths of a people. They are the first, and highest; the basis of their futurity; and determine the future development of a country. These principles realize themselves, but these realizations act, in the course of time, again upon the original principles, as in time a country develops and perfections itself. The original principles

---

[17] The term "side" is apparently a translation of the French *côté*, meaning aspect.

are realized; and the different sides and classes spring out of them. There stands a country developed. After that, some side becomes preponderant; harmony is lost, discord arises, and change takes place. It may fall, or revolutions may restore harmony by crushing [22] the preponderating power. I should like to know what effect one particular side of society might have upon the general spirit in the course of time. For example, what effect the Navy spirit, constantly in contact with a country, may produce in the course of time.

In observing a country, you might note the most marked activities of it and the most preponderating classes or sides of its society; that is, you might see what activities of the mind are there the most developed. Then, by studying the nature of these activities and determining their effect upon the general spirit, you might have the result of a people, but you must observe closely, for there [23] are many sides in general to a people, more than to the best individuals; so that the individual should first have developed in himself, at least the spirit of these activities; he might let the mechanical part go, and not miss his judgement. A branch of industry pushed to a high degree must affect the general spirit of a people.

Sunday 17th October

In the night a breeze sprung up, so that we made fair headway. This morning it is quite fresh, and we passed Cerigo[18] {between} about 8 and 9. We have gone 8 miles an hour at times; the weather is cloudy and damp, at times rain. The wind has continued good all day, but the weather is disagreeable. Towards [24] evening it became slacker and in the first part of the night we made no great headway; it was squally and changeable. The day, although Sunday, has passed away about as the others. The most material difference was that the people shaved. There were no prayers or any religious ceremony. In the evening we did not, however, play whist. Consequently it was rather tiresome. I have felt lazy and stupid all day, so that I have done scarcely anything.

---

[18] Cerigo, modern Kythera, is an island off Cape Malea, the southernmost tip of the Peloponnesus.

Monday 18th October

This morning we have a fine breeze again. The wind a little east of north; but there is a disagreeable swell which impedes something the vessel's course. About 11 there came on a strong shower of rain. [25] After that the wind became rather faster, the sky clear, and the weather fine, and we are now going on five or six miles; the rain had the effect also of allaying somewhat the swell. At twelve o'clock we were latitude 36-30 N. by 19-53 East, 266½ miles from Malta.

The breeze lasted till evening and went down after dark. We made some slight headway however, during the night. In the evening we had a game of whist. I have had today a great hatred for doing anything, and I have done about nothing. I have read but little, and thought none at all. A sea voyage is a tiresome thing, take it any way. The sea effects me in such a way that I have no feeling for study on board of ship. I [26] feel lazy and sleepy, particularly when it rocks. I must have land, freedom to be alone when I wish it.

Tuesday 19th October

This morning the wind sprung up again about 6 or 7 o'clock and became rather fresh about 10. We have been going 8 miles an hour. At noon we were 36–20–15 N., 17–27–46 E., 147 miles from Malta. The wind kept strong, and lasted all day, and through the night.

The name of the Captain is Triescott, and {he} lives at Portsmouth, or rather at a place right opposite to it, and but a very short distance from it. He is a man who has quickness and activity in his motions and who has the faculty of commanding. He [27] makes things move, but take him in the reign of ideas and you find him nothing; he believes in all the religious superstitions etc. He reads but little, as I presume, for I found no books on board. He has thought but very little upon that which is created by thought. Otherwise, he is a smart, active, and persevering fellow.

The English officers of the Navy do not appear so hospitable and polite, as those of the Russian Navy. The difference is this: in the first place, the latter give you a passage and they think but very little about {it}. They are not difficult, whereas with the English, it is difficult. [28] They don't like to do it, and they consider it as a great trouble. Also, with regard to eating, if you make something of a passage, they expect you to join in, and make part of the mess, which is very just. This the Russians, however, never expect, but then, they have very fair table money, which the English have not. The differences are naturally to be explained. The Russians are fond of novelty, because they are yet new in the thing, and thus they carry into the Navy the land spirit, and that is very hospitable. The English are not so fond of strangers and novelty; those of the Navy are impregnated with its spirit, which is quick [29] and decided, and has less urbanity in it than the land spirit.

With regard to talents, you find the English more hardy. They are better sailors, but the greatest difference is between the sailors; it is less between the officers. The English sailors are better, they will do what the Russian ones cannot; there is more spirit, more enterprise among them. They are also more obstreperous, less obedient, and less manageable. They get higher wages, and when they are punished, it is much more severely so. I have seen men of talents among the Russians, but the English are better adapted, however, for good Navy officers. That certain mechanical enterprise and tact, so [30] peculiar to the English, is better calculated to make good seamen. But it now requires interest to a great degree to get advancement in the Navy, and I think it sours and tends to damp the Navy Spirit. Everyone speaks of it as a thing well known and the only manner of rising.

I think there must, before a great while, be a revolution in England. The general organization of society and the light in which one class stands in, with regard to the other, must produce some change. I am surprised only it has lasted so long. When it {the revolution} begins, it will have different principles for its movers. Aristocracy, and inequality of property, and the principle of individual material welfare, [31] will however be the leading ones. I should, for one, like to see it come. The general advancement of the spirit of nations interests me too much to wish to see it stopped for individual welfare. England must be baptized with the spirit of the new century, behind which it is lagging. She has too much of the middle age in her; she holds too much to old forms, usages and practices. There is more mechanical than spiritual about her, more exterior than interior.

Wednesday 20th October

The wind continued brisk all night, and this morning early, Malta hove in sight, and before 9 o'clock A.M. [32] we were there, and cast anchor in the quarantine bay. The land of Malta is not high, so that it is not seen at a great distance. The island spreads itself out before you, with one or two little adjoining ones. You see the city, with houses scattered along the shores to the right and left of it. You see no trees, but the shape of the buildings and their light colored stone shining in the sun produces a lively and handsome effect.

In arriving I wrote a note to our consul, requesting him to call down to the Parlatorio[19] on the city side. My object was to get money from him. He came down, and I found him a good looking and gentlemanly [33] man. He gave me the money immediately that I had need of, without any hesitation; he took me upon my looks. The Captain has been hurrying very much to arrange his officers to start their evening. Everything has been in a state of constant command and confusion, but I doubt whether he gets off tonight.

I spent a part of the day at the Parlatorio, walking about and doing nothing. The first thing I did was to get some fruit, which I ate with the greatest pleasure, as I had been without since leaving Nauplia. The young midshipmen bought a good many things but particular brandy and spirits.

At the Parlatorio was quite [34] a large number of people, some to sell, some to do errands. The noise they made was terrible, all talking together, bawling out if you wished to buy this thing or that; they showed at heart an eager desire of gaining money. I dined on board, and left about 5 o'clock for the Lazaretto. It is a complete prison. At sunset they lock you in, and you might as well be a felon, as suspected of having any contagious disorder.[20]

---

[19] The American consul in Malta was Eynard, later mentioned by name. Italian *parlatorio* usually means the visiting room of a prison, or the parlor of a school or convent. Here it seems to mean a promenade or market place where the inmates of the quarantine are permitted to meet outsiders.

[20] The Lazaretto (quarantine) was a Venetian invention for the prevention of the spread of plague and other infectious diseases. Arriving passengers were required to be quarantined for a certain number of days, depending on the ship's port of origin, to determine if they had any infectious disease. At the time Brisbane was incarcerated there, a scaffold used to hang those who attempted to escape quarantine stood near the Lazaretto.

I passed the evening in writing and reading but went to bed a little after 9. It will be rather tiresome, but as I have plenty to write and something to read, besides, as a person can think everywhere, I hope to get through [35] the thing without much *ennui*.

Thursday 21st October

I was not up very early, as I had nothing to hurry me, and you are as well off with your head on the pillow as upon your feet. The weather is fine, and the vessel I came in has already gone.

I have something more to say to say about the Greeks, and I will begin with their physiognomy. You find among the Greeks a difference of face, as is the case with every people, but in their differences you however find a resemblance, so that the Greeks have a national physiognomy. Their cast of looks approaches perhaps nearest to that of the French, but it also differs [36] much from {it} in many respects. You rarely find among the peasants of either sex a handsome face. Among the richer classes you find a clearer physiognomy; the features better marked, more harmony in the face, and more regularity, but it is still the same face, only perfectioned. You find in the Greek face, a great many lines, but they are not those of expression, they are dry. I have remarked them in very young children, and they become more distinct as they grow older. Between the eyebrows, about the sides of the nose, upon the forehead, around the mouth, you find these dry lines. Why they are there, and whether it is a thing in the flesh I cannot tell, but it is very general, [37] although you find many exceptions, and that mostly in the richer classes.

Discontent, so peculiar to the Greek character, hard life, and their constant uneasy desire of bettering their individual situation, may in part account for it. Among the peasants you find a great many ugly faces; without harmony, without any characteristics of finer feelings, with discontent and miserableness marked upon them, but you rarely meet a stupid, unmeaning face, as among the Austrian peasants. You always find the features of their face more or less characteristically marked, in order to save them from the appellation of stupid.

You find in the eyebrows [38] and the eye, mostly, something which gives an expression to them. The eyebrow is the best thing you generally find in their faces, and it is mostly clearly defined and has a determined form, that is, it is not formless and indistinct. You scarcely ever find red in the cheeks of a Greek, either man, or woman. The women are of a pale brownish hue, and the men a deeper color. You very rarely find among the Greeks a strong, open countenance. There is always something that is wanting, something out of harmony. It is the same thing with their character.

You find the aquiline nose the most common. The blue eye, or rather dark blue or grey, [39] is also common. The hair generally brown, rarely very black, or very light. The form of the head is not so marked as the European head. They seem very often too far back and not broad enough on top, the forehead even, that is, without projections, or bumps. This is very often the case, although there are exceptions, as well as there are men of mind and talents among the Greeks.

The Greeks are laborious when they have a reward immediately before their eyes. Still, it is said, they are lazy, but as they have a great desire of gain, I think they will suffer and work for it. The Greek is fond of [40] pleasure and enjoyment, but a material kind of pleasure. If they can escape from work, and eat well, amuse themselves at games, and boisterously, they are contented. You find very rarely among them that higher pleasure of finer feelings, or of the thoughts, which shows that a material miserableness surrounds them. They try to escape that, and plunge into its contradiction, that is, into material enjoyment. They produce nothing with regard to sciences, arts, or any kind of learning.

Perhaps a people must be materially happy, that is, they must have their wants easily satisfied, they must not have the picture of material miserableness constantly about them, in order to go [41] above it and search the pleasure of higher, (or, as I might say, of exterior) feeling, such as exists in the arts. There it is exterior to us. It is not in ourselves, as is the case with the enjoyment of the senses, or to search the pleasure of the thought as it is developed in the sciences, etc. We must pass beyond the pleasure arising from the immediate satisfaction of the senses, so common to a people surrounded by great material wants, in order to feel the want of, or wish for, this higher pleasure of exterior feeling and the thoughts.

The Greeks do not feel this pleasure. The material one, the enjoyment of the senses, [42] is as yet the degree which they are in, and their civilization is also at that point. Material wants are so great, that the individual satisfaction of them demands all their efforts.

The Greeks are great talkers. They are always gabbing. When there are several together you will hear half of them talking at the same instant, one louder than the other and making a great noise. In this respect also, they resemble the French. The Greeks talk generally very loud, and when they dispute about the price of anything, which appears one great occupation of their tongues, their manner of reasoning is most noisy and violent. [43] The peasants are very fond of telling you their hardships; how much they have to work, how heavy taxes etc. they have to pay, and their misfortunes, if they have had any. They are always complaining, and are not in harmony with government. Some regret these persons or those, many the Turks even; but they all wish government to give them plenty to eat and drink, and put money in their hands. The aim of government and liberty appears to them only that.

As yet the Greeks take no interest in what is exterior to themselves. Individual welfare is the direction of all their efforts. No side of the mind, nor [44] of its activities, are developed with thought. Whatever is done, is not done for the thing, but the satisfaction of some individual want is its ulterior object. You find but very little strength of character among the Greeks. They bend easily; they are also easily won with money. They are said to possess but little bravery; in the open field or in single combat they will stand but little force. They also have great fear of authority.

I have passed the day and evening in writing and reading. I hope to get through with the fifteen days without much trouble, or *ennui*, particularly if I can get a girl [45] in quarantine with me, which I have set about. If she comes, it will be under the pretense of working, or making some shirts, or something of the kind.

Malta: Friday 22nd October

The weather is remarkably fine. There have arrived three vessels from different places in the Quarantine harbor. Also, yesterday, one American one from Boston. It has to perform five days quarantine; the quarantine jackasses!

I have sent a man off to see about getting a girl in quarantine with me. It is perhaps a foolish business, but as I have the desire, and as there is no society, I will do it. It is very probable that in a day or two, [46] after she is here, she will bother me, and I will wish to get rid of her. Although I think it, still I will do {it}, if it is practicable. Virtue is a thing for women, but it is well for everyone to follow it. Should I catch a ———— {disease} by sleeping with a girl, then I would praise virtue. Virtue is also one of the "going to heaven" principles.

Those who consider this life as only a preparation for the eternal, but individual one, that awaits what is termed the soul, which is neither the body nor the mind, generally search for her {virtue's} protection. I don't know, myself, what virtue is. I am not aware that a distinct definition is given of it. What society may often term virtue may be something [47] else. What is contrary to the forms of a society is unvirtuous, so that the affirmative principles of society are virtues, what it forbids the contrary. A virtuous man is {he} who acts according to the principles of society in which he lives. When we consider the merit of the world, we see it has advancement as one of its great principles. Whatever tends to restrain it and keep it stationary sins against it.

In all affirmative forms of society there is some vice, because those affirmative forms tend to preserve that particular form and retard progress. The virtuous man develops the affirmative principles in his own circle. [48] The vicious man affirms that the negative principles are also right, and that his society does not contain all the principles, known with regard to the present, but not with regard to futurity. The spirit of the world contains all principles. The virtuous man gives the lie to those which are not among his society, thus the virtuous man is good but finite; and the aim of finite goodness, virtue, etc. is to give man an eternal existence, an existence of pleasure, but at the same time it is individual, consequently an independent particularity in itself. What is eternal is general; individuality is finite. Thus the theory of giving the soul an individual [49] eternal existence is incompatible with itself.

But men rarely conceive that there is any pleasure for the individual unless he feels individually. The individual is the expression of a general principle. He expresses it by how it exists, but he only expresses it. The individuality stands there, not to contain the general principle, but to give it a form, an expression.

Thus with man the individual passes and comes. Its existence or per-ishableness with regard to man is indifferent, for its principle always sends new ones {individuals}. The individuality strives to retain its existence, but it [50] feels that it can only be finite, thus it makes a finite eternity. Thus the punishment of the individual who will not be interested with man, is to pass away and perish.[21]

Search the great and measure yourself upon the scale of your efforts!

I have passed the present day as yesterday. I have written various com-mencements of letters, etc. and read some. It was near eleven when I went to bed.

Saturday 23rd October

It rained very hard this morning for about an hour, then it cleared off and the weather again is beautiful. In the sun it is quite [51] hot, but the rooms of the quarantine are very large and entirely of stone, and I think that they must be cold, and rather damp. I don't feel it particularly, but I expectorate more phlegm since I am here. For two or three days back I have had an ani-mal excitement upon me, that is, I felt elated. At present, it is passed. I don't feel quite well; any little movement makes my blood run faster than com-mon through the veins. I don't feel much like writing or doing anything.

–at night–

In thought, we may become men while yet boys; but with regard to the body, years only can bring us to manhood.[22]

---

[21] Brisbane's moral philosophy consistently concerns itself with what is general, with the devel-opment of humanity as a whole, rather than with the condition of individuals or even indi-vidual communities. Perhaps this is why he preferred to operate on the most theoretical and abstract level. As often in these diaries as he expresses a longing to devote himself to some great work, he never became involved in the operations of any of the Fourierist communi-ties whose existence was owed in great part to his rhetorical efforts. Brisbane held noble sentiments towards humanity *en masse*, even though in his personal relationships, especially with women (particularly notable in this diary), he does not always seem to have observed the conventional morality of his day, or paid very great attention to the feelings of the object of his passions. Many of his philosophical digressions on virtue seem to occur at moments when his adolescent sexual drive is getting in the way of his plans for study and self-improvement. It is necessary to remember that he was only 21 when this diary was written.

[22] This remark and the attack of "animal excitement" mentioned above, may be related to the girl he has decided to procure (although we hear nothing more about her).

[52] *Sunday 24th October*

Today is Sunday and I have kept it holy by lazyness. I have done but little. However, I have had two or three ideas in my head, which I will later put in writing. I have read six numbers of the *Constitutionnel*. I think there will be rough waters still in Belgique. At least that country will succeed in getting great concessions, if not by pacific means, then by hostile ones.[23]

Monday 25th October

I have not felt myself very well today. I have a slight stiff neck, or pain in the muscles there. My body also is in a relaxed state. I have had but little feeling for any kind of activity. I have, however, read [53] a part of the *Logik* I took with Michelet over again.[24] I began also today the *History of Philosophy* by Rixner.[25] The method which he applies to the result of all philosophical methods has a great resemblance to the principles of Hegel. They both develop the principle that all philosophers, when classified, and their starting point, and their fundamental idea considered, hold a part of the truth in them, and that a constant progression, in harmony with their civilizations, has been going on; although with regard to time it may have receded back, but, however, afterwards to pass itself farther on. I find also, that some of [54] the earlier systems, as represented by Rixner, have a resemblance with some of the categories of Hegel's *Logik*. The Indian philosophy, I think, must be dressed up somewhat by the translators, for it strikes me as being too profound for that early age of the world.

Tuesday 26th October

The past night was very stormy; there was a very strong wind, accompanied with violent rain. This morning the sky was covered with vast volumes of

---

[23] The *Constitutionnel* was a prominent French newspaper of the liberal opposition to Louis-Philippe. Brisbane had probably become familiar with it at the Sorbonne. On the heels of the July Revolution in France, the Belgians revolted from the Kingdom of the Netherlands in August of 1830. Just three weeks before this diary entry, on October 4, 1830, Belgium had declared its independence, causing great alarm among the crowned heads of Europe.

[24] During his first winter in Berlin, Brisbane followed Hegel's lectures and studied his writings, including the *Logic*, under the guidance of Professor Michelet of the University of Berlin. See Introduction: 12–13, nn. 31, 34.

[25] Thaddeus A. Rixner (1766–1838) wrote widely on philosophy. His three-volume *Handbuch der Geschichte der Philosophie* had appeared in 1822–1823.

heavy clouds, but in the afternoon it cleared up and seems to promise fairer weather than we have had for a few days back.

I have [55] been reading Rixner nearly all day. I have got as far as the 63rd page. I am, at the present time, thinking again upon the plan of my play. I have a part of the ideas, but I cannot compose a plan for developing them.

Nature is governed by laws. Man governs himself by thought. The laws are applied to her exteriorly, and she follows them because her nature is susceptible of being acted on by them. Man finds in his own interior the thoughts which guide him; and, as he has conscience {consciousness} of them, he guides his activity by them.

[56] *Wednesday 27th October*

The weather this morning is fine, the wind has changed, and I think we will have a clear sky again. I have not felt very well for some few days past, but I got better again with the weather. I have been writing and reading today as common.

In the evening I read a part of *Don Carlos*. It pleases me better than it did at first, but Schiller cannot be compared to Goethe. There are some very handsome things in it, but there is not that ideal you find in some of Goethe's plays. The language is not so simple and is more worldly; with Schiller there is more studied effect of feeling and passion. [57] With Goethe you find interior nature and thought flowing abundantly out without effort. I think {no} thought upon anything could be deeper, no long detailed account could equal, the few words in *Don Carlos*, where Princess Eboli says to the Priest: "*Obschon Sie mir bewiesen, dasz Fälle möglich wären, wo die Kirche sogar die Körper ihrer jungen Töchter für höhre Zwecke zu gebrauchen wüszte.*"[26] Nothing can equal it. In Schiller, as well as in Goethe, you find that idea predominant, that high individual perfection and an inte-

---

[26] "... though you proved to me there were some cases possible in which the Church knew how to use the very bodies of its youthful daughters for some higher goal." Schiller, F.: *Plays; Don Carlos*, tr. A. Leslie and Jeanne R. Willson, New York, 1983: 175-76. All German translations and references are courtesy of Professor Harry Piotrowski of Towson University. Here Brisbane refers to the great German Romantic poets, J. C. Friedrich von Schiller (1759-1805) and J.Wolfgang von Goethe (1749–1832). Brisbane had been deeply impressed by the aged Goethe, whom he met in June of 1829 in Weimar. (*MB*: 79–80) Goethe's *Italian Journey*, published in 1816, may well have provided a model for Brisbane's diary.

rior constant striving to reach that perfection should be our aim. I think with them, but often forget it, as I forget myself.

[58] *Thursday 28th October*

The weather fine; saw the American consul, who was at the Lazaretto upon some business. He is to send the newspapers tomorrow. I am leading such a still quiet life in this place, that if I don't mark down the ideas that pass through my mind, I will have nothing to write, for there are no actions. I go to bed about 10, up about 8, breakfast at 9½ or 10, dine not far from 5, and the rest of the time is passed in reading and writing.

Friday 29th October

Some extracts of a letter to my father:[27]

With regard to antiquities, there are but few in the Morea, {the Peloponnesus} and do in no degree repay the [59] trouble of searching them out. I performed that journey in order to see the actual state of the country and get an idea of the futurity Greece may offer, but there is no striking futurity reserved for her. She will not take a part again in history, neither will she meddle more with the general affairs of the world. She will exist interiorly, supporting her inhabitants, but she will create nothing; she will produce no exterior results.

There is more mountainous land in Greece than plains. The former is incapable of being cultivated, and the soil of the plains and valleys, even, is far from being of the first [60] rate. It seems to have but little strength in it, as if exhausted. The crops it produces are thin, and want weight and substance. The general characteristic of the soil is stoniness. You always find gravel, hard yellow clay, or quantities of little loose stones, and the soil is very much intermixed with these. The mountains in general are nothing but rocks, and oppose an insurmountable barrier to internal improvements. Besides, there is but little water in the country; there exists scarcely a stream that is not completely dried up in the summer. [61]

When I consider our country, the vastness of her soil, the great facilities and rewards she offers for gigantic internal improvements, the force of

---

[27] Brisbane's father, James Brisbane, settled in Batavia, New York, in 1801. See Introduction: 7–9.

nature that reigns there, and the spirit of enterprise and activity that animates her inhabitants, capable of developing all that force; when I take that general view of her, and find it so vast, Greece like a speck vanishes from the sight, and in every wish towards her you become indifferent, her highest result being in comparison too small to interest you.

With regard to a republic, Greece is as yet a [62] good distance from it, both in fact and in principle. Capodistrias is called President, but he is in reality dictator. The republican form of government as we understand the thing, at the present day, requires various conditions of political knowledge and improvement among the people. France is immeasurably before Greece in civilization, and the late events show that her political education is not yet great enough to support that *forme*. [28]

Saturday 30th October

Further extracts from the same:

There exists but little general feeling among the [63] Greeks. Each one seems to strive individually for himself and, as I said, I believe, in one of my former letters, the thing that least interests the public is the public itself. Capodistrias is liked by some and disliked by others. Those who are in office and employed by him, praise him up to the skies. Those, on the contrary, who have met losses in the revolution, or for other reasons wish to be employed and are not, are very much dissatisfied with the present government. Among the peasants, again, you find many who regret the Turks! They would rather see them back, for under them, which is true, their taxes were less.

This individual interest seems to be the rule of judging, the [64] scale upon which everything is measured. The lower classes look upon government and liberty as things which should put money in their hands without their troubling themselves much about earning it. But the peasants are industrious when they have a reward directly before their eyes. They will work hard for money, but as money is not always to be worked for in the country, you find a good many of them lounging away their time. Added to that, they have a great many holy days of religious ordinance, which they keep scrupulously. The living of the peasants is very poor. Brown bread and

---

[28] Brisbane frequently uses the French word *forme* to mean convention or system.

cheese, both bad in their way, together with a few onions, form [65] their common nourishment.

You never find beds in their houses. They sleep on the floor, with a piece of carpet or mat under them. In short, their state is {so} much inferior to that of our farmers, both mentally and materially, that they cannot be compared together. I was searching for a standard of comparison between them, but it is not to be applied. But the physical formation of the country is one cause of this; the Turkish system, under which they have grown up, another.

There are no internal improvements whatsoever. They have the worst possible agricultural machines and the worst system of agriculture. When they have raised their crops they cannot carry them to any market at a [66] distance, because there are no roads, except for mules and horses, and the portage would take off the profits. Thus the productions of a valley are consumed there. They bring but little from the exterior, and send less in return. In the interior the few boards necessary to build the floors, etc. of a house, must often be brought twenty miles distant, and two at a time upon jackasses. There is not a wagon in all Greece. This gives you an idea how completely everything must be done in the most difficult manner. Consequently the country must be very poor. Machines are like banks; you get double the interest of the force employed.

But, notwithstanding all these difficulties, the Greeks [67] stand up against them with a good deal of courage. If they have a resemblance with any people of Europe it is with the French; and they have some particularities of the French character in them. Their manner of talking particularly strikes you. It is loud and quick, and when several are together, they talk all at once, making a great clatter, very much like Frenchmen. A Greek is generally noisy when he talks, and has a good deal {of} swagger; this is observable among those who are rather {well} off.

With regard to classes, there are three principal divisions: the peasants, who live in the interior, and cultivate the land; those who live near the water, and lead a sea-faring life; and another [68] class who inhabit the towns and make a living by shopkeeping, and various trades. Among these you find those individuals who are the best off. There are also a good many priests and some soldiers, but they cannot be said to make a class. They are a branch only. You also find some few individuals, who have received an European education, and who might be said to be of the European civilization, but their number is small. Many of them are not employed by the present government, because they have the ambition themselves to be the rulers.

There are but very few persons in Greece who are rich. With the exception of three or four merchants in the islands, who are known to possess considerable wealth, you will very [69] rarely meet a Greek who is worth a thousand dollars.[29] A country must be very poor when it offers so few resources to its individuals.

You will be surprised, perhaps, when I tell you, that in all Greece, there is not a town or city, which with regard to beauty, the goodness of its houses, its resources, taverns, travelling facilities, etc. is equal to our village of Batavia. More newspapers are printed there than in all Greece, there being only two in the latter country. The smallest tavern in Batavia is better than the first one in Nauplia, the capital. Nauplia contains more inhabitants. It is also a seaport, but notwithstanding that, Batavia possesses more resources, and does more business. [70] Consequently, when the capital of Greece is not equal to Batavia, you may imagine what Greece is in comparison with the United States!

Malta: Sunday 31st October

The Turkish civilization at the present day is uninteresting, a mere blank.[30] The reason is because there exists among the people no intellectual activity or movement. (If it interests us, it is in a negative way. It is to see a civilization, in which intellectual activity is replaced by the principles of habit, and religious rules.) The Turks perfect nothing, neither do they try to perfect anything. Arts, sciences, all kinds of improvements, etc. are neglected; whatever is done, is done by habit. They have [71] necessity and the instinct of man to guide them. With such principles to act from, a people can develop nothing with perfection. Higher activities of the intelligence

---

[29] A successful farmer of Batavia, such as James Brisbane, might be worth several thousand dollars.

[30] The Ottoman empire in 1830 included Turkey, central Greece, the Balkans, Syria-Palestine and Egypt. The ruler was Sultan Mahmud II. The empire was politically and militarily in its decline, constantly obliged to fend off European and Russian attempts to interfere in its internal affairs.

are forgotten, because they require higher principles than habit and neces-sity. They require mental activity.

Consequently when you look at the Turkish civilization, you find noth-ing going on there. It is a void. There is no one point you can seize hold of, and say, "Here is one side of the intelligence they are developing; they are bettering their national constitutions; they are improving their politi-cal state, or are making internal improvements, etc." No, all is a dead calm, undisturbed by the movements of a higher [72] civilization. Such is the Turkish civilization.

Exteriorly there is a resemblance between it and the Greek civilization, although interiorly different principles have coincided to produce that effect. The latter civilization resembles the former in as much as it has, so far at least, produced nothing; I mean in arts, sciences, institutions, and such exterior things. We find no intellectual movement in the people tending towards higher objects. We find activity there, but it is the activity of each individual trying to better his own condition. This was the principle of the Greek Revolution.

By driving off the Turks, they thought to come in possession of all their [73] property. Religious prejudices were also active, but spiritual objects were not the moving principles of that war. Liberty of opinion, freedom of conscience, election rights, inviolability of the laws, freedom of the press, etc., such things as characterized the late events of France, were not what they fought for. As they had never had them, they had not conscience of the want of them; or, rather, their civilization was not advanced enough to reach those particulars, or feel those wants.

Greece will produce little in the intellectual world, (that which is in opposition with the material one, or existence). To live will require all the efforts of the individual, [74] and leave him no time for other objects. Material wants must first be satisfied, before men go to look for those of a spiritual nature. Since Greeks imagine, with a kind of enthusiasm, that their country may return again toward some epochs of its former glory, if future favorable circumstances arise. But they are not aware that a country is a continual development, a continual progression, be it towards perfection or degeneration, and what it has already once done, it will not do or realize a second time. An epoch, once passed, remains with the time in which it once existed. It is a bad thing for a people to have [75] a passed world behind them. They turn their backs to futurity to look at its brilliant epochs, and forget the present, to strive to return to them again. With us {America} the passed does not yet exist. We must face futurity; we cannot look behind, and all our efforts tend to create that world of realized intelligence, (which is the arts, sciences, laws, institutions etc.) that lies before us as a nation to accomplish.

Architecture has no model in nature like sculpture and painting. It is a complete product of the mind. It might be called the science of lines, for you have nothing [76] but lines to attain and express its beauty. Feature and coloring do not help you here. That beauty which should be found in the fine arts in general, is not so easily to be judged of, and appreciated, as is commonly supposed. The individual does by no means find in his natural feelings, or uncultivated taste, a standard of judgement; very much the contrary. For that real beauty, which should animate a work of art, is not the result of simple imagination and unpolished fancy. It is the result of something higher. It is the result of the Thought having conscience of, and contemplating the beauty [77] in nature, but going out beyond it and idealizing it. It is the result also of something else besides this, even. But that something, I do not myself know how to define.

It requires a great deal of study to understand the theory of the fine arts, and to know what the artist should endeavor to attain in them, but more still to execute. The arts are always in harmony with the intellectual cultivation of a people, out of which they spring. They are one of its developments. So for example, in very religious times we see most pictures painted to represent scenes of Hell, Heaven, the saints, and all such [78] religious machinery. By observing their progress we have one of the signs of that civilization. Considered in this light, they occupy a higher place and have more value than this world commonly gives them. We do not, then, look upon them as mere casual products of a willful fancy, having no other rules before it than to create what pleases and no higher aim than a simple imitation of the natural objects around it.

Capodistrias is a man about fifty, I should judge. His hair is perfectly white although his eyebrows remain black. His face is thin but well formed and indicative of talent. [79] He appears to be still a very active man. At the Russian court he filled a high station for ten or eleven years, so that his manner of speaking and manners are polished and easy. The first time I saw him, I had a conversation of about two hours with him. He talks a great deal. He appeared to be frank to quite a high degree, for he did not seem to hide his views, and he spoke very plainly upon subjects in general, political as well as others.

One great difficulty, he said, was to find men capable of holding public offices. As the grown up persons had been brought up in the Turkish school, they had no system, nor knew nothing of it. When he wanted a man he had to educate [80] him again, and from the highest clerk to the lowest under him, he had to be training them constantly. Thus he had to overlook everything himself. He said he wanted time to educate men to put system and regularity in the government, for at present he could not find civil officers, capable of taking charge of a department, and managing it properly. He praised very much the youth of Greece, but did not seem to think much of the present generation of grown up people.

Against the politics of England he seems to have distrust. He does not think she is open, and frank in her views towards Greece. Capodistrias has always led a diplomatic life, and I think he has management [81] and address rather than a strong character. A man, to push forward a people, must possess energy and force of character. He must throw himself, as it were, into the spirit of that people, and drag it along with him in his progress, but Capodistrias looks upon the Greeks as a people to correct, and the position he takes, as you no doubt will feel, must hinder him in a higher or less degree from entering into their spirit. Having him accustomed to the organization of the European states, and the contrast between it, and that of the Greeks, has impressed him most probably with that feeling.

Monday 1st November

Today is the beginning of a new month. I have but three days more to remain in [82] this place, that is, in the quarantine, and the idea of being released so soon gave me quite a gay feeling. The weather has been fine, but I observe that at this season of the year there are very sudden, and very heavy, rain showers.

During the past month I have changed scenes often, and some new ideas have come into my mind, but still I have been stationary a good deal. Taking it all together, however, I have not gained or advanced much. It has been rather a quiet month. Where I shall be the first day of the coming month I don't know precisely, but I set down Naples, or within a few days of it.

[83] *Malta: Tuesday 2nd November*

The day is as beautiful as I ever saw one. The sky is cloudless, the sun shines brightly, but without scorching heat. More lovely and more agreeable weather could not be found. I would like to be out to enjoy it. The temperature of the present day, is the most delightful, the most to be wished. It is equally poised, a gay day, and lovely without overbearing heat.

What is the reason, that it is so difficult to realize in a practical institution the theoretical principles of the same? How is it that, more than two thousand years ago, theories of institutions were in the world which required that length of time after them to make them [84] practical?[31] To realize an idea practically among people is no doubt very difficult. To realize the theory of an institution requires that all the inharmonious interests of the different individuals should be leveled, before it can go into effect. To go from a monarchical government to a Republican form; what a step it requires! When we think, what a change must take place in a vast quantity of particular interests! All these interests are so many ideas, which must be leveled and brought in harmony with the great idea, before it can {come} fully into effect.

The difficulty of realizing institutions lies often with the individuals who are charged with rendering it practical. Their ideas are not in harmony with the [85] head idea. Consequently in order that they may not destroy it, it is necessary that they should be shut up in *formes*. Thus the institutions must take *formes*, which remain indifferent to circumstances. Thus {you} can often find stupid formality in them. The reason, more or less, is because the individual cannot put them in practice. Thus, an institution must have the principle of existence and application within itself. It must first act exteriorly, that is

---

[31] Presumably Brisbane is thinking here of the length of time it has taken for a republican form of government to be realized in Europe, two thousand years after it had first appeared in Rome. The problem of the practical versus the theoretical would play a great role in his final decision to embrace Fourierism in place of Saint-Simonianism.

its aim; but its interior arrangement must be so, that it must act exteriorly, and in such a certain manner. If *formes* were not forcibly given to men to act in, there [86] would be a terrible confusion in the world, so few are the persons, who have an idea of the relativeness between them, and objects around.

Formes are, in a great many cases, realized ideas of good, but these are *formes* for the different activities of the mind, for the thought will develop itself. Men will consent to walk in any *formes* to gain their object, but they will not consent to not gain it.

Malta: Wednesday 3rd November

The present day has been as fine as that of yesterday; tomorrow and my quarantine is ended. I have been today uneasy, impatient. I have not been able to study or pay attention to anything steadily. It is my old feeling of impatient [87] uneasiness, which costs me a good many hours.

I think in my future life I shall have that disease called the gravel, or stone. However, I consider that I should not have it; according to the chances of hazard and luck it does not fall to my share. I have already lost one eye,[32] and have gone through different bodily infirmities, so that I think, according to the chances of hazard, I should be absolved. Several hazards have been realized upon me; it would be singular should that one also.

Thursday 4th November

Today the quarantine is ended. Tomorrow I leave. When they brought in my bill, they had put me down [88] for the whole sum, although two persons had come at the same time. I asked, why I had to pay the whole amount? They answered, because the others could not pay, they were poor. "Then," I said, "let the government pay for them. I, as an individual, am less bound to do it than it." They did not relish it much, but as I kept firm, saying, "Show me the written rules, and I will comply." As they would not

---

[32] This remark is extraordinary. Nowhere else does Brisbane record that he had "lost an eye." Two weeks earlier (Diary I: 15, October 16, 1830) he complained that his eye was bothering him, but his portraits show him possessing two eyes. In 1833 his use of a glass eye seems to have been regarded by his acquaintances as an affectation. Beard: *Letters*, volume II: 371. The only support for Brisbane's loss of an eye is his brother George's characterization of him in later years as a "one-eyed pimp." R. Pettitt: "Albert Brisbane, Apostle of Fourierism in the United States 1834-90," Ph.D. Thesis, Oxford, Ohio 1982.

show any such law, they had to give in. I paid two thirds, but they afterwards made one of the other persons pay the other third.

I paid, for the room: $4. My part for the guardian: $6, less one shilling. He has two shillings and six pence per day. I paid [89] eighteen pence of it per day. The length of the Quarantine is 14 days.

The days you arrive and go out are reckoned, which leaves 15, net.

Malta: Friday 5th November

I left the Lazaretto at about seven this morning and came to Valletta, the city's name, and am staying at Miralif's Hotel. The first thing I observe is that the streets are regularly laid out, running crosswise, some wider than others, also not all of a length. They are well paved. The houses are well built, and have a good deal of uniformity. They are plain, all of stone. When ornaments are used they are in the Italian taste. The walls are generally plain, having a crowning sinus and the sinus on the windows.[33] The houses are high, having almost all balconies. [90] The second observation was that there were a great many churches and that their bells make a great clanging. The third, that there are about as many priests as whores, and the number of the one is so considerable, that you have difficulty to imagine the other can be so numerous. You see images stuck up everywhere, at the corners of streets, and other places.[34]

Of all things I hate is the Catholic religion, and the priestcraft spirit. Respect the prejudices of others, they say, but I say no! Cut to the quick, where there is stupidity, and obscurity; and those who have loaded themselves with prejudices, let them suffer for [91] having them.[35] Up to our present day we have seen there must be some religion, or the name of some, in a country. Since there must be something of the Lord, then let it be in the Protestant *forme.*

---

[33] Sinus: a rounded molding at the top of a wall or around a window.

[34] These were the Maltese *nicci*, holy images erected on building facades, which included a receptacle for coins, to ensure the answering of prayers.

[35] Brisbane's opinion of Catholicism fluctuated. He expressed strong dislike for Catholic superstition in Malta and Italy, but later, in Germany, seemed to find Catholic architecture inspiring. See Diary II: 90–92, November 9, 1831. He ended by marrying a Bavarian Catholic, Adèle LeBrun, whom his parents at first refused to receive. See Introduction: 16, 19, 21.

There is less *forme* and nonsense in it, it is more in harmony with the present state of intellectual cultivation, the priests have less influence, they are not so sectical. In short, the Catholic religion disgusts me most completely. I have the completest aversion for those priests and friars, often vile minded, and full of passions, base and low, and restricting them mechanically, according to certain rules, which are followed, not according to the spirit, but to the word.

Malta: Saturday 6th November

[92] I have today been walking about the city. I also have ordered some articles of clothing, a pair of pantaloons {for} which I pay $8, a waistcoat $3, etc. I dined again with M. Eynard, and went to the theater with him. He appears to be very polite towards Americans. The play at the theater was without interest, and some of the things applauded were the most foolish and miserable. There is but little higher cultivation among the Maltese, a superstitious, religious, money-catching race, with more priests, whores, and beggars in their city, than in any other of its size I ever saw. It is a complete hotbed for such plants.

[93] How rare it is to find among men a feeling for something higher than existence! How rare is it to find those who seek objects for the mind, and work at matters in the regions of intellectual activity. The people have to work hard to earn money. That is, there are so many of them, and every kind of industry is resorted to. You see a great many miserable objects in the streets, and you don't see many signs of riches among the native inhabitants.

The physiognomy of the man is without intelligence; you see bad formed faces, vacant ones, and also, as I would term it, those of compact unconsciousable flesh. [94] You observe faces, with deep black eyes, black eyebrows distinctly marked, and they seem to have but one look, as if but one idea could find places in their mind. The inhabitants are of a bad blood, and bad race. There appears no elasticity in their nature, no flexibility of mind, superstitiously religious, linked with other circumstances, makes them without elasticity of intellect. They produce, and have produced, but few men, I believe, of distinction. The Greek peasants, for example, are much superior in intelligence, quickness and action than the Maltese.

Malta: Sunday 7th November

[95] The weather has been rather changeable. I have done nothing in particular, walked about some, looked at the women, there being a good many people in the streets. I saw some handsome female countenances. Dined with Eynard. There were several persons invited to dinner, among the rest two sisters, one of which was handsome, and she appeared in her nature good and pleasing. She had a pretty face; the features well formed, no complicated beauty; no lines in the face. Smooth, simple of shape, denoting a good nature within, but also simple, that is, kind, obliging, affectionate; but not a nature of feelings of a rarer kind such as [96] the feelings of the thought's nature, as for music, painting, or other certain activities of the thought. I talked with her with pleasure during a part of the evening. Carlton, is, I believe, the name.

Malta Monday 8th November

Today I have been to the old city, as it is termed.[36] It is a place offering nothing interesting, with the exception of the catacombs. They are passages hewn under ground in the rock by the Saracens.[37] You see how the rooms are disposed to receive the dead, but all the bodies have been taken out. The thing offers otherwise no particular interest. I saw the churches, which the inhabitants look upon with admiration, but there was nothing [97] worthy of notice.[38] There were some paintings, but of not much merit. There were

---

[36] Mdina, or Citta Vecchia, 7 miles west of Valletta, was Malta's capital before the Knights of Malta built Valletta in the sixteenth century. The Order of the Military and Hospitaller Knights of St John of Jerusalem, (the order's full title) was originally founded to care for pilgrims to the Holy Land. The Knights took vows of celibacy and poverty, and only Catholic noblemen could aspire to join the Order. They ruled Rhodes until driven from the island by the Ottoman Sultan Suleiman "The Magnificent" in 1522. Their control of Malta lasted from 1530 to 1798, during which time the island was a Christian bastion against the Ottoman fleet as well as the Barbary pirates. The Knights lost Malta to Napoleon in 1798, and it became a British colony in 1800. The Order still exists, and its present Grand Master is a Scot.

[37] The extensive catacombs of Mdina were built as Christian burial places from the first to the eighth centuries AD. (The Saracens took the island in AD 870.) Brisbane later describes his visit to the monastery crypt: ". . . the skeletons of the departed monks, stuck up upon their feet in prayerful attitude, were about as fascinating as they could reasonably be expected to be under the trying circumstances of the case." (*MB*: 136)

[38] This may have been the Cathedral of St Paul in Mdina, built at the end of the seventeenth century. (*MB*: 136)

a large number of {illegible} and images of Christ and his mother, very badly done, perfect monsters, which the fellow who unlocked the door took great pains to show me. Seeing what they were, I took no notice, nor would look at those he showed me afterwards, at which he was very angry. He saw I had a contempt of the things, and he grumbled a good deal.

I returned home after about six hours ride, very much fatigued, and a kind of stiffness in my back, at the neck, and a lame feeling across the hips. I don't know what is the matter with me, it may {be} rheumatic affliction. [98] The quantity of beggars you see is astonishing. You find as many in the country as in the city; you pass but few persons who don't cry out, miserable, little children as well as men, and both healthy and strong looking. Last night as I was coming through the street, a fellow, a young lad, asking me if I did not want a girl, and seeing I paid no attention to him, followed me to the door of the hotel, and asked me if I would not give him a penny to buy some bread, which I did.

Malta: Tuesday 9th November

Last night passed the evening at home, as I did not feel well. My body seemed bruised and lame. The day has been fine, and [99] I have been running about doing nothing in particular. I have bought some articles, wrote a letter to Manesca,[39] and sent one already written to my father. I have done nothing intellectual today, in fact, for some days back. I have had no new idea, or at least my mind has been employed other ways.

I said this to myself today in German, *"Gefallen ist bei mir nicht das Wort denn was uns gefällt ist uns ähnlich, uns gleicht, und anderen zu gleichen, das heisst, sich selbst nicht sein; was gerade die Aufgabe ist."*[40] Dined with Eynard, went afterwards to Mr Carlton's. I went to see his pretty daughter. She is pretty, but I should know that I was not [100] made to live with a woman. I am too easily put out of the idea of the thing, too accustomed to change. On sleeping with any woman one night, I consider three must pass, before the desire would take me again, and so on, until it would not take me at all.

---

[39] Jean Manesca, Brisbane's former teacher.
[40] "The word is not to my liking, because what is to our liking has a resemblance to us and is like us, and to be like others means not to be oneself; that is precisely the task." If this is a quotation, it has not been identified.

The desire is strong before possession, and possession destroys immediately its value. I never slept with a woman whom I could support afterwards.

I talked with Miss Carlton, and, as the custom is to shake hands here, her shake was warm, a press, a squeeze. There was feeling in her fingers' ends, and her look was so clear, so entire, so feeling! What would be her kiss?

[101] *Malta Wednesday 10th November*

Goethe says: "*Der Mensch ist dem Menschen des interessanteste, und sollte ihn vielleicht ganz allein interresieren. Alles andere, was uns umgibt, ist entweder nur Element, in dem wir leben, oder Werkzeug, dessen wir uns bedienen.*"[41]

So say I, and so am I in feeling. To me, the landscape looks void; it is only color and shape. It is still. It produces but a smile, a feeling of bodily pleasure, whereas a thought well developed excites in you a deeper pleasure of surprise, of satisfaction. You find a new view upon the mind. The principle of acting, the view on the aim of life is widened. [102] Thinking about the rules of conduct, I said to myself today, "Act as you think, and think nobly."

Today I have done nothing but buy a few articles. My neck has troubled me a good deal. Going the least in the wind makes it worse. Dined at home, went afterwards to Eynard's who certainly is a very clever man, and his wife is a good natured woman, and also a certain natural force.

Went afterwards to Carlton's again, but the stiffness of my neck hindered me from being at my ease. The girl has to a certain degree a passion for me, not yet strong, but such a one as youth, [103] with its warmth, and imagination, is ready to bestow. Touch but the cord; the thing is there, and ready {to} expand itself. In later years, and after various cases, it is no more so. Then you must create it. You don't find it in her; it must go from you. Habit, and want (intellectual perhaps) are these principal ingredients. The first is the only true feeling. The latter is taste. I have known myself in a case, where I would have given anything to have possessed a woman, and when I asked myself if I loved her, I found that feeling did not exist in me.

---

[41] "For human beings, it is humans who are of greatest interest. Everything else that surrounds us consists of either the environment in which we live or the tools we use." Goethe, *Wilhelm Meisters Lehrjahre*, in Trunz, E. ed.: Goethes Werke, vol. 7, Munich, 1973: 101.

[104] *Malta: Thursday 11th November*

The weather is and has been uncommonly fine. It is as warm as spring, but there is something however, in the atmosphere, which has not that mildness, and renovation.

I was at the theater in the evening, they played the two Peters, but the thing was badly got up.[42] During the day I have done nothing except walking about a little and buying some few articles. The life I have led since I have been in Malta is the most inactive, unproductive. I have done nothing. I have been employed with nothing that was worth being employed at. The stiffness of my neck has in part [105] hindered me, but without it, it would have been nearly the same.

Malta: Friday 12th November

I requested M. Eynard to find me a passage for Sicily, and tomorrow, he informed me, a vessel was going. I will go first to Syracuse, and then to Messina perhaps. Today has passed like yesterday, a nothingness. But this kind of life could not last long. Were I for some time to be plunged into this inactivity, I would then rouse myself up, and the contrast would force {me} to double activity. In the afternoon I feel unwell, a kind of fever takes hold of me, although it is slight, and then my stiff neck begins.

[106] I was this evening at Mr Gat's. Eynard went there and introduced me to that gentleman. I went to Carlton's but did not find them in. My neck has troubled me more this evening than any other. The blood pulsing through it causes a throbbing pain.

Malta: Saturday 13th November

The weather is fine, as usual, and I was to leave this evening, but the captain has put it off till Monday, which does not please me in the least. I ought to have been in Sicily and nearly finished my quarantine by this time, but see what procrastination does. Not to delay is a rule hard to be followed. I dined with Eynard and went again to Carlton's, but the father had left that afternoon and they did not receive anyone. [107] I have a strong desire to see that girl. There is something in her which excites in me that feeling, and

---

[42] The theatre of Valletta was the Opera House. The work Brisbane refers to as "the two Peters" is unidentified.

when I once get that desire in my brain, why, I must satisfy it. I find here nothing to interest me, she interesting me more than anything else. She draws me more than any other object, but I am a being, who, when he has an idea or a feeling he wishes to execute or satisfy, must follow it. I must have it. I cannot keep myself from possessing it. Reasoning, calculation, etc. produce no effect; it is a gravitating power, toward which I must slide.

Malta: Sunday 14th November

The weather has been good, but my neck has been bad. I have done nothing; dined at 1 o'clock, [108] and in the evening went to see Miss Carlton; found them this evening at home. They were alone, and I passed a most agreeable evening. I was reading some parts of Byron[43] which made tears come in her eyes, the idea of her father ever present. I stayed there quite late, talked about a great many things and passed a most agreeable two or three hours. There is something in the look of her eye, in her glance, which is full of feeling. Her voice also is very melodious. I am sure she is full of feeling. Could I but find an occasion to kiss her, could I find her alone, and were I to say a few words of love to her; a squeeze of the hand; a look, and then take her into my arms, and [109] then imprint one kiss on her lips, I am sure she would melt away with feeling, and forget herself in the trance of the embrace.

Malta: Monday 15th November

The captain does not leave. I have been running but little about. The weather is very bad and my neck also is on a par with it. I had in the afternoon twelve leeches applied, and though they produced no immediate effect, still late in the night I began to feel better.[44] I passed the evening again at Miss Carlton's but I felt rather dull and the evening was not so animated as yesterday. But I left late. Perhaps the mother does not wish the daughter to let herself be interested with a person who must [110] so soon leave. I have touched the cord to the girl's heart, I have awakened her feelings.

---

[43] George Gordon, Lord Byron (1788–1824), who had died a romantic death in the Greek War of Independence just a few years earlier, had left many passionate poems perfectly calculated to bring a tear to the eye of a sensitive young lady.

[44] Thinning the blood by the application of leeches was a standard remedy for fever, which was thought to be caused by an overabundance of blood.

Tuesday 16th November

Today French newspapers arrived, and I had the pleasure of reading them. Nothing particularly new has happened in Europe. My neck, I think, is well again. That, in part perhaps, and reading the papers, set me into one of my overstrung fits of feeling, and excitement. After exhaling it out again for about three hours, I came into my natural state. I dined at Eynard's and went again to C.{arlton's} but they were not in.

The idea came into my head to go and find a girl. [111] The more I have anything to do with those women, the less I get accustomed to them, and I always feel myself lower after it. (Lengthy crossed-out passage). It is difficult to act to the thought. Habit leads you by its chains. Early instilled feelings make a slave of you. I wish I could break all their bonds.[45]

Malta: Wednesday 17th November

Today the Captain is to start. I settled some bills, bought some few articles more, and arranged all little matters. During my stay in Malta, including the Quarantine, I spent nearly $100. I bought some articles of clothing, but otherwise I had little to spend. [112] The weather is fine, and quite warm. I have been running about the city, but nothing in particular has engaged my attention. I have rarely spent a time so empty in mental work, so passed in nothingness, as the time I have spent in Malta. I have done nothing, I have wrote no letters, neither read, nor made any observations. I should have left here five or six days since. That time has been lost, and the Devil take me for a fool for losing it. Besides, the lying captain who was to start Saturday has been the cause of the loss of four days.

In the afternoon I went to bid adieu to Mme. Carlton. I found them in the act of walking out. I met them in the street, and said I would call again in [113] an hour, at which time they were to return. I returned, and found them in. We talked about various indifferent subjects. My mind was running about at its own pleasure. I was alone with Miss Maria a few minutes. I ought to have said something in them, but I know not how it was, I did not; I was out of character there. I would have said something; it was a moment. It was in my mind, but my tongue forgot to say it. Those moments rolled

---

[45] These cryptic remarks seem to indicate that Brisbane feels himself controlled by his intense sexual drive, which he attributes to early habit.

on. Had I then have taken her hand even, and said a word or two, but other thoughts, and at length the mother came.

After some general conversation I bid them adieu. Her squeeze was warm. A wish or two of health, prosperity, or something like it, fell from her lips. Her look was full, and [114] seemed to double itself, as if to double time. Her voice was clear and bell-like, and I turned and parted from her and forever, who, it appears, knew how to make me take a strong interest in her. It is she only in Malta I leave with regret.

I went afterwards to dine with Eynard. I had already sent my trunk on board. About half after eight, they accompanied me down to the little vessel and bidding them also adieu, I bid goodbye to Malta and left.

(Change of scene)
The following were the persons I knew in Malta: Mr and Mrs Eynard, Mr Carlton's family, Mr Gat, Mr Lewis, a Scotchman (merchant lately from America) and some other persons.

The wind was fair, and we receded fast from Malta. Here is another change. Impatient for it, but [115] nevertheless a melancholy feeling overshadowed my thoughts. There is something left you regret, which at the moment of leaving presses upon you; but the wide scene before you hurries you to start and points out the necessity.

Mr Eynard has been remarkably polite to me during my stay at Malta. I have dined at his house nearly every day. Mrs Eynard also has been very polite; we got great friends. If I squeezed her hand she was not angry at it.

At Sea: *Thursday 18th November*
A fair but light breeze is wafting us towards Sicily. The weather is fine; summer clothes were worn when I left Malta, and you find the weather warm when you walk. I perspire quite strongly. I saw the coast of Sicily, as we were passing along. The [116] land seems high, and I observed some villages on the coast. Between one and two o'clock in the afternoon I arrived at Syracuse. You cannot see the city until near, as a point hides it. The vessel entered the harbor, which is very large and runs into the interior of the land. The city is situated upon the side of it.

The place has but an indifferent appearance from the water, and the recollections of what it must have been, and what it is, gave me a melancholy
feeling. Everything around oppressed me, and I wished that the quarantine
I have to perform here, and what I have to see, might quickly pass, so that
I could leave. I would like to speed over these scenes, and get at length in
some place, where I can [117] find harmony again with myself.

There were no rooms empty in the Lazaretto for the present, but for
Saturday morning I was promised one, as the Bombard I am in is very small.
The cabin not large enough to stand up in, about five feet broad, and six
long, a mere dog's box. I was not much pleased with the idea of passing a
couple of nights more on board. I shall be delighted when this quarantine
and my business in Syracuse are finished, and I can leave again. on – on
– on –

Syracuse: Friday 19th November

This morning I was once or twice to the Custom-house, about health declarations, etc. Very particular questions were made about books and letters.
I had [118] three different declarations to make of the books I had with me,
and they wished to take the letters from me; but assuring them they were
simply for money, they consented to wait until I had finished my quarantine,
and then examine them, together with my books. All letters sent to Sicily
are opened, and they are very rigid with regard to books. They wish to shut
out all kinds of knowledge and light as if their inhabitants were already not
enough plunged in ignorance. A miserable principle, is that which can live
only where ignorance darkly reigns. Ignorance must surround it to hide its
defects. If light was there, they would shine too perspicuous, and would
wither [119] away before the force of public commonsense.[46]

I have done nothing today. It is impossible to feel free where you can
scarce stretch out an arm and leg, and such is the case on board the little
Bombard.

---

[46] The treaties agreed upon at the Congress of Vienna had resulted in the termination
of Napoleon's Italian kingdoms and the restoration of a Bourbon monarchy in the
Kingdom of the Two Sicilies, which included southern Italy. The repressive nature of
Bourbon rule, as described by Brisbane, triggered numerous revolts in the 1820s which
required the periodic intervention of the Austrian army to restore order.

There is no kind of order on board these little vessels. The Captain eats with the sailors. No one pays attention when he orders, and they all dispute together. There appears to be no ordering, but if anyone says something to be done, he does it. There appears no distinction between Captain and soldiers. I never was on board a place so confused. So many persons, and consequently so little freedom. To be alone is, for me, to be free, to enjoy liberty. [120] Nothing is so disagreeable to me as to be forced to remain with persons. I like society, but I must be alone when I wish it. If I have constantly to remain in society, as is the case on board of ships, I dislike it excessively, although it may be composed of agreeable persons.

But the quarantine is particularly disagreeable to me. Everything is so miserably arranged. It appears as if the Italians have neither the idea nor feeling of arrangement, and right execution in their heads. How superior is the American manner with regards to enterprise, undertaking, execution, arrangement, etc. In everything is, or will be, the American spirit superior.

[121] *Syracuse: Saturday 20th November*

They promised me a room in the Lazaretto for today, but it was not emptied of the goods that fill it, consequently I must wait till tomorrow. This is in harmony with Italian enterprise and arrangement. On board of this miserable little vessel, it is impossible to do anything. Although thinking seems to require no room, still I have a proof on this occasion that when you are a slave with regard to exterior objects, the mind remains also enchained. I have done nothing today, nothing in the force of the term, except about half an hour, that I was walking alone on the place allotted for those in quarantine to [122] talk with those out of it, there feeling myself free. My thoughts run off, taking a double start from the contrast they had felt. In that short time a vast number of thoughts, feelings and sciences passed through my brain.

It is to me an absolute necessity to be free, that is, to be alone, to be where I am not disturbed, where people cannot break in upon me; where I can read, write, and be with myself, and know that I will not be disturbed. The mind must often be with itself, because it is a thing that cultivates itself. It wants solitude where it can work at itself undisturbed. If certain objects, over which you have no command, are presenting [123] themselves before you, and disturb your attention, it is impossible to get at any harmony and unity with yourself; and how vast is the proportion of individuals that are constantly living out of that harmony with one's self, till at last, of all things they become the least interesting to themselves and are constantly calling upon those exterior objects, however trivial, to attract their attention and fill the void within them.

It is difficult to make thoughts the object of our actions instead of exterior things. To gain a thought appears nothing gained, the tuning of the interior. The giving it a direction seems to offer the least advantage. The slightest exterior gain, even the satisfaction of some [124] useless want, appears to the great mass of individuals as having more solidity in it. Seeing nothing of their interior, whatever may go there appears lost. The exterior is the only thing seen, and they don't know that whatever is produced and effectuated there is but the realization of its interior. How very few are there who work at their interior cultivation, who consider the perfectioning of their interior, and ennobling of their aim as necessary. It is so difficult to act to the thought, to work for an idea, and when executed, so little seems gained. Perhaps this is my case. I describe it with truth.

[125] *Quarantine, Syracuse: Sunday 21st November*

The weather is fine and has been so. This morning they began getting the things out of the room I am to have, and about noon they finished. The place is small, and, but for contrast, it would be very disagreeable, but the Bombard is so much worse than anything else, that comparatively, the place must be good. I got a bed from the hotel and other necessary things, so that I am once more in a room. About one, I came on land, and took up my residence in the room, so that I am now in it, and at this present moment am engaged in posting up my journal, which for [126] a day or two I had neglected.

It is night. I am writing by candle light and am alone, consequently with myself. Thus, I am in very good company, which, if there was another here, would be broken in upon, and I could not then answer for its goodness, because I would then be with some one else. But to be alone is agreeable. I don't like to be looked at and observed. I like to be free and follow the fancy of the moment. When I have done with this cursed quarantine, then, thank God, I shall have no more to perform in a hurry.

The occasion of this quarantine is the smallpox at Malta, but the [127] precautions taken here are very imperfect. He, who has just arrived, touches him, who is just going out, and no attention is paid to it. The appearance, the outside of the thing, is regarded, and nothing else, but I doubt whether these people here could do anything better. There is no order, no arrangement in them. The Malta quarantine is a thousand times superior; and the accommodations are palaces, in comparison with the shanties here.

Some remarks upon Malta, which I have delayed placing here. Malta is a rocky island about 60 miles in circumference. A good deal of art is used in [128] collecting earth to cultivate. Every spot is put to use. Above 100,000 inhabitants live upon the island, so that it is very much overpopulated. A large number of people are out of the island, as sailors, etc.

Valletta, so called after the Grand Master who built it,[47] is the capital of the island, the residence of the Governor, military etc.[48] It has large and excellent harbors. All public buildings, such as arsenals, barracks, quarantine establishments etc. are remarkably well built, the fortifications immense and superb. The streets are mostly very regular; well paved, kept clean by the prisoners, the dwelling houses well built of stone, and [129] high. Rent is cheap. The interior arrangement of the houses is often bad. The architecture is in the Italian taste, but in building the city they never thought of it, I presume.

There are a great many churches, and the clattering of the bells is very great. St. John's is the first, the others are less worthy of attention, but this one is very handsome.[49] There are chapels there for the different nations, with their respective emblems about them. In the French chapel I observed the best piece of sculpture. The floor is covered with slabs, which represent tops of tombs. Upon these slabs are figures, which are made by inlaying different [130] colored stones. Each Knight, or distinguished personage, has his grave there, and on the slab that covers it are his arms, and some emblem,

---

[47] Jean Parisot de la Vallette (1494–1568), Grand Master of the Knights of St John, founded the city in 1565.

[48] Malta became a British possession in 1800. In 1830 its governor was Major General Sir Frederic Ponsonby.

[49] St John's Cathedral was built in 1573 as a conventual church for the entire Knightly order. Each *langue*, or national group, had its own chapel; Knights of distinction were buried under the nave.

such as a skeleton, etc. Although there were two or three fellows following me around to show me what I could see myself, to catch a few pence, still the church in parts was left dirty and not much attention paid to it.

The hotels are good, and not dear. I paid eighteen pence English per day for my room, and their other charges were reasonable. I stayed at Micalif's in Strada Stretta (Strait St.). English manufactures are also cheap in Malta; only [131] 1 per 100, is paid on English, and 2 per 100 on French goods. There are livery stables, carriages, boats and all such conveniences cheap.

The overcrowded population of Malta must produce several effects. There are in the first place a great many beggars, both in the city and in the country. There are a great many people, who have nothing to do, and are ready to do anything. There is a great greediness for gaining money; anything will be done for it. There must also be a great many whores, and female virtue is sold at a cheap price, that is, among the needy classes. There are a great many of these women and many handsome ones, [132] but they don't appear to run much in the streets. *Macarels*[50] replace them. The English and strangers support no doubt that branch of commerce, as the Maltese in general are too poor to indulge in such extra luxuries.

The government of the Knights has left the people with two curses: firstly, with a very fervent Catholicism, secondly, with an overwhelming quantity of priests. The priests swarm round the streets in as large numbers as the beggars. Even young lads you see equipped in complete priest's dress with breeches and three corned hat. But there is a law at present existing, which prohibits anyone from becoming a priest [133] who has not the means of supporting himself, but there is also another regulation which makes him leave his property to the church at his death. This puts me in mind of the Turkish *wakfs*,[51] but the priests generally transfer secretly their property to their relations, but now and then a sudden death sends them to the devil, and their property to the church, leaving perhaps some very poor relations behind. The Catholic religion, or superstition rather, and the priests, I hold in the greatest detestation. There is nothing, for which I have at the same time such a despisal, and such a hate. I despise it for the hurt it does [134] in enchaining the minds and filling them with prejudices.

---

[50] *Macarel*: procurer.
[51] *Wakf*: Islamic charitable institution.

A commercial life is the highest in Malta, that is, among the Maltese. The English military think themselves, most probably, above it. The society does not demand arts and sciences, so that you do not hear the Maltese spoken of as producing distinguished individuals in the arts, sciences, etc. There appears to be naturally but little intelligence in the people. The physiognomy denotes it, in a measure. You find among the women of the higher classes some very pretty faces, and the English and Maltese blood mixed together produces often handsome countenances. [135] The men's physiognomy in general is less good, there may be some good looking faces among them, but the beauty of a man should be different from that of a woman; it should be the beauty of intelligence. His physiognomy should indicate mind, and that precisely is what is most wanting in the faces of the men.

There is a great deal of want and poverty in Malta. As not much commerce is done by the place, and as its interior resources are small, such must be the case. The English spend a good deal of money, and they are, I think, better off with them than they would be with any other nation. It is said however that the English [136] manner, and their principle of conduct, tend to anile[52] the spirit of the inhabitants, but I don't know how they would get on without them. They cannot defend themselves against foreign power, so that they would be the prey of those who came to take them, and I suspect the government of the Knights did much more to anilify them, than the English line of conduct.

The island of Malta is very rocky, or rather the body of the island is one entire rock, which is of a soft nature, yellow ocher color, and hewed with the greatest ease. It is not much harder than hardened clay.[53] From this, everything is built, all the houses and [137] all the fortifications, but the stone easily rots, and crumbles away, so that the facility of preparing it is counterbalanced by its little solidity.

There is a theater in Malta which plays three times a week, but it is small and is not enough encouraged to enable them to produce anything brilliant. The pieces are small generally, and not well got up. It is an Italian opera.

---

[52] Anile: senile. Anilify: make senile (fr. Latin *anus*, old woman). Could Brisbane mean to say "annul" and "nullify"?

[53] The island is mostly underlain by yellow *globigerina* limestone.

Everything with regard to living in Malta is done well and comfortably by those who can afford it. The English no doubt have influenced this. The hotels, for example, are well furnished and have every necessary, and are as complete as in Paris. Private houses also are well arranged, and as rent and living are cheap, it can be done.

[138] The language of Malta is the Arab, mixed with some Italian and other terms, but the Italian is in general use and is the business language.[54] The English is also much spoken at present.

With regard to the Maltese spirit, it appears to have no particular direction. The people try to gain a living and make money. That appears about all. Nothing of an interior nature to the wants of society is produced. The physiognomy of the peasants in particular is heavy and unintelligent, and in the Maltese nature there is naturally, I suspect, but little intelligence. That is, they don't appear to be a people of quickness and sharpness. Their origin hangs on them. [139] Every spot of ground in the interior is cultivated, and the inhabitants are contented to work hard for a little money, and all kinds of industry are resorted to.

Had the French the government of this place, I think the greater part of the women would become kept mistresses. The French are great amateurs of that kind of thing, and where they would wish to have a *maitresse* (mistress) the English would rather choose drinking and horse-racing. But the English officials, however, have not a very good reputation among the mothers, the latter call them "a wicked set."

There is only one Knight that is generally known for one, remaining in Malta. He is an old Frenchman and receives a pension [140] from the British government. The institution of these Knights appears to me to be a miserable affair; it is the same of religion. They take the positive part of it and produce an institution from it, of which it is the interior moving principle and at the same time the exterior object. All such institutions are completely out of joint with the spirit of our times. The climate must kill them, if nothing else.

---

[54] Malti, the language of Malta, is a Semitic dialect with infusions of Phoenician, Arabic, Italian, and French. At this date, Malti existed only in spoken form and would easily have been mistaken for Arabic. Italian was the official language of Malta until the twentieth century.

In Malta the priests have not much power openly, but as there is a great deal of superstition among the inhabitants; they have, no doubt, secret influence. In the time of the Knights it was otherwise. They could post a man's name upon [141] the church door, who let a certain time go by without confessing. The Knights could not marry, which was the cause of so many public girls perhaps. At least, they all had their mistresses, which laid the foundation.

You find a great many of these public girls, who pay strict attention to their Catholic prejudices. You will see them wear a ribbon, or tape around their necks, with a square bit of cloth, or paper pasted on cloth, with a Christ, or Virgin Mary pasted on it. And of all disgusting things, is to see Catholic prejudices and a whore united in one person, as if one went to the other for help. However much in harmony they may be, in the Protestantism there are no such forms to seize [142] hold of. You cannot tell a man's religion there by exterior signs. The forms have at least the merit of being interior. The Catholic religion makes me, as it were, contented with the Protestantism.

Syracuse, Quarantine: Monday 22nd November

Today is the first day I have been entirely in my room at the Lazaretto. I have got my books out, and have occupied myself in reading, writing etc. I also have had the pleasure to be alone, and am relieved from the disagreeableness of being constantly surrounded by persons. The weather is remarkably fine, but it is rather warmer in the sun. The sky is clear, and the country that spreads around the [143] bay, or harbor, of Syracuse presents a handsome and pleasing prospect to the eye. It is a plain which is bounded by high land raising up, the top of which runs in a horizontal line. The plain appears covered with trees and verdure, and extends some distance from the water into the interior.

At about the time I left Berlin and during a part of my stay there, a great question that was running in my head was whether character, that is, a spontaneous manner of feeling or acting, or thought, that is, a line of conduct, which should be the result of thinking and calculation, was the most preferable. Whether it was better to have a character [144] that made us act spontaneously, without calculation in a certain manner, or whether it was better to obtain that line of conduct by thinking? Was a thinking person, or a person of character, the most to be admired?

These questions occupied me a great deal. I was striving to obtain a certain manner of feeling and acting, and as I considered I did not possess it naturally, I endeavored to obtain it by the thought. At that time I leaned in favor of character, but at present this question has gone out of my head, and what I was then striving for, I have now lost sight of. It was first excited in me by the society [145] that surrounded me. Removing from it, I lost it gradually out of sight. I now am more occupied with exterior things. My thoughts turn now when judging people and deducting from exterior data the spirit of different societies of people I may pass through.

A person who is constantly travelling is necessarily so much taken up with exterior subjects that he forgets himself or has not time to pay attention to interior objects when so many exterior ones demand his attention. Also when I am more tranquil and leading a regular life, exterior objects require less attention. I then very often criticise myself. I examine my conduct, and blame, or rather despise my faults and errors, but [146] in travelling, you have the stupidities of so many other persons to correct, that you can escape yours.

The fine arts, and architecture in particular, have occupied a portion of my attention for some time past. I don't mean the mechanical part of them, but their principle, and the beauty that should be found in them. After reading *Wilhelm Meister*, I could not help from trying to think in that manner.[55] It pleased me so much that it drew me on with it.

For the Catholic religion I have at the present time the greatest dislike. A priest excites in me a feeling of the greatest detestation. It is difficult for me [147] to keep from detesting all religion in general. It is only when I consider it stripped of all its positiveness, and think it independent in itself and apart from men, that I can be the friend of it. For religion, when filling low and vile minds, always seems to me as getting dirtier by the contact.

Religion, pure in itself, is the development of the mind searching out some spiritual or intellectual cause, as the creating, moving and enlivening principle of the universe. It is always in harmony with the state of develop-

---

[55] Goethe's *Wilhelm Meisters Lehrjahre*. See above: Diary I: 101, November 10, 1830, n. 41.

ment of the society out of which it springs. Consequently there may be people without religion, if they are too little developed to raise above nature, and search for [148] causes for natural objects. The substance of religion is the subjective thought conceiving the universal thought of the universe, and at the same time this relation between the subjective thought and the universal thought in the Christian religion is the symbol of the truth, since they made the mind of man of the highest nature. Christ, I presume, did not understand half of what has since been understood for him, but that is of no consequence, for if later times understood it so, it is a sign that those times comprehended it, which is the same thing, or better, since it shows [149] the principle was more general in the minds of men.

I have a great mind to make out a list here of my bad qualities. There is a good number of them. I have also conscience of them. They are in part natural, the part the effect of early habit of acting, and early impressions and manner of feeling. The defects of the objects I proposed myself when very young still hang upon me. I have conscience of my defects, and see them in the light they deserve. I also correct them gradually to a certain degree, but they very often have mastery over me. The natural ones, I think, are easier to be corrected than those produced by early habit.

[150] *Syracuse, Quarantine: Tuesday 23rd November*

The weather is remarkably fine. I have done nothing today of an exterior nature, except eating and walking across my room. I have been reading, writing, and leading an interior life. I am not very impatient in this quarantine, since I have a room at the Lazaretto. With study and speculating the time passes without *ennui*.

Some extracts of a letter to Lechevalier:[56]

J'ai passé presque deux mois dans la capital des Mahometans. J'ai tâché d'observer ce Peuple qui ne joue plus aucun rôle aujourd'hui dans le progrès de la civilization, et du Monde. La civilization Turque est à [151] present un vide; rien ne s'y élève, rien ne s'y vient. Elle ne produit absolument rien qui soit intérieur aux besoins de la société. Il n'y a dans ce peuple point de l'activité, point de mouvement intellectuel. Il a le nécessité, l'habitude, et l'instint natu-

---

[56] Jules Lechevalier was a fellow student of Brisbane's in Berlin, who would later introduce him to Saint-Simonianism and the works of Fourier. See Introduction: 2–3.

ral de l'homme pour le guider. Mais aux de pareils principes, on ne sort pas du monde physique et du ses besoins pour travailler dans le Monde de l'intelligence. Il faut la pensée pour moteur, et c'est de là seulement qui découlent les institutions, la force morale, ou, pour ainsi dire, l'ame d'une Nation. Mais chez eux la pensée active est morte, aucun coté de l'esprit n'est developpé avec pensée. [152]

Arts, Sciences, Institutions etc., tout est négligée; ils n'ont pas conscience même de leur Nature. La force d'une Nation; ce sont les opinions, les objets interieurs qui animent le peuple. L'homme agit toujours en harmoni avec le contenu que son esprit a reçu. Pour rendre son activité grande il faut lui donner des buts extérieurs à, et audessus de, son simple individu. Pour ses opinions et ses sentiments il est actif, et il souffre pour les réaliser.

Mais dans une peuple où on ne fait aucune attention a l'education, où aucun contenu n'est donné à l'esprit, où il n'est qu'une vide, dans lequel il n'entre que la pensée, ou plutôt le sentiment des petits besoins individuels, [153] où aucune vue extérieur à l'individu ne trouve place, où aucun moteur intérieur ne lui est donné pour le fair sortir de lui-même! Quand la masse des individus d'une Nation est dans cet état, alors il faut nécessairement, que cette Nation soit sans force.

C'est là le cas avec les Turcs. Ils sont aujourd'hui totalement sans force morale; il y règne une faiblesse qui ressemble au sommeil. Décidément, il ne faut qu'un petit choc pour fair disparaitre ce peuple de l'Europe.[57]

---

[57] "I have passed almost two months in the capital of the Mohammedans. I have tried to observe this people who will no longer play any role today in the progress of civilization, and in the world. The Turkish civilization is at present a void. Nothing will rise from there, nothing will come from there. She will produce absolutely nothing which is interior to the needs of society. There is, in this people, no activity or intellectual movement. It has necessity, habit, and natural human instinct to guide it. But on such principles, one does not depart from the physical world and its needs to work in the world of intelligence. Thought is necessary for a motivating force. From there only {from thought} flow the institutions, the moral force or, so to speak, the soul of a nation. But with them {the Turks} active thought is dead. No aspect of the spirit is developed with thought.

"Arts, Sciences and institutions, etc, all is neglected. They do not even have consciousness of their nature. The might of a nation; these are the opinions, the interior objects which animate the people. Man always acts in harmony with the content which his soul has received. To make his activity great, it is necessary to give him goals outside of, and above, his simple self. For his opinions and feelings he will be active, and he will suffer to realize them.

"But among a people where no attention has been paid to education, where no content is given to the soul, where it is only a void, in which only the thought or the sentiment of little individual needs enters, where no view exterior to the individual finds

Syracuse, Quarantine: Wednesday 24th November

The weather has changed and has been cool today; the wind is also strong from the northwest. The exterior movements I [154] have been engaged in today are as customary, eating, and walking, nothing farther. Having but little to do with my hands and feet, not distracted by exterior objects, the mind must naturally go to itself to find objects for its attention and activity. The mind is something like the stomach, except that it is in constant digestion, and is constantly demanding something to satisfy and support that digestion. Most minds find food in exterior objects, and those who are satisfied with the most trivial objects approach nearest the animal. I am of opinion, however, this state tends to bodily health. There are some minds that turn upon themselves, and become their own food, they oftentimes consume themselves. This I [155] think is against bodily health. But, let bodily health disappear in consideration before the result of the mind working upon itself.

Syracuse, Quarantine: Thursday 25th November

The weather is this morning still cool. I saw a few flakes of very light snow, which reached the ground, but in the middle of the day it was fine weather and agreeable.

The two books I am reading at present are Rixner's *Geschichte der Philosophie*,[58] and Schiller's *Wallenstein*.[59] The systems of philosophy represent the thought striving to comprehend the highest principles of the universe, and its own nature, and its source. But besides that effort, the mind produces a quantity of societies, their various [156] differences, regulations, institutions, in fact the whole construction of the general relations of men to men. Now by examining, and correctly defining, the various feelings, as it were, or fundamental faculties of the mind, such as its interior strife of

place, where no external motivating force is given to him to get out of himself! When the mass of individuals of a nation is in this state, then necessarily this nation will be without strength.

"This is the case with the Turks. They are today totally without any moral force. A feebleness which resembles sleep reigns there. Decidedly, only a little shock will suffice for this people to disappear from Europe." (French translations by A. B. Stallsmith.)

[58] Rixner. See above: Diary I: 53, October 25, 1830, n. 25.

[59] Schiller's historical play *Wallenstein* was first produced in 1799. See above: Diary I: 56, October 27, 1830, n. 26.

development and advancement; the interest it is capable of taking in exterior objects, as well as its power of satisfying itself, with itself, or with a mental object, and various other mental determinations; as well as those more properly arising from the body, such as love, hate, desire of pleasure, etc.

These determinations have often a high degree of spirituality in them, but what proves them not to be entirely [157] so is that they are in harmony with, and molded by bodily differences. They are things that are also in different degrees in almost every mind. By making this examination and correctly defining these fundamental faculties, would we not have a clearer view, and better be able to comprehend and determine the various activities of the mind in its developments in societies, and the particular activity of individuals? Has the mind faculties of different natures? That is, are there some that have their root in the mind itself, and others of a bodily extraction, or which are influenced and directed by the physical part?

This seems to suppose that the body and mind are distinct and separate, whereas they are both one.[60]

[158] *Syracuse: Friday 26th November*

Today is the last day of my last quarantine and certainly it is a pleasure to think I have got over these imprisonments. Although I support this kind of thing much better than many persons, still it bothers me a good deal, more perhaps on account of the various botherations attending it, such as the difficulty of getting what you want, and as you want it. It is not so much in being confined; but by being confined, you {are} subjected to serious contrarities.

The weather is delightful, and warm. That coolness has passed. Today I have not done much. I could not apply myself. The greatest misfortune with me is that I have not command [159] over my mind. When I am studying some subject, which requires attention, it {my mind} flies from the thing, and I cannot direct its attention to such and such points as I wish.

This afternoon one of the custom house officers came to pay me a visit. He made some few compliments, said they treated strangers like friends, and that

---

[60] In this passage Brisbane seems to anticipate something of Fourier's theory of 810 capacities and attractions (see Introduction: 3). Brisbane's inclination toward systematizing individual capacities and differences may partly explain the intensity of his reaction on first encountering Fourier's work a year and a half later (see Introduction: 20).

they would give me *pratique* (liberty from quarantine) as early as possible. This was in order that tomorrow morning, I would not forget to give him *la buona mana*, (the good hand) as they term it, that is, some little present in money.

As the duties on everything are exorbitantly high, a vast deal of contrabanding is done. By bribing the custom house officers, which is very easy, you get anything in you choose.

[160] *Syracuse: Saturday 27th November*

This morning about 9 o'clock I left the quarantine, and more circumstances have passed before my eyes today than during the last ten.

On leaving the Lazaretto, I took my trunk with me in the boat and went to the health office about a ¼ mile distant. There they wished to make some trouble because I had brought my trunk away without permission. However, recollecting that the person that came yesterday evening to pay me some compliments had told me to do it, I soon shut their mouths. I, however, had to return with it on board the vessel, where I opened it, and a person who had come with me, took three [161] letters I had, for different persons in Sicily, and after they were read at the police, were returned to me. I then got permission from the Custom-House, which {is} a small concern near the water, to bring my trunk on shore. I sent for it, and opened it before them. They took all my printed books, making, however, but a slight search, and having my manuscripts, no doubt in hopes of a reward, which, however, the Vice-Consul, who was with me, hindered me from giving. For, having no money upon me, I applied to him, and he insisted upon not paying them.

As I went to the health office another *cicerone* (guide) came to offer his services, asked [162] me if I had need of anything. I answered no. However, as I returned to the vessel, he took a boat and followed after me. He said the Consul had sent him, etc. On returning on shore he followed me, and meeting the consul, he walked on with us. In a few minutes I met the other one, who had sent me his card the first day I arrived and who had come to pay me a visit once at the Lazaretto. Consequently I had two following around after me. I decided upon taking the elderly man the consul had recommended for today, and the other for tomorrow.

After getting my trunk through the custom-house, [163] I came to the hotel. They sent my books, however, to the police. As I was standing in the court, the first person that addressed me was a *Macarel* (procurer), who inquired if I wanted anything in his line. Ten or eleven days confinement did not make me averse to his proposition.[61] I breakfasted about ten, and then went out with my cicerone, the old fellow. As I was walking down the street hearing something like guns or pistols shooting off, I inquired what it was, and was informed that it was some *festa della Virgina* (feast of the Virgin), I forget which, where it is necessary to fire a kind of pistol in order to render the ceremony more imposing.

[164] I stopped into one of the churches. As I was going down the street, and among the diverse uninteresting forms that struck my attention, there was one, however, which I looked upon with a certain degree of interest and pleasure. The church was tolerably full, but not far from the door, where I was standing, were three young girls, of eighteen perhaps, kneeling down, and their faces turned towards the altar. Consequently I could see only their backs. The middle one struck me, from her form and from her dress. I thought she must be handsome, and the idea of a young and handsome girl at her prayers, and the idea coming in my head, that she [165] resembled Miss Carlton, made me look at her with an interest and certain pleasure which held me on the spot. But, as she continued in the same position and did not turn round, I was at length forced to leave the church without seeing her face, which most probably would have destroyed the illusion.

The first thing I went to visit was a bath found a considerable distance under ground, hewed in the rock. It was hewed in an arch-like form and supported by square pillars of which there were four. I believe the bath was another room cut in the rock, which was about large enough for one person, and it filled naturally by water, [166] which has a kind of brackish sulphurous taste. You descended into it by three steps. There was a place to let in also warmer water. The whole thing, however, is without any kind of art. The work is coarse, and common, and no attention has been paid to beauty. I don't think, myself, that it is of Greek construction.[62]

The next place I visited was the temple of Minerva. You see on the outside about a quarter of the columns projecting out beyond the walls,

[61] Brisbane's quarantine actually lasted from November 21 to November 27, 1830.

[62] Brisbane was probably visiting the ancient underground reservoir of Ortygia, still called, inaccurately, *Bagno della Regina* (bath of the queen).

which have been built between them, in order to form it into a church.[63] The architrave and frieze is still preserved.[64] The style is heavy, and the forms have not that delicacy [167] and beauty of the Athenian monuments. The columns have a *plintus*,[65] which is a square piece of stone, and of a few inches in height.

The columns, with regard to thickness and height, and the cut of the abacus,[66] with three lines at the neck, have a great resemblance with the few remaining columns of the Temple of Jupiter at Corinth, which is much more ancient than this one; nearly all the columns of each side are standing, but walls built up between them; and in the interior they have been so often whitewashed, that the exact forms are not distinct. However they are easily well seen from the exterior.

Towards [168] the west, before that front of the temple, has been built a new one with all the tasteless forms and ornaments of the Italian-Roman architecture.[67] In the interior two columns of this front are still seen, probably those of the *pronaos*.[68] I did not examine the thing closely, and for that reason, I intend to return there again.

I also saw what appeared {to be} two antes,[69] on each side of these columns, with a very plain capital. These two columns have a kind of base, composed of a square *plintus*, an oval *gleet*,[70] and another smaller one above it, but excessively bad{ly} made. The shape and forms are clumsy and ugly, so that I think [169] there is no doubt of its being a later addition. Also, instead of the three indentures under the *eichinos*,[71] there projects a little oval rim and a small flat one under it, also no doubt made by some fool, in working at the church.

From the Temple of Minerva, I went to see that of Diana, but a law suit having taken place between the relations with regard to the house in whose

---

[63] The fifth century BC temple of Athena, in the Piazza del Duomo, was rebuilt as the Cathedral in the seventh century AD.

[64] Architrave: the lower part of the entablature of the temple. Frieze: a band of relief carving.

[65] Plintus (plinth): the flat stone base of a column.

[66] Abacus: the flat stone slab above the column capital.

[67] By "Italian-Roman" Brisbane means baroque. The church facade was built in 1754.

[68] *Pronaos*: the porch of the ancient temple.

[69] *Anta*, pl. *antes*: a flat column set into the wall.

[70] *Gleet*: no definition of this term, which recurs below, can be found. It seems to mean an architectural ornament carved in relief.

[71] *Eichinos*: the element of the column capital below the abacus.

walls the columns are enclosed, it was shut up and I could not get in. I then visited the celebrated fountain, in which were kept, I believe, the fish of Diana.[72] It now serves as a washing-place. The water has a slightly brackish taste, with a kind of sweetness or softness, and is warmer than cold.

[170] From there I went out of the city, to view some few things, but I saw over them with a good deal of haste, as I intended to return again. I saw the Roman amphitheater.[73] The seats are cut in the rock, and are tolerably well preserved, but parts are broken away, and the area is filled up with earth. You see the subterranean galleries for the people when it rained, and under that is the subterranean gallery, where the wild beasts were let loose, and the door is still there where they entered into the area.

From there I went to the Greek theater, the one built in earlier times.[74] This is much larger, the seats [171] constructed more comfortably, there being a space left for the feet, so that those above should not incommode those below. The work is very good. It is executed with care. There are a great number of seats one above another; and the number of persons the place could hold must have been immense. The theater is very large and is much superior to the one I saw at Argos {Greece}. About in the center, on the steps or seats, a mill has been built, the water for which is furnished by ancient conveyances.

From there I went to the great stone quarries, from which the stone was taken for buildings [172] and all kinds of constructions. It is said that Dionysius[75] kept also his prisoners here. In the center is left a tall piece of rock standing, which reaches as high as the original surface. It is of considerable size at the base, and grows smaller at the top. On the top is said to have been a guard house for a soldier to observe the prisoners below. In the northwest corner is the large excavation called the "Ear of Dionysius." (See Illustration 12.) The profile of the opening seen from the outside resembles something a jackass' ear, but certainly nothing that of a man. The excavation is in the solid rock, the width of the place is at the bottom several yards, [173] and closes in an oval slant at a considerable height from the surface. There is an

---

[72] Today called the Fountain of Arethusa.

[73] This amphitheater was built in the fourth or third century BC.

[74] Built in the sixth century BC, this theater saw the first performance in the west of Aeschylus' *Persians*.

[75] Dionysius I was the tyrant of Syracuse, 407–368 BC.

astonishing echo in the interior. A pistol was fired off, and the noise was frightful, but what is singular, it is said this echo has become weaker by use. The cicerone says he recollects when it was much stronger.

The Ear of Dionysius at the top of the entrance of this place is a little kind of chamber, but very small, where it is said Dionysius would go to hear what the prisoners said who were confined there, the echo being so great that he could hear the smallest sound. But that, I suspect, is all nonsense, for the little openings hewed out in the rock are very small and [174] not calculated to stand in with ease. Near the Ear of Dionysius is a large quarry, which is cut under the surface, consequently has a covering, which is not the case with the exterior one. This place resembles a cavern. It is quite large and several large supports of the rock is left standing. The sparrows have taken up their lodgings here. Water drips from the rocks and there are some little pools, but no stream of living water.

After that, I walked about upon the site of the ancient city. The land rises up directly from the water until at the theater, and {at} this place it becomes quite elevated and the foundation is all rock. I saw some [175] of the aqueducts, which the cicerone said extended eighteen miles. It appears that there is one made above the other, and he explained it by saying that if the enemy stopped the one, in order to deprive the city of water, that the other was left. But I doubt very much that the thing is so, for there was no need of bringing the two, one above the other, so far into the city.

I returned home after four. I dined between five and six, and the Captain, coming in, dined with me. After that I wrote this, and about eight I went, and found a very pretty girl, whom the fellow of the morning showed me. She is the daughter of a poor family, who thus sell their children to [176] get bread to put in their mouths. In going there, considering my action in an individual light, I did them a favor; considered in a general light it was a curse, because making them whores destroys them. Thus the general action is destructive. But, since they are so, the individual action, considered in itself, is a favor. It does not make them more, or less so. Had I not gone there, they would have been the same tomorrow, consequently that action was indifferent. But what I gave them puts for tomorrow, and day after tomorrow, bread in their mouths. This part consequently is not indifferent.

The mother held a [177] little child in her arms, a girl, which she kissed tenderly. The action seemed strange to me, for as she only had the prospect before her of bringing up the thing to follow the same path, the object to be attained struck me sooner, as being more of a nature calculated upon drawing forth tears, than kisses of affection. But such is the poverty here, that mothers, finding themselves without bread to put in their mouths, sell their daughters, first as virgins, for a few dollars I was told they were got, then afterwards as common girls. I don't make these remarks without a general aim. It shows strikingly various results in society; and to what [178] point continual oppression, mental as well as material, will bring a people.

The mind is the mind in all countries, but the body is not the body in all countries. There is a great difference between the physical individual of America, and this country for example. The difference of the mind is also full as great, but the mind does not seem to change its nature, it changes only its object, direction, or aim. The body changes its nature. I was told that the taxes were so heavy upon lands, that respectable people have been known to have to sell their daughters, to be able to keep their possessions, and to live. Such a fact gives distress to the mind.

[179] The contrast between the desire of retaining the means of living, and the necessity of making the sacrifice of the first object for keeping those means strikes you to the heart. It is a damned alternative. But he who does it, no matter his circumstances, must reach that point by the steps of mental degradation.

Syracuse: Sunday 28th November

From the fortress Exapelo, that is, of the six entrances, is a superb view of the entire site of the ancient city.[76] The plain spreads out before you to the southeast and south, and its large surface is covered with rocks and stones. You see ruins of walls running in various directions, and [180] their square blocks of stones scattered in various directions. First comes the city of Tiga. The whole surface is rock with various indentures of roads. The whole of the site of that city is covered with shapeless recesses of stones. Here and there a small patch of ground is cultivated. After that, farther to the southeast comes Agradina. Parts of it are now cultivated and covered with trees,

---

[76] The Euryalos fortress was built in the early fourth century BC by Dionysius I.

but no vestige remains of temples or any such thing to mark the shape of the ancient city. The catacombs are there with some stone quarries. Down near the large port is seen the situation of Neapoli. Its site is lower than those [181] of these other cities.

The general view is extensive and superb. You see the sea forming a half circle around you, beginning at the southwest and intending to the northeast. Ortygia, the present city, and the large port, lie before you. Facing the south to the right spreads out an extensive and beautiful plain, covered with trees, and cultivated. It is lower than the site of the ancient city, which presents nothing but a surface covered with formless masses of stones. To the northward Etna rises in its magnificence, and you can trace the coast in its windings for a long distance. Catania, like a white spot, is also to be seen.

[182] I went this morning with the cicerone to see the site of the ancient cities of Tiga, Agradina and Neapoli, and to see the exterior walls of the cities and those built by Dionysius.[77] They {are} all in ruins. There are some few parts standing, but nowhere the entire height. The smaller stones used to fill up between the outside layers are mixed, and cover the hewed stones of those layers. A subterraneous military passage commences in a stone quarry near the fortress of the six gates, and runs a long distance nearly down to the sea. It must have cost great labor, as it is hewed in the rock, but the catacombs are the most surprising thing of the kind.

There are rooms after rooms, spreading out in all directions, and a long street runs straight, from which [183] other passages branch out. The length of this long and straight passage has not been determined. They have proceeded about a mile and a half in it, but did not find the end. There are chambers hewn in the rock. A passage passes before them, and in these chambers the graves are hewn one behind another. The breadth of the chamber is about the length of the grave. The graves lie lengthwise with the breadth, and so behind each other. There are various round rooms at different distances, with a hole in the top for light, which were used to sacrifice to the dead, perhaps.

Near the catacombs is a church cut in the rock underground, where the Christians in early times performed their service. There are four columns in

---

[77] The quarters of ancient Syracuse were Tiga, Agradina, Neapoli and Ortygia.

it, in Byzantinish style. The plan is not very large. It has one or two smaller side rooms.[78]

[184] What material misery, and what mental degradation coupled with it! I have almost got into a fever with having the image of the thing in my mind. What fatality is it, or what principles in a people may it be that create such a social state? Was it possible to better the thing? Could not some change of government amend the present state of the people? How much to be desired, how godlike to be longed for! Could but the head of power see and comprehend it, should he sacrifice all his power were he a man, he would find, in the thought of having raised the condition of so many individuals, a thousand times repayment of his sacrifice. He could exist in the thought of the world of improvement he had created.

[185] *Syracuse: Monday 29th November*

I went this morning to see two columns, parts of which still stand at the capital, and a portion of the top of the shafts are broken away. They stand upon a little rising ground, at some distance to the right of the river Anapus. They are those of the temple of Jupiter.[79] The columns have sixteen flutes only, and what is singular, they have a kind of base, that is, the flutes do not run out, leaving a space of about 8 inches plain, smooth, which looks like a flat band running around the base of the column. The columns are in one piece, but as the tops are broken off, the proportions are not to be determined, but I think they must have been heavy. {Brisbane includes a drawing of this column.}

[186] The river Anapus is a little stream full of weeds, and the banks covered with reeds and grass. Little boats can be rounded up, as the water is a few feet deep. The stream runs tolerably fast. It is on the banks of this river that the Papyrus plant grows. It is a tall reed, six or eight feet high, growing in one straight green stock, of which the green bark or skin, taken off, presents a white substance of a fine pithy and fibrous nature, which can be cut in fine shavings; and these shavings put together side by side form a sheet. But the precise ancient process is not known or at least not understood.

---

[78] This may be the church of Santa Lucia, beneath which are the largest catacombs outside Rome, as well as an underground chapel.
[79] The temple of Olympian Zeus was built in the fifth century BC.

I was in the museum today to see again the handsome Venus; that statue [187] delights me. I do not think it an original. It is copied from some of the Grecian masters, but it is well executed. She holds a robe or covering, used on leaving the bath, in one hand, the two ends of which pass around the thighs, and meet in her hand. It then falls behind her, forming a support. A dolphin at the left side serves the same purpose. This statue gave me a particular pleasure. I fell in love with it. The perfect beauty of its form, the highest degree of female perfection in form reigns in it.[80]

There are some tusks of elephant that have been found near here, underground, and some teeth. The former are much decayed, the latter are sound. There are also in the museum some vases [188] {and} some other statues, etc.

Sent today a letter to LeChevalier, to Mr Brisbane and to Mr Eynard.

I could say a good deal upon the people of this part of Sicily, and a vast deal of the impression that has been left upon me. How completely, from top to bottom, does the same spirit reign. The lower classes are a vulgar development of the higher ones. The same spirit is everywhere; it has for its differences polish and coarseness, not the difference of direction and object. There seems no point to hold on {to}. You find no persons (at least they are so few, that they are lost) animated with a higher spirit.

The common direction seems [189] given to all minds. None seem to get out, and soar above the aniling circle.[81] There seems here a thirst for money that astonishes you. Misery and want no doubt exist, but that to escape them resorts should be flown to, which show a high degree of moral debasement; does not seem to me as a necessary effect. There are other means to provide for the wants than by low and degrading employments. The thing must be in the people. By tracing out principle, you could explain effects, but that would require thought.

As the government is against all, each one is against the other. Everything is done by low vile intrigue, each working secretly against the [190] others as much as possible. No open and firm dealings, all twisting and underhand. The procuring and satisfying of the mere wants appear to be

---

[80] The Landolina Venus, a Roman copy of a Hellenistic Greek work, currently is in the Museo Archaeologico P. Orsi.

[81] Aniling: see above: Diary I: 136, November 21, 1830, n. 52.

the only end, and aim, of the mass of individuals. As this is the only object, it having in itself no intellectual principles, the means taken to procure them may be of any nature. An unintellectual object being the aim, no intellectual means are used to obtain it, and the intellectual guide once thrown from us, we seize everything, as it were, blind.

All resorts are resorted to, to gain money. No kinds of debasement of the mind is an obstacle in the way. He who suffers his wife to become [191] the mistress of another, and makes a whore of his daughter, reaches the lowest step of total self disconsideration. If a superior demands it of a clerk under him, over whose place he has power, he is as vile in feeling, as he who accords it, and this supposes a passiveness on the part of the women. That is, everything with them, that is, woman, is valueless. They cast it from them, and possess no esteem for it. But doubly cursed be the government, which by its principles and nature, forces the willing victims in such paths.

The poorer classes sell their daughters. It has become a traffic. They sell them first when still young and virgins, for a few dollars, and afterwards they become common [192] girls. These poor little creatures sometimes have a natural horror for the thing, but then, the fiend-like mother drives them on to it. She sends her daughter in the street and lays, as it were, an admonition not to return without some fruit. Thinking of the thing has put me, the latter part of the day, in a fever. I completely lost balance of myself.

Night before last, I went to a house and found there a little girl, of about seventeen. Last night she came to my room without, however, my wishing it. When she went away, I made pretence that I had no money. She believed it, and seemed in great distress. At length she exclaimed, "O! what will [193] Mama say?" In a few words I saw the whole history of the poor girl, and the hellish nature of the mother. I said to myself, what interior demon-like thirst governs such a woman? The desire of money is the outside appearance, but there must be some deep principles in the interior nature, which push them thus on to move {act}. I am sick, and overcome with these images. They follow me around before my thoughts like a fatiguing devil. I could not live in this place. I should die of mental consumption.

I wished to leave Syracuse this afternoon, but it was late before I returned from the River Anapus.

[194] *Syracuse: Thursday 30th November*

The weather is cloudy, and I think, is on the change. I have nothing to do today. I have seen what is to be seen, and have not the spirit, nor desire to visit them again. I have been in a growling humor yesterday and today, and I wish to be off from Syracuse this afternoon. I shall go today about the mules, and the rest tomorrow. This however, is not my choice. The consul here, Horatio Nicosia, imagined it so, and stuck with such a pertinacity to his ideas, that it was impossible to arrange the thing otherwise. Of all the damned things I hate, is to bend my ideas to those of another. I must be [195] free, at least in my calculations.

Today is the last day of the month, and during it, I have done nothing. It has been an idle, unproductive thirty days. Part of it has been spent in quarantine, part at Malta, which had but little result, and another part of it at Syracuse. These few days have not been lost. I have seen a good deal in them, and more conceived. I had no idea there was so little intellectual movement among the people. All political feeling, that is, the desire of the individual to see himself that the general laws and forms that guide him are in harmony with the state of society, all that feeling is crushed.

If some news gets into the place, one [196] person, meeting an acquaintance of his, asks him if he has heard any news? "Yes," answers the other. "Well, what is it?" "No, tell me yours." They go to work about it something like freemasons, letting each other know by signs and roundabout questions. If they talk the least about political subjects, it is in a secret place, and with well known friends. They whisper the thing out, as if the open skies should not hear it.

I was asking the consul some few questions. He seemed to have a great dislike to touch upon the forbidden ground. How miserable must be the forms, which, in order to make men enter into them, must first crush intellectual liberty, that they [197] may not see, or feel those forms. Horatio Nicosia, our consul, {is} the only person I know in Syracuse.

I stayed at the Hotel of the Sun. For my room I paid half a dollar, and for eating about three quarters {of a dollar}. Left Syracuse between 1 and 2 P.M. The Consul had given me a letter for Signor Don Gasparo Vinci, who has a counting house and possessions about ten miles from Syracuse.

On leaving the city, the road passes over the site of the ancient city. After getting outside of its boundaries, the surface still continues nothing but rocks. For the first part of the way the land is not cultivated. You then [198] descend a little, coming into lower ground. You meet one or two country houses, with the land cultivated around them. You pass an obelisk raised by the Romans to commemorate their taking of Syracuse, but a good deal of it has fallen down. It is constructed of blocks of hewn stone. You afterwards come to a little hamlet, which lies within the possessions of this Signor Don Vinci. The land from the water back some distance is very flat, and is plains. There then suddenly rises a chain of high hills, on a bank of high land, whose sides towards the sea are very bold. It struck me that the water once had covered this plain and that [199] its banks were these hills. The surface is here everywhere rocky.

After passing the little hamlet, we continued on a short distance and soon came to the house of Signor Don Vinci. I discovered, however, that he is a priest, and I did not like the idea much of having to thank one of the race for a night's lodging, but the novelty of the thing recompensed it. On arriving at the house, which is a tolerable good one, I found he was out, and that he would not return before 8. It was then half after 3. But I found one or two servants who got the things from the mules, and I came into the house. The interior appearance said of itself that no [200] women were there. It was dirty and badly ordered.

An old servant with a blue kind of velvet roundabout,[82] a pair of tattered patched breeches, and a face that did not express an idea, showed me a room, and after arranging the bed, went to see about preparing the supper, as I had determined upon waiting {for} Signor Don Vinci. At each interval of doing something, the old servant would begin whistling very methodically and continue until something else fell under his hands. Everything in the house appears neglected.

Living alone and without society, there is nothing to induce a person to pay attention to his style of living. [201] When the individual lives alone, without interior objects to make him act in different manners, he generally sinks lower and lower within himself, until he comes to perfect rest and then remains without activity.

---

[82] A roundabout was a short close-fitting man's jacket.

My room here is not bad, except the floor is very dirty. A little table stands near the bed, and over it is hung a cross, with a little bronze image of Christ crucified, badly done, as is everything in the way of arts under religious influence.

Signor Don Vinci came about 7½ {7:30}. He was in a jacket and breeches, and large boots with a white cotton bonnet. He is a strong look-ing, good-natured countryman, not as intelligent as [202] one of our farm-ers. He said all men went *all'inferno*, (to Hell) who did not believe in the Pope. Tomorrow morning he is going about two miles, he said, on my route, and we are to start together very early. We supped together and very well, and went to bed about 8½, {8:30} as we intended to leave at five.

From Syracuse to Catania: Wednesday 1st December

During the night it has rained, blowed, thundered and lightened. Sig. Vinci was up and left at five, although it then rained. I left at seven, it did not rain at the time, but in about an hour it commenced and continued with a good deal of force during the rest of the time. Today is the 1st December, and [203] it is the first rainy day for a long time, and by accident I have been condemned to trudge through it, which was no wise agreeable. However I put the guide's cloak around me, giving him mine, and by that means kept the best part of me dry.

The country, for some time after leaving the house where I slept, has the same appearance as between it and Syracuse; that is, the surface is rocky and not much of it cultivated. I saw among the stones one or two pieces of shells petrified, which were of a large size. Further on, I observed great quantities of black stone or lava, which resembled that I saw in the ground to the west of the ancient city of Syracuse. [204] This black substance or lava is buried in the earth and there was here, formerly perhaps, the crater of a volcano. The weather, however, hindered me from observing precisely. It was so rainy, and I so uncomfortable, that my curiosity was drowned.

Not much of the land was cultivated for more than half way from Syra-cuse. It is stony, and a coat of soil only covers the rocky foundation. This rock is of a yellowish color, resembling that of Malta, except it is much harder. There is between Syracuse and Catania only a little footpath and but little travelling is done.

The appearance of the peasants is unintelligent, their faces ugly; indicative of the [205] absence of any such thing as thought. Their physiognomy in general {is} decidedly dry, unharmonious, unintelligent, and without any beauty, regularity, etc. The Greek peasants are superior to them and the Grecian spirit finer, more independent and less slavish than the Sicilian one.

About twenty-four miles from Syracuse the country begins to change. You descend still, however, and you leave behind that rocky surface. The land is better, or at least there is more soil, and you meet now cultivated grounds. You pass the mouth of a little stream, the country for a long way in the interior is flat and low. You then come to a river, which is crossed in a large boat.[83] The [206] same plain continues. It is, no doubt, more or less overflowed when the heavy rains come on. Only parts of it are cultivated. As you approach nearer Catania, you see the houses and parts of pavements etc. built of lava, which is a large coarse black substance, resembling something compact cinders, such as come from a blacksmith's forge. It appears hard and durable.

There is only one miserable inn between Syracuse and Catania, and the houses and appearance of the peasants denote but little comfort. This country is richer in soil than Greece, but there is more activity and quickness in the Greeks than these people, but there are very [207] natural reasons for it. I arrived in Catania, not fatigued, and I entered by the large Street Ferdinanda. The city appeared larger to me than I expected. The large number of the people in the street surprised me.

The houses have an oldish look and a certain appearance of neglect, and absence of enterprise seems to reign in the city. As I was coming in at the gate, I was stopped, and was told that it was the custom to examine the what entered the city, but that if I chose to give him some little *regalo*, (gift) I could pass on; so I gave him two Taris.[84] I went to the Locanda della Corona d'Oro (Hotel of the Golden Crown). The *locandiere* (hotelier) gave me soon a book in which was written a [208] thousand and one praises of all kinds, and in many languages. There were many more English than any others, then Germans, then French, and Americans, then

---

[83] The confluence of the rivers Dittaino and Simeto was a few miles south of Catania.

[84] A Tarij was a bronze Maltese coin, worth eight cents.

Italians, etc. I got a dinner which, notwithstanding the thousand and one recommendations, was not over good. I asked the chamber maid to sleep with me. She stood a moment, and then said very coolly, *"bene"* (all right).

Catania: Thursday 2nd December

The weather today is tolerably fair, but cloudy. I have been running a good deal about the streets to see the place. The lava-principle is decidedly predominant here. Everything, almost, is built of it: the [209] houses, the pavements of the streets, etc. The streets are strait, some very long, broad, all edifices in the Roman-Italian style of architecture, the dwelling houses tolerably large, and not badly built, but a general appearance of neglect is visible. They don't keep them clean, and as there are a great many balconies, and almost always flower pots on them, the seeds fly into the crevices and plants sprout out from there, which adds to the appearance of neglect.

Catania has the appearance of a city that exists within itself, that is, there is no foreign or exterior impulse to add to, and enliven, its antiquity. Each one works to make his living. Those who have it pass their time as agreeably as [210] they can for themselves, but it could be sworn to *a priori* that no activities of a nature exterior to the individual animated the mass. But little content is given the mind. It remains within itself, and with a simple direction. It does not spread out its activity exploring different sides of itself, because "itself" is the thing that least interests it. It is easy to see from the general appearance of persons and things that the country around Catania offers more resources than that of Syracuse. There does not appear that general poverty, and the thirst for money seems rather slackened. When I arrived here, I was neither assailed by *cicerones* (guides) nor *macarana* (procurers), neither do I see so many [211] beggars in the streets, although the place is so much larger.

I am decidedly better contented with this city than Syracuse. Priests are not wanting here, but I think there are less whores. The churches are built in the worst taste possible. There appear fewer monks and friars here than in the above city. I had to go to the Police at 12, in order they should make out a *carte de sejour* (passport). They are taking all possible precautions since the affair of France, which has distilled in them a fear that goes to their very marrow.[85]

Besides that, I must get Signor Tomaselli, a person for whom Mr Eynard gave me a letter of introduction, to answer for me, or at least to say he knows me, and that I am [212] no suspected character. *Il n'y a rien que craignent les gens autant de l'Esprit.*[86] It is better to deal with the devil, he is less subtle.

The port is small, and larger vessels do not find an anchorage proper to induce them to come in. This is a considerable detriment to the city. There are in Catania some few remains of antiquities: a Grecian theater, a Roman amphitheater, a bath. The Grecian theater was of a large size, and remains show that it was well and costly built. The seats are of the stones of Syracuse, brought from that city, but they were all covered with slabs of [213] white marble about two inches thick, as were also various other parts. I observed the pavement of an entry ornamented the same way.

There are various large galleries for walking in, when rains force the spectator to leave the open area, but I observed that these galleries were arched, and by means of pieces of lava, cut out for the purpose, but made firm with cement. This may be of later addition. The larger part of the theater is under ground, and houses built over it. It has been excavated down to the last seat, but the scene[87] is still covered. I observed a large slab of marble commencing a little distance from the lowest seat, forming consequently [214] the pavement, but the wall stands upon it, and hinders further inspection. Perhaps could the ground be entirely taken away, the entire scene of the theater might be found preserved, which would be something interesting. I think this theater in later times has undergone reparations or changes.[88]

The amphitheater is much larger, and what you see of it shows it must have been of great interest. The corridors running around it are very long.

---

[85] By the affair of France, Brisbane presumably means the elevation of Louis-Philippe to the French throne in July of 1830. The King was a constitutional monarch, and therefore a fearful example for absolutist states.

[86] "People fear nothing so much as intelligence."

[87] The scene-building, from which the actors appeared, would have been behind the orchestra.

[88] The structure visible today, built above the Greek theater, is of Roman date.

You see the one for the animals, at every few feet cages for them branch off from it. Everything here is of lava. The interior here is still filled up. The capitals of the pilasters you find in [215] different parts rising above the surface. They are also of lava.[89]

There is a bath of considerable extent, also under ground, but parts cleared out. There is nothing in all these things, however, for the architect. The bath is of very common construction. You see several rooms, the ovens, and places for heating the water etc. Also some round stone balls, used also when heated to put in the water. All these excavations have been made by the Prince Biscari.

Another thing which is curious is one of the ancient walls of the city, over which the lava ran in 16 hundred and sixty something.[90] Although the wall is of considerable height, 30 feet perhaps, it is extremely covered over with lava, and in one spot they have [216] excavated down to its foundations.

The police are very particular with regard to strangers, and as I said before, they are very strict in the means they take to know what they do. The Innkeeper has to send twice a day to the police to say what the travellers have been doing. In some countries every man is held to be honest, until he is proven to be the contrary, but here every person is looked upon as a rogue until he turns out to be an honest man.

Catania: Friday 3rd December

The present day has been clear and fine. I went this morning to visit the Museum of the Prince of Biscari.[91] There is a [217] large collection of antiquities, but none of Grecian production, except perhaps a part of a Jove. The number of little Roman bronze statues is very considerable, as well as of lamps and such things. There are a large quantity of marble statue busts, and some bas-reliefs, but mostly out of Roman times and that later even, or of the lower Empire. I went through them quick, because I found nothing of much merit, and of superior execution. The collection of Etruscan and other vases is quite extensive, and there are some large and handsome ones

---

[89] This amphitheater, built in the second century AD, seated 16,000 people. .
[90] Etna's recent eruption in 1669 had covered the city in lava.
[91] The Biscari family's archaeological collection is now housed in the Museo Civico in Catania.

among them. These are by far the best things of the museum. There is also a collection of lavas, some few objects of natural history, etc.

[218] I decided, together with a Mr Allen, a Scotchman whose sister I recollect to have met, also by accident, in Cologne last year, to go up Mt Etna. We determined upon going first to Nicolosi, a town about two and a half hour's distance, and sleep there for the night and proceed on the next morning to the summit. We set off about three with two mules, the weather fine and everything promising fair. As you begin to ascend Etna (the road however is very little slanting, the ascent being very gradual) you meet cultivated lands, some little villages, poor things however, fruit and other trees, wheat and different grains seen growing. The land looks rich and good and has accumulated over ancient lava, but it requires [219] several centuries to form.

You, however, find in this lowest part of Etna a good deal of land destroyed by lava and fields of it spreading out, the top of its blackish surface diversified by quantities of shapeless masses of different sizes, both large and small, blistering, as it were, up from its level. The road, for halfway up to Nicolosi, is very good. You pass some few scattered houses, one or two towers and some poor little collections of houses. In every part you find traces of lava, so that the whole mountain has been buried up, and that strata of lava covered over and reburied again.

The country is cultivated as far up as Nicolosi, except different considerable large portions of land destroyed by [220] the lava. Nicolosi is about the highest village, but its temperature is very moderate.[92] There is no snow within a long distance from it still up the mountain, and you can easily do without fire in the daytime. In the night it is more agreeable. I saw there Signor Geniellara, a very obliging man, which is of great aid to travellers, and no doubt very much bothered by them sometimes. We passed the night at the *Locanda Nuova*, (New Hotel) although it is an old and poor concern.

Etna: Saturday, 4th December

We were to start at four. However, on looking out at that hour, we find to our great sorrow and disappointment that the weather since last eve-

---

[92] Nicolosi is 698 meters above sea level. See the map of Brisbane's Italian route, Illustration 10.

ning had completely changed, and that [221] it was an excessively foggy, a cloudy and windy day, and at the same time it was raining very fast. We soon got back to bed again, and remained until nearly 8. We then got our breakfast, and not finding the weather changing any, we determined upon setting out and going as far as possible.

After leaving Nicolosi, the first part of land you pass over is a little desert, as it were, of fine black sand, or rather between sand and small pebbles about as large as the end of your finger, and decreasing to dust. This was just up by the Mt Rossi, at that time they made that irruption which destroyed part of Catania, and so many villages.[93] [222] This sandy level lasts some distance. You then enter into fields of modern lava (that is, such as have not been grown over, or not covered with soil) or streams which have flowed down, and across which you pass.

The land here is completely covered with lava. It has in general a black appearance, but when it has been long exposed to the weather it becomes grayish, gathering a thin coat of a mossy substance, or something of the kind. Irregular blocks and points of lava are projecting everywhere from the main surface, resembling huge cinders from a forge. Consequently, the surface is very irregular, which is found by the lava boiling up, as it were, or by passing over resisting surfaces, throws up [223] numberless points and blocks and unformed shapes which cool in these various shapes. You see vast fields covered, which resemble something a dirty sea dashing its short irregular waves in every direction.

After passing across this track you continue, entering the *Bosca* (woods). This covers a very extensive surface there. Formerly at some distant period were also fields of lava here, but time has covered them with a deep and rich layer of soil, upon which grow a vast quantity of large fine oaks. It is a forest. You find, however, brush wood, and not many plants. If cultivated, it should make no doubt a fine grain country and would be very productive. The climate is by no means frigid, there being [224] yet no snow on the ground in that part. The ascent in general from Catania is not steep, but very gradual. In the *Bosca*, however, you have to go up one or two little hills, rather steep. At the upper end of the *Bosca* is the *Casa della Neve* (House of Snow), and it is about here that the snow commences.

---

[93] The Mt Rossi craters were produced by the eruption of 1669.

We proceed little farther on with the mules, and then sent them back there, where a fire was made to await our return. After the *Bosca* commences the snow country, which is immense fields of lava not covered by any soil, and on which only a few plants or shrubs grow, starting out of the crevices. After leaving the mules, the labor of walking on foot was very great. In part, [225] we walked over the points of lava, which was like scrambling over heaps of stones, and in part across the snow, but it was not hard enough to support us, and we would sink in.

The wind here was strong and raw, the weather excessively foggy, so that it was impossible to see far before you, and every now and then torrents of rain would pour down. In consequence of this, it was necessary to have on a good deal of clothing, which made it very fatiguing. We proceeded above an hour or two on foot, and then came to a halt, being convinced we could not reach the top, or rather, being there, that we could see nothing on account of the fog. The guide once stopped and said we could go on no farther, but I took the lead, and we ascended a considerable distance still. We then commenced returning, and after traveling through the most abominable weather, heavy rains and wind, we reached Catania at about 9 at night. We gave the guide two dollars.

[226] *Sunday 5th December*

Left Catania about 11 o'clock, having taken, together with the Allens, a carriage with four horses which had to return to Messina, and for which we paid $3 apiece. I stayed at the Corona d'Oro in Catania, the charges of which were about as follows: 3 Taris = 24 cents, for breakfast, 1 dollar for dinner, and 4 dollars per day for room. The dinner was too dear. $1 for servants. I went to bid adieu to Signor Tomaselli. He is a liberal feeling man, and above the prejudices of the society that surrounds him. After leaving Catania, the road ascended for a while around the side of Etna, passing through cultivated lands, the soil of which has grown over the lava.

The road is good and the [227] rise gradual. After a few miles you begin to descend, having passed the ridge of the mountain. The land is in general well cultivated, although there are strips covered with later lava, which are barren. You have Etna at your side, and as the day is tolerably fair, its white summit was to be beautifully seen, now and then obscured by floating masses of clouds. The country is uneven and presents many handsome prospects. You pass through several villages and one or two tolerably larger places, but these towns are no wise worthy of note. They generally have a neglected appearance, as if their inhabitants were without emulation and enterprise, which is the case.

Everything is done in a manner, as it were, simply to satisfy [228] the need of it. You see but few handsome faces among the people, and that particularly with regard to women. Their physiognomies are without beauty and showing but little intellectual character, which is natural, where the principles of the government tend to a regular moral degradation by the means of material deprivation, and the government, from its nature having no want, or in fact the contrary, of intellectual activity, among the people.

After leaving Catania, you pass over the beds of ancient and later streams of lava for about twenty-three miles. The sides of Mt Etna present many little rises of land here and there, or hills, in general of a reddish brown color. [229] The ascent is very uneven, being valleys here, rises of land there and little plains in other parts. Giardino, where we stop tonight, is about half way.[94] We arrived there a little after dark, and before coming to it, we passed a plain of some distance in breadth, of which the land is very low, and which has not been overflowed with the lava. The inn where we stopped was not bad for a little country village. The eating was good, but I was annoyed by the fleas, which served to put me in mind of Greece.

To Messina: Monday 6th December

Left about half after seven. I proceeded on foot to see the Theater of Taurominium, which is situated about a mile and [230] a half from Giardino. The coast all day has been very steep, and running near the sea; it rises up very steep and very high, forming hills cut in every direction by deep ravines, presenting consequently a very irregular appearance. They are covered with a certain degree of verdure. They offer many very handsome and picturesque views, and bold scenery.

Taurominium is situated on the top of one of those high hills, the ascent of which is long and fatiguing. The present town is a miserable dirty and poor place. A little to the east of it are the remains of the theater, which are

---

[94] The ancient Naxos, near Taormina.

quite extensive, but which are not out of Grecian times, unless it be [231] the seats, and they are so much covered and ruined that it is difficult to distinguish them, or at least to see their ancient form.

Around the back part of the theater runs a wall of brick joined with mortar and the entries arched. Before the theater, which forms the scene, are also walls standing, and remains of columns unfluted, and Corinthian; not well done, at least without much beauty, as is all the bit of ornaments you find remaining, which are walled in to preserve them by some person or other. Their execution as well as forms show them to be Roman and without much care and taste. Probably the theater was originally built by the Greeks and injured by some earthquake, and afterwards repaired by the Romans.[95]

[232] The view from the place is most magnificent. You see Etna; and the day I saw it, its top was covered with snow, shining brightly in the rising sun's rays, and a pale body of smoke, looking something like a cloud lightened out, was raining from the crater. You see also its sides, diversified with little hills, at one time craters, and outlets also, scattered over with villages and houses, all receiving a lustre from the rising sun. The general color of the sides of Etna is a reddish brown, not much heightened however, but in some parts it is darker, in others lighter.

You see also the coasts winding in the distance and some picturesque scenery immediately in the neighborhood, a part of which is a little valley, running from the sea-coast [233] with trees, and closed in by very high and steep hills. It has a bold and picturesque appearance. The road after this, nearly all the way to Messina, lies near the sea shore. The scenery in many points is very handsome. A little distance from the edge of the water rise very steep hills, of which I have spoken above. The road in many places has been cut through the bottom part of them, and they produce layers of limestone, sandstone, clay etc.

In entering Messina, you pass an outside gate, and quite a long line of houses before getting into the interior. We arrived about 4½ {4:30}. I went to see the American consul, Mr Payson, and I passed the evening there. There were several persons besides, and *écarté*[96] was [234] played, at which I

---

[95] The theater of Taormina was built in the third century BC, and reconstructed by the Romans in the second century AD.

[96] *Écarté*: a card game.

lost a *pezzo e mezzo* (a piece and a half). It was about 1 when I returned home. So much for the day, and so much for the four or five last days. In them I have run about, been occupied in visiting places. Outside scenes enough have passed before my mind, but there has been but little intellectual work.

I have been for four days past traveling with Mr Allen, a Scotchman. Consequently I have not been traveling alone, and I find I gain nothing by traveling in company. Although it may be in certain cases more agreeable, because I am too much taken up with the conversation of the other, and I think it more profitable to [235] be engaged with oneself, the thought being only worked upon by itself, and its expansion is effected by its own effort to dilate itself. I consider it better to travel alone.

Messina: Tuesday 7th December

Today I have been walking a good deal about the city, to see how it is built, laid out, etc. and the appearance of people and things. This place in its outside appearance differs considerably from either Syracuse or Catania, but the spirit is the same, it only containing more activity and expansion, consequently, more developed in certain directions than in the above place. It does by far more commerce, possessing a large harbor, and having certain privileges. This principle [236] explains the difference of things. It has been ruined by an earthquake, and within forty years rebuilt anew, and owing to that circumstance, the houses have a better, newer, and more modern appearance, and are better built, than in Catania for example.

The place is large, containing about 60,000 inhabitants. There are some large streets. The others are of not much consequence and many of them narrow. Neither are they very regular. The larger ones are broad and long, well built, many well furnished shops in them, and a great many people passing. The people seem to possess more activity, they look more modern, and it is easy to observe the [237] effect commerce produces upon the people, in comparing them to the Catanians. There are no want of priests, but I think monks are scarcer. There must be, in a society, some movement towards some objects. If it be towards commerce, it produces a certain effect, if towards sciences, arts etc. a different corresponding effect, the same with military feeling. The object or determination of the movement produces an effect harmonious with itself.

Here there is no particular determination towards much else than commerce. Commerce consequently produces a certain effect. In Catania the same is the case, but there is less commerce, consequently the people are more sunk within themselves, within the individual. [238] Exterior principles of movement are even more rare, which leaves the individual much deeper in himself and in his individual existence. In a society there is a religion; its forms and prejudices become a part of existence. There is also the manner of living or existing, and their forms are the method of existence, or its exterior or realized existence is consequently in them. Consequently they are existence. These forms are different in different societies, consequently determinations towards the same objects realize themselves differently, and these effects are in harmony with the forms. The effect is in itself the same, but its realization is tempered and toned by the society on which it works. [239] Commerce here does not realize itself in the same way; still, it produces an effect. Messina, having more of it than Catania, makes it also a more agreeable city, it being about the only exterior activity they have.

There are also a good many strangers here, also foreign merchants, etc. which tend also to give more diversity to the place. Messina is well built, large, some handsome streets, does a good deal of commerce, but it is otherwise uninteresting. The opera is the only public amusement. People seem to go but little in society, that is, there is not much sociability among families. I am speaking of the natives, which is generally the case in commercial towns. You find nothing to do, nothing to attract your attention, for as [240] one is, so are all the others. Things seem to stay within themselves, they don't branch out to catch your attention; you find but little to lay hold of. A simple uniformity, amounting to a void, surrounds you.

Messina: Wednesday 8th December

There are two buildings here that I have seen, which are very worthy of attention, consequently they have not been thrown down by the earthquake. The style of architecture is nearly Gothic, but it is still somewhat mixed with Byzantinish forms. You find, for example, tall thin columns. There are only two of them on each side of the door. In many little particulars you still perceive remains of Byzantinish taste, [241] but the arch has disappeared and the Gothic outline in general has replaced them. In the interior you find Byzantinish granite columns. There are no windows in front, no *strebepfeilers* (buttresses).

The front presents a striped appearance. The layers of stone one above another, running horizontally, have each a different color. One of the layers, for example, is of a reddish marble, another of white, another layer inlaid, forming various black figures, upon a white ground. These layers are of but little breadth, so that they give a striped appearance to the building. There are many of these stripes of inlaid stone. On each side of the doors are twisted pillars, of very long proportions [242] in comparison with the diameter, and having a large capital in pairs in the Byzantinish taste. The rest of the door is in Gothic style. Its arch is not quite pointed enough.[97]

The building is a passage from the Byzantinish to the Gothic. In the sculpture and the ornaments, there is much more of the Gothic, although there is something in them which is of foreign taste, but not Byzantinish. Grace and care of execution are stamped on them. The large masses of the building, to resume, are not Gothic, neither is the interior, but the details are so. The top of the building has been thrown down, but along the top of the front, which formed the largest mass, projects a gleet[98] of white marble, simple in shape, under which runs the whole length [243] of the building, a round gleet projecting independent from the wall, and about the size, and twisted like the columns. The vine, and various leaves are used as ornaments, and it is the one twisted in the others that form some of the capitals. The interior of the church has nothing of the Gothic.

Messina: Thursday 9th December

I went this morning to San Giovanni, a little village opposite to Messina, to see if I could find mules to go to Monteleone.[99] When I was about halfway across, the boatman said the sum he was to have was larger than that which he had asked on shore. At my refusing to give him more, he turned the boat about [244] and said he would return. He went a short distance, but soon wheeled about again on seeing me laugh at him, and pursued his course. The servant I took with me engaged mules to Monteleone for five

---

[97] Possibly Brisbane is describing the thirteenth century church of Santa Maria degli Alemanni.

[98] Gleet: meaning unknown. See above: Diary I: 168, November 27, 1830, n. 70.

[99] That is, across the strait of Messina. See the map of Brisbane's route, Illustration 10.

and a half, *pezzi*.[100] On arriving at San Giovanni, it was necessary to go to the judge and show my passport. The servant also had to get a passport to be able to come with me, so very particular are they with regard to these things.

I returned about five o'clock, and after dinner, about 7½, {7:30} I went with Mr Payson to Mr Cloyson, a German. There was a tolerably large society and *ecarté* was played. I won six [245] dollars. In the early part of the morning, I was searching for a large boat to go to Naples, called "Spirinaro," if I recollect, by sound. The prices they asked were sixty and seventy dollars.

During my stay in Messina, I have done nothing particular. I have looked at the city, seen the little theater in which prose, or rather comic, pieces were performed. It might be called a pocket-theater. I have also spent one or two evenings in a small society. I have played a little *écarté*, of which they appear to be fond, and won more than I lost. I do not know how much the natives go into society, but foreigners seem to be quite [246] sociable. I have known at Messina: Mr Payson, Mr Cloyson, a German, Mr Kettel, American, Walker, two of them, Signor Fowls, Italian.

Left Messina: Friday 10th December

Had my account made out by Mr Payson, and gave him a draft for 593 francs, or {illegible}. Breakfasted at his house. He is a man of a good deal of natural force, which, from his education, is without result. Mr Fowls, who is the Neapolitan consul general for the United States, gave me a very polite letter of introduction upon a person in Naples, whom he instructed to introduce me to various persons. I will see how it serves me. The landlord's bill was very [247] reasonable. Breakfast 3 Taris, dinner 6 dollars. Room, 3½. We were two in it, which makes in all 7.

Left Messina about 12 o'clock. The wind was rather high, and it was with difficulty I found a boat to carry me across. They asked at first five dollars. I gave them however, two dollars within a few cents. We started off, and as we began to get into the middle of the passage, we found the waves high and strong for the size of the boat. The boat rolled most prodigiously. All of the sailors were a little uneasy. Twice we saw two waves very large, rolling right upon us. Had they have struck us on the side, there would

---

[100] *Pézza*: a piece of money.

have been danger, but by the dexterous use of an oar, and [248] the helm, they got the prow suddenly round to the wind, and we mounted it without further difficulty. We had to do this several times, letting it also take us by the stern. She would not go straight to San Giovanni, but was forced to go around a point into a little bay a good deal further down. This crossing produced no fear in me, but I felt a kind of nervous feeling for half an hour afterwards.[101]

I had the mules brought but found them miserable beasts, and no saddles, except a kind of wooden thing. However, as the weather was fine, I did not mind these inconveniences, and I started off, intending to reach Palmi. The road runs along the [249] shore. The coast rises up into steep high hills very near the water's edge, as between Giardino and Messina, and has the same appearance, and same character. You see some fine villas, and some bold scenery.

The land appears in general well cultivated. The towns and villages you meet with are not well built. They are in general ugly, dirty, and but little care is taken to make things better and more comfortable, which with a little trouble might be made so. Neglect and indifference is visible, but in many cases without the reasons of physical want. With the Turks, the same thing is to be observed. The reason is a certain moral listlessness. The want of comparison, and stimulant [250] in part flowing from it.

Although the land is very high, it is cultivated in the highest parts. Its soil is very fertile and not rocky. The physical construction of the country is very different from that of Greece. Two towns through which I passed on the coast are quite large, Scilla,[102] near to San Giovanni, and Bagnara, further on. A carriage might pass this road, but there are some few places not quite finished yet, at which they are working. This road has, it appears, been lately made. There are several large bridges, with 1830 marked upon. It surprised me that the thing had been so long neglected. The present road they are making must be expensive, as they have to cut away sides of hills, often rocky and a considerable distance down.

[251] We reached Palmi about 8 in the evening, and before arriving there, we had to cross a tract of country uninhabited and desolate, which

---

[101] See *MB*: 138 for a more dramatic version of this incident.
[102] Legendary home of the monster Scylla mentioned in Homer's *Odyssey*.

is considered as one of the dangerous places, with regard to robbers. The guide requested me not to call out loud, or make any noise. We went quietly. I descended from the mule and went afoot. The night was dark, but we arrived at Palmi without any incident.[103] I had no great fear of robbers, but the place looked desolate, and about dusk one or two common-looking fellows passed, with arms. The muleteer told one of them that *gens d'armes* (armed men) were coming at a little distance behind. I have heard since, that this evening or the morning following, a man was robbed on the other [252] side of Palmi, of 3,000 ducats,[104] at another place which is considered as a dangerous spot. Consequently, passing the straits of Messina and travelling across this place in the evening, might be termed {a} ticklish affair.

Calabria: Saturday 11th December

The wider part of the tavern where I slept last night is a stable, through which it is necessary to pass to get in the upper part. The fleas devoured me *à la Grecque*, which put me in mind of some of the nights in that country. I found the people very obliging, and a desire to please, but they had nothing scarcely to give me to eat. The keeper of the place made me pay the things, however, as dear as in the best hotel in Messina, as poor as they were.

[253] Left this place, which is but small, with fresh mules for Monteleone at 8½ {8:30}. The road here leaves the sea, and you pass more through the interior. The land is very high situated, far above the sea, but it is not rocky, the soil is fertile, is very well cultivated, and appears to produce everything in abundance. After leaving Palmi you enter into a tract of country which is very beautiful. You see high lands, with some lower ones among them, all well cultivated, and covered with various grains just growing. The sides of the hill are also cultivated or covered with trees. There are some very pretty prospects which were the more pleasing to me, as I have not of late [254] seen so much fertile and well cultivated land.

This portion of country is finer than any I have seen in Sicily, perhaps the neighborhood about Catania and Etna may in some respects be better, but it is not at least so to the eyes, and I rather doubt whether it be so in

---

[103] Also described in *MB*: 139.

[104] The ducat was the currency of the Kingdom of the Two Sicilies, equal to about 80 cents.

reality. At a little distance from Palmi you pass an extensive grove of olive trees. Oil is sold here for about 16 *granis*[105] for 36 ounces, or 14 in large quantities. Wheat at 20 *Carolini*[106] for a *Tumolo*,[107] which is about 50 *vololi*. Each *vololo* is 33 ounces. Oats {are} 11-12 *Carolini*. When the grains are harvested, they are sold, I have been informed, much cheaper.

At some distance further on from the olive grove, you come to a quite a large forest of different kinds of trees, with [255] a good deal of under-brush. This is the other suspicious place that the man was robbed, of which I have spoken a page or two back. The weather is fine. The country appears everywhere well cultivated and possessing a good soil, much better than I expected. I have seen but few beggars, and although the people are not rich, and have rarely money, still, there is not much material want. This country is much finer, the soil is much better and less want among the people, than I expected to find.

The approach to Rosari is very handsome. It is situated upon the top of a hill, the sides of which are covered with trees so that you see it through them. You also pass through a little grove of olive trees to come [256] to it, but when you come there, you find it a miserable little place. I have observed today that the physiognomies of the people in the country I have been passing through are much better than those of Sicily. The difference is quite great and easy to be remarked. The women's faces in particular are much handsomer, the men's also, in proportion. You find some well delin-eated and pretty features. It gave me pleasure to look at the young girls that passed, although they were in tattered petticoats and barelegged. There are a large number of villages in this part. I counted toward the sea on my left hand, nine that laid within sight, not far from each other.

Mileto is another little village through which I passed. This is of [257] antique foundation.[108] It is a small place. In a square in the middle of it is a large circular fountain or well, where I observed women washing. I saw also the remains of a tomb. The side, and the two ends were remaining, but the other side was broken, and part wanting. It has been placed in a little open spot, upon a little pedestal of stones, by some of the inhabitants. It is not of

[105] A *grano* was 1/100 of a *ducato*.
[106] A *carlino* was equal to 10 *grani*, or 1/10th of a ducat (about eight cents).
[107] A *tumolo* was a dry measure equaling about 100 pounds.
[108] This may have been the ancient city of Miletos. See *MB*: 140.

large dimensions. Its sides are sculptured, which represents a battle between men on horseback and men on foot. Its general execution is not bad, but it is not finished with a great deal of care. The proportions are good. The work is no doubt Greek. I observed also a fragment of Byzantinish work, and some other few signs, which showed the place to be antique.

[258] The country in general bears about the same appearance. I passed in the morning some low land of some extent. But here you find long and very deep ravines, running in crooked directions. Their sides appear less fertile than the top of the high land, which might rather be called extensive ridges. I picked out of a bank, which has been cut down to form the road, two little shells, of which there were a large number in it. The bank was formed of a hard yellowish sand. Arrived at Monteleone about six. I found the innkeeper of the inn I stopped at, a most honest and outgoing man. I paid him more than his bill. He gave me supper, coffee in the morning, and sleeping for 8 *Carolini.*

[259] *Calabria: Sunday 12th December*

The innkeeper came with me this morning to show me what he thought to be pieces of ancient work. It is a castle, built in quite modern times, but in the situation of the ancient ones. I saw something of it, that I took to be Roman work, and one piece of wall left, which I took for Greek. The stones are without mortar, and nicely formed together. Monteleone is situated on the side of a hill, on top of which is this castle.

There are a great number of villages in this neighborhood. It is about four miles from the sea, containing several thousand inhabitants, seven perhaps, but it is like all these inland villages [260] uninteresting, still rather neglected and offering but few resources. There is but little traveling by strangers in this part of Italy, and the inns and accommodations in general are but poor. Monteleone is such a situation as the Greeks would have chosen, and no doubt the neighborhood of the place, and Mileto, has been a particularly inhabited part. The scenery of the country is handsome, and the soil good.

Left Monteleone between 8 and 9, took two horses there for Cosenza, 13 miles distant, for 7 ducats. The road begins to descend, and after some distance you reach the low land, that is, a little strip laying between the sea and the range of regular high hills, which probably formed the ancient [261] coast. Between San Giovanni and Bagnara this strip of land is much narrower, and in some places it does not exist at all, the high coast rising up immediately from the water, but here is of considerable breadth. From the water up to the high and steep hills there is a slight and regular ascent.

I passed one of the *fiumari* or streams of water. There were about a dozen persons around it to help those who came across. I thought it was some dangerous place, but I found that the water scarce reached up to the horses' knees. Not having any small money, I wanted my half dollar changed. No one could do it, and I am sure I passed half a dozen houses and a change [262] of post before I found someone capable of giving me small money for it. They had not half a dollar laid by. This shows they have no surplus, at least in money.

The guide left the main road after 18 or 19 miles, and took a small road, for horses only, as it was shorter. We arrived at Nicastro, a town containing 5,000 or 6,000 inhabitants, about dark. They showed me the best hotel, which was a poor concern, containing two or three rooms, with half a dozen beds in each, at a *Carolino* a piece. I got a room to myself, and after dinner commenced writing a little. They brought me a paper where I wrote who I was, where I was going, etc. A while after that, there came two *gens d'armes* who asked [263] divers questions, examined my passport, etc. About half an hour after that, there came still another, who went through with the same ceremony. They have, it appears, a particular suspicion of strangers.[109]

Calabria: Monday 13th December

Left Nicastro some time before it was daylight, and began picking our way in the dark. The guide {took} a small path which is much shorter than the main road, but which also is bad, and passes over the hills and through the valleys. On the plain, I did not find the weather at all uncomfortably cold, but on the mountains the wind was rather fresh. The country through which I have been passing today is different [264] from that of the former days. It is more mountainous, bolder, and the mountains rockier, and less

---

[109] As Brisbane mentions above, the Kingdom of the Two Sicilies was known for its use of spies and police to guard against rebellion.

cultivated The tops of a good many of the hills are covered with trees, and the sides of some grow the vine.

When we started the sky was perfectly clear; the stars shone brightly, but as the sun rose, it became cloudy. However, we had no rain. I have crawled today over a good many of these mountains, and generally by bad paths. From the tops of many, you have very handsome views. You see some low land of some extent, but nowhere enough to call it a plain or a valley. These mountains are in general separated by very deep ravines, which [265] are wide at the tops, but which are very narrow at the bottom, forming now and then the bed of a stream. Some of these mountains are very rocky, particularly the sides. They seem formed by layers, one above the other. The soil is less abundant, they are fewer inhabitants and the land is not near so generally cultivated.

This part of the country is said to be dangerous on account of the robbers, at least they say that there {are} *brutti luogi* (rough places), but I was no wise disturbed. There are too few persons pass this way, I should think, to give encouragement enough to the trade. The sides of these mountains are very steep, and the ravines between them run in winding [266] directions. About nine miles from Cosenza we came again into the main road. As I was proceeding along, I met about a dozen *gens d'armes* conducting three men chained together. Someone behind told me they were robbers, and their countenances made me already suppose it.

The country here becomes level, or rather you pass through a plain. You see the mountains still at some distance on both sides of you; the sides of these hills are covered with a large number of villages, and particularly on the right, there appears nearly a continuous chain of them. The country is here well cultivated and the land good.

We arrived at Cosenza about seven. It is situated low and upon sloping ground. [267] It is well peopled and there is a garrison of a thousand and some men there. The Hotel I was at was, however, a poor thing. There appears no activity and enterprise for bettering things in this part. They live in order to exist, consequently anything superfluous to it is not searched for.

On arriving, I sent to see if there was any carriage going to Naples, and found one is to leave tomorrow morning. I made a bargain with the man, giving him twelve ducats, which was two or three too many. He asked at first fifteen *pezzis*. Cosenza is a place of rather more activity. It has a theater and the travelling in carriages rarely extends farther than this, but there are a considerable number that [268] come here.

At San Giovanni, the country appears poor, as well as the people. Their physiognomy is in general ugly, and the difference between the faces of the people here, and of those between Palmi and Monteleone is very striking. There appears harmony between the inhabitants and the soil that nourishes them. The country between Palmi and Monteleone is very handsome, the soils excellent, and is everywhere cultivated. I have rarely seen a more beautiful tract of country. The mules I got at San Giovanni were most miserable, and terribly abused. Those I found at Palmi were much better, were well fed and fat, and the prices lower. This also is a little sign.

[269] In this part of the country there is but little travelling by strangers, and the people consequently seem more honest with regards to them. I found the country people strong and healthy looking, many taking off their hats, and bowing as we passed. They appear to be hard working, but mental activity does not exist among them. Religious dogmas are strongly impressed upon them, and you scarcely find a person who does not go through all the rites, as if they were in the Middle Ages, for example. I had no idea, that there was a country, where the Catholic religion was in such perfect bloom.

The people have the bad habit of carrying packs upon their heads, [270] and this is done by quite young children, but mostly by the girls and women. It was between Palmi and Monteleone that I remarked the best-formed physiognomies, and this more so in the girls. Their faces are without those dry lines, and there is generally something pretty in the features. After leaving Monteleone, the road descends towards the sea, and does not pass through the interior of the land. Consequently, I have not been able to see the interior, the strip between the sea and high land is in parts cultivated but there are but few houses.

After leaving Nicastro the country becomes very mountainous, of which the soil is not so rich, [271] and there are none of those broad strips of high land. The sides of the mountains are often quite rocky, and mostly not cultivated, but more or less covered with trees. The country is poorer, and you see that it produces an effect upon the inhabitants. They don't look so well off, and I have remarked a difference in the physiognomy. It was easy to observe that there were not so many regular and well-shaped faces.

At ten, eleven miles from Cosenza, you leave these mountains, or rather you enter into quite a large plain, chains of hills rising up on each side. There are no villages in the valleys, but great numbers on the side of these hills. The plain is well cultivated. This land is low, at least [272] much more so, than that about Monteleone.

Calabria: Tuesday 14th December

Left Cosenza about 10, without having seen much of the place, it raining abominably, and being the most disagreeable weather possible. The road lays through the plain, and the country in general is much lower than that I have left. It is not so handsome, and the people do not look so well. You see hills at a distance, and you raise now and then higher land, but the mountains have in a measure disappeared. We passed two or three streams without much difficulty, but about which they make so much trouble. I observed [273] some grottoes hewed in the rock on the sides of two or three hills. They were ancient, and the entrances in part filled up. The place we stopped in for the night is called Spezano. We found a poor inn, where there was nothing but macaroni to eat.

This part is inhabited by people who speak a language different from the rest of the inhabitants. They call themselves Albanians, and are said to be remains of the Greeks of *Magna Grecia*.[110] They have become gradually Catholics, but their priests can marry, by a permission obtained from the Pope. The inn is kept by one of these families. The mother is a very tall woman, two of the daughters also, having blue eyes, black hair, and a certain form of physiognomy different from the Italian inhabitants. [274] There was one daughter, however, short and resembling the generality of Italian inhabitants. These people do not carry loads upon their heads and there is a difference between their dress and the Calabrian one. The whole day has been damp, wet, rainy and uncomfortable, disagreeable and abominable.

---

[110] Beginning in the eighth century BC, the Greeks founded numerous settlements in Sicily and southern Italy. The area was known in antiquity as *Magna Graecia* (greater Greece). In Calabria there still exist people called *Grecanici*, who speak a dialect of Greek and practice the Orthodox Christian faith. What relation they might be to the Albanians, who settled in parts of southern Italy during the middle ages, is unclear.

Calabria: Wednesday 15th December

The present morning is such a one as that of yesterday, and we did not leave until nine. I paid my bill, which was only four *Carolini*. Had I been alone, I would have paid more than double that sum, but I paid at the same time with the other persons travelling in the carriage. The country has continued about the same. The road [275] has been terribly bad, and the land has not been very high.

Before arriving at Morano, where we were to stop, and only eighteen miles from Spezano, we approached some very {high} hills, the tops of which were covered with snow. We passed today one or two flat plains surrounded by hills. They are cultivated, but no houses built on them, as the *Malaria* is said to be there. The *Malaria* appears to me in many cases as a kind of humbug.[111] This part of the country has a different appearance from that between Nicastro and Cosenza. The land is not so high, more sloping; the hills not so separated by deep ravines, and not so stony.

Arrived at Morano quite early, and might have proceeded farther, but for some [276] stupid chickenhearted reason, that it might be too late before we reached Rotonda, or something of the kind, we did not go on. This place is built upon the side of a hill, which is nearly circular and runs quite steep up to a point. Upon the top are the ruins of some old fortifications or castle. It presents a singular appearance, as you see one row of houses rising above another. There is a good deal of poverty, it is said, in this part, and I observed a good many beggar boys, asking for charity. The inns in this part of the country are poor and dirty places. I was again eaten up by the fleas. The room through which you pass to go into the bedrooms, was occupied by a cobbler, and served for other purposes. [277] In the room beyond that, and the first you enter from the stairs, were a number of hogs eating acorns, and other things in the same style.

Calabria: Thursday 16th December

The weather is the same as it was; it could not be worse. We did not get off till late, and we have this day only gone eighteen miles. There is no spirit of activity and enterprise in these people. Everything is done slow, and with

---

[111] *Malaria* (Italian: bad air), far from being a humbug, made many low-lying plains uninhabitable in Italy in the nineteenth century, and accounted for thousands of lives.

so much caution and lack of promptness, that it might as well not be done at all. There is no energy in the people. When the moral, the intellectual are not called into activity among a people, you see its effects [278] in the most trivial circumstances of life. It leaves ruin with a spring of action, and they are never prepared to execute any little undertaking, which is out of the lines habit has put them in.

After leaving Morano, the land begins to ascend, and for four miles you have to travel up a slanting road. The ascent is gradual, and along the sides of the hills. These hills are different from any I have seen, they are excessively stony, uncultivated, and no trees growing upon them. The land appears a bluish limestone; I have remarked a good deal of it in Greece.

Before the hill on which Morano is built spreads out a little valley, well-cultivated and enclosed in hills. These hills are very rocky [279] and not cultivated. These hills form a different kind of country from any I have seen in Calabria. After having crawled up the sides of the hills for four miles, you begin to descend, but not so much as the rise. You first come into a plain, stony, gravelly, and uncultivated. It is quite flat, and surrounded by those rocky, barren hills. You also see detached hills, not very large, raising out of the plains.

This tract of country resembles very much some I have seen in Greece; the formation of the ground and the stones resemble each other. This plain is uninhabited, uncultivated and dreary. There are two guard-houses for soldiers, to keep the road [280] clear of robbers upon it. The road in some places here is not good, but they make as much fuss about it as if it led over precipices. It was necessary for us all to get out of the carriage two or three times, to pass places over which an American stage driver would have trotted his horses, without looking at the thing. This stony tract lasts for some time, until you get really to Rotonda, twelve miles distant from Morano. You make one or two more descents and then come into sloping land, which is again cultivated, and on which you see habitations.

This part of the country is in general poor. Physical nature seems bad off here. You see plenty of beggar boys in the villages. Rotonda is a dirty [281] little village, over all the rest of them. No pains are taken to better things. The interior of the habitations of the poor are dark, blackened with smoke, and appear dirty and uncomfortable. The country after Rotonda becomes quite well cultivated, and the land appears good. The vine is particularly attended to. I saw a great many of them growing. The country here is not flat, but uneven and sloping hills. The road still descends.

We arrived about 4 o'clock at Castel-Luce, where we were to pass the night. I found one of those dirty and uncomfortable looking inns, (the best in the place however) which appear to be peculiar to this country; they gave [282] us, however, a tolerably good dinner, and the place could be made better, had the people themselves the wish to be any better than the places they inhabit. These habitations are the mere expression of their indifference. Those who have their interior cultivated wish to make the exterior, or physical, life as much in harmony with it as possible.

Calabria: Friday 17th December

The morning has been raining and bad weather. About noon it cleared off and was fine but cool weather. For a time after that, it began raining again, which turned to snow and for an hour or two there was a hard [283] fall of snow.

On leaving Castel-Luce, you pass at the foot of a large mountain on which is another town of considerable size called Castel-Luce Soprana. The country through which I have passed today is mountainous and in general bad. The mountains are divided by strips of lower land, which are not flat, forming little valleys, but which also slope away, forming uneven surfaces. These mountains are uncultivated, except the sides of some very few, and they are also for the most part bare of trees. Some few have groves growing upon them. The lower lands are mostly cultivated, but there are also [284] parts of them which lie barren.

You see but few villages, and but few isolated habitations. This part of the country is much inferior to the country near Monteleone. The inhabitants also please me here less, but it is to be observed, that there is more communication in these parts, the dresses of the people are rather different in some respects, and that more so with the women. I have remarked but very few good-looking faces, and there is but little beauty in the general physiognomy of the people.

We set off rather earlier this morning but have come but a short distance, about twenty miles. The villages in this part of the country, or in what I [285] have seen of Calabria, are nearly all situated upon high land, in the Greek fashion. The streets also are narrow and crooked, and both of these things are no doubt remains of their ancient situation and shape.

There are three persons travelling in the carriage besides myself, but they form the least interesting, and as stupid a society as I ever fell in with. The one is an old fellow with a stupid, lazy, sleepy look, and a monkey laugh; dressed very dirtily, not washing himself; and his manner of speaking the Italian in harmony with his other qualities and appearance. He said today, in entering the tavern, *qua sta bo* instead of *qui stiamo bene*, (here we are well lodged), about [286] the only of his words I have understood. The other, a seafaring man, good natured, but a mind without the least content. The other is a lad of fourteen, who has as much beard as I, whose body will soon be set, and corporeally he will be a man before he is mentally a boy.

This perhaps is one of the results of a warm climate. The body gets set, before time is given to the mind to expand and develop itself, and get rid of its prejudices, or at least gain general views of things. The body, as it were, springs up and takes the mind before it has had time to apply itself to different views and feelings. When the body is once set, it is difficult to change direction, and shake off prejudices.

[287] They talk a good deal upon the price of things, but much more upon where they have got, or where they can get, a certain large quantity of some eatable of which they are fond, for a small sum of money. The old fellow wears only one glove at a time alternately on each hand, keeping one in his breeches-pocket.

Calabria: Saturday 18th December

The morning is bad again; started off early, as we have thirty-three miles to go today. The country after Lagonero, where we slept, is about the same; mountainous, and stony land, but little of it cultivated. There are very few houses; and the products of this tract [288] of country appear comparatively nothing. On the sides of some of the mountains grow trees, but scantily, but there is underbrush. The rain after a while turned to snow and there was quite a hard snowstorm, but which melted on touching the earth.

After travelling about twelve miles, the road commences to descend into a plain, the hills glide away gradually, and you find yourself in a large level plain, of considerable breadth, and about sixteen miles long. On both sides of it rises the chain of mountains, which I have been in, and the two branches of this chain are tolerably parallel with each other. Their sides are rocky, and uncultivated, and their tops covered with snow.

[289] This plain is large and very level, and most all its parts cultivated. Grain and the vine I observed growing. Upon the sides of the mountains that border it you see a number of quite large villages not distant from each other, which show that the soil is productive again here. The villages are built high up upon the sides of the hills and you don't find a single house in the plain, except a *Locanda* (Inn). The land of this valley is more or less gravelly. It does not appear to be a thick coat of earth over a foundation of rock or clay, as in parts of Southern Calabria.

Three or four miles before arriving at the place, where we stop for the night, the plain ends, and you pass a very deep [290] ravine, over which an arched bridge of stone has been made. Just this part of the road must have cost a great deal of labor and money to make it. Besides the bridge, the road is cut in the rock for some distance, and it appears hard. You find a great many rocky sides of hills cut away, but the stones there are not united together in large firm masses, which renders it much easier to blast, and break them away.

I have a great desire to get to Naples. I hope to find letters there from America and Prussia. Some months ago I was hurrying to get to Constantinople for the same thing, and there received none. Had I then thought that, months after, I would be hurrying to Naples for the same [291] letters, I would have felt most disappointed. It is so long since I have received none, that I have become accustomed to it, and were I to find none in Naples, I would be less disappointed than I was in Constantinople.

However, I cannot help but speculating upon the nature of the letters I shall receive. I try to divine what their contents may be and imagine them sometimes one way, sometimes another, but I suspect in fact that I will find commonplace letters, speaking about nothing of much importance. I also hope that such may be the case. What I ask is that all may be going the old track. Two persons I think must be dead, Mrs Stevens and old Mrs Cary.[112]

---

[112] Mrs Stevens was Brisbane's maternal grandmother. Old Mrs Cary was probably his great-aunt.

With regard to exterior things, and to other persons, this existence is not of much importance.

[292] The place where we slept last night is called Laputosa. The inn was like all the others, a neglected looking place, nevertheless you are not badly served. You observe here some slight traces of the neighborhood of a great capital. They will be found much stronger at Salerno, thirty-seven miles nearer to Naples.

Calabria: Sunday 19th December

Left before light. The weather fine, though cool. The road passes through a country of sloping hills. The mountains at a distance on both sides. The hills are stony and bare, the lower land in general cultivated. Dined at Eboli. The inn was formerly a convent, and I remarked some Byzantine columns, supporting [293] arches, which however were nearly all walled in.

Before Salerno, towards the south, spreads out a large valley, which runs from the sea shore into the interior and is bounded by highlands in the same manner as the valleys in Greece, that run from the sea shore into the interior. A part of this plain is covered with high brushwood, which is a celebrated hunting place of the Royal {Bourbon} family. The rest of it is cultivated in all its parts and it is a most valuable tract of country, more so, as that behind it, is mountainous and poor. There are a number of villages on the sides of the hills that bound it to the north. The road passes near this end. To the south I could not see. [294] There is also a large number of single houses scattered for the most part on the borders of it. I observed large numbers of mules and wagons on the road, going and coming from Naples.

I saw this morning a singular piece of superstition performed. We met three crosses posted up on the side of the road, as customary, but the middle one, which was also the largest, had an uncommon number of symbolic ornaments, such as ladders, hands, hammers, pinchers, etc. On it also was a box, to hold the money the passengers might throw in, and I observed that all the company with me, as stingy as they are, scrupulously gave, each one something. Under the money box [295] hung an oil-pot, the oil of which has received the benedictions of the priest. The postillions of the three carriages that were travelling together took the pot, and dipping the feather or bit of stick that was in it, in the oil, made a cross upon the forehead of each of the horses. They did it very gravely, and the horses stood very quietly, which was very well, for could they have comprehended the nonsense of those who governed them, they would not have suffered themselves to be driven by them farther.

Tomorrow I am in Naples and shall see whether at length I get some news from America. The weather has been fine, and we arrived at Salerno a little [296] before six. You see here the neighborhood of a large capital, or of a town in itself large. The dress of the inhabitants, their number, the quantity of people walking in the streets, the goodness of the hotel, the better care in which it is kept, and the persons playing on some instrument in the street to gain a few grains.

The living in Calabria is very cheap. It costs me for supper, or what might be termed a dinner, lodging and coffee in the morning, between four and five Carolini, but often four, and once or twice even less. Had I have been alone, however, they would have made me pay about three or four times the amount. But being with these people, I paid no more than they did. [297] The innkeepers did not much like that I should pay with the rest. Considering me as an Englishman, they wished to get more from me and the servants always begged me for *buona mano*, (a tip) although they did not do so with the others.

Passed in the afternoon a funeral. It was an old woman. She was carried upon the shoulders of four persons, and laid uncovered upon a kind of bed. With the French, when a dead body passes they take off their hats, as a sign of respect, and it is a very natural feeling. When a corpse passes, it presents us the symbol of ruin and death, and a kind of feeling of fear, and fear always commands a certain feeling of respect, arises within us which must find its expression. This expression of it may be very [298] different. With such a feeling in the mind, the body voluntarily must do something, and seizing the hat and raising it from the head seems one of the most natural manners of doing it.

Arrived in Naples: Monday 20th December

Left Salerno at about light, and arrived at Naples between three and four. Went, as soon as I could change clothes, to my banker, to see if at length

I should not receive some letters from America, and to my great delight I found one from my father, one from my mother, and one from Henrietta.[113] It is now seven in the evening and I have not opened them yet. Having [299] something to do, I did it first in order to be perfectly at my ease, and to read them without being interrupted, consequently with more pleasure.

It is a kind of fête to me to receive these letters, and I make it such. Upon the seal of Henrietta's was marked "Henrietta." I kissed it. I will now read my father's first, and then the others. I think the contents will only be commonplace; let me, however, see. What a delight to commence breaking the seal. I had to replace the letter upon the table to make these remarks. Let me commence again.

My father's letter is read. It says but little, but a certain style says more. He speaks of completely indifferent subjects, but I see there is [300] growing a difference between us in our manner of seeing and thinking. It is a letter different from me, and as I would not entirely wish that, it leaves a kind of uncomfortable feeling. To live in one way, and the same places, is a bad thing for a mind naturally active as is his. It brings us into exclusive views and exclusive feelings. Let me read my mother's. I find within it another from my father. I will read this one first.

This pleases me better. It is in his usual style, cool and calm with regard to all subjects. There is nothing particular in it, no advice. A hint or two, with a "perhaps" placed before them. Now then, for my mother's.

[301] I have read it, and it pleases me. It is better written than my father's, and some expressions are very good. She flatters me a little, which I would rather see out. It is written without any cast of melancholy, and my letters from Constantinople seem to have pleased her very much.

Now for Henrietta's. What a different world; what a different relations exist between us! In looking at her letter there is an entirely different feeling. Let me open it. It commences, "Absence, my dearest friend, is a terrible thing, especially when one goes too far, and in remote countries where no letter can reach him."

I have read hers. It pleases me very much. It is written with truth of feeling, and tenderness. [302] It is not so long as I could wish, but she does not

---

[113] Brisbane had become close to Henrietta Solmar in Berlin the winter before. See Introduction: 13, n. 35, also Diary II: 34-39, October 12, 1831; 107-09, November 15–17, 1831.

seem to think it will reach me. There is a tender tone of feeling in it, that gives me pleasure. There our correspondence shall become new; life, vigor, and tenderness on my side.

The road from Salerno to Naples shows that the traveller is approaching a large capital. You pass several quite large towns. The road first passed along the water. High land bounds the coast. The solid rock has been cut away in some places to a very considerable depth. After some distance the road leaves the shore, and passes through a vale. Every point of land possible is here cultivated. You pass one or two towns, and the [303] road soon enters into a level valley, which continues so until you reach Naples.

It is at first quite narrow, a mere strip of land running straight between high hills, whose stony and bare sides are uncultivated, but not as much of the valley is lost. This narrow strip continues for some time, it then widens out, or rather enters the broad plain, which spreads out to the south of Vesuvius, and the road then passes along the northern part of it. Houses are scattered on the sides of the hills, and the road is covered with numerous wagons and people coming and going. You first pass through Portici before arriving at Naples. It is a large and good-looking town, and joins almost with [304] Naples. By giving a trifle, my trunk was not searched at the Customs house.

As the carriage entered the city, and passed up along the *quai*, the place seemed to resemble something a miniature likeness of Paris. It did not meet my expectations. The physiognomy of the people in particular did not strike me as having anything particularly characteristic in it. I had thought that the Italian countenance had in general something delineated in it, but I find a great many broad flat faces. They resemble something the French, but there is far less character in their general appearance.

I went to the Hotel of Russia, which I found [305] a very large and well furnished, well arranged establishment. I went to see a woman, whom I had met at Cologne, and to give her a letter. She recognized me immediately, and was surprised to see me. After that, came home, read the letters I received and wrote till late at night.

Naples: Tuesday, 21 December

Bad weather in the morning. Wrote some; about 1 went out. Could not walk much, as my foot troubled me. I rub the skin off of one of the toes, and having since caught cold on it, the rubbing of the boot against it lames me when I walk. I went to see some tailors about clothes, but I engaged none. [306] I have done scarcely anything. I was at home in the evening. The weather bad. I leave till later some of the remarks I might make upon what I have today observed.

Naples: Wednesday 22nd December

I found a tailor today for making me clothes, and his prices are very cheap, one third less than one of the tailors I saw yesterday. Bought also a hat, paid 2½ ducats for it = $2.00.

I have been running about a good deal looking at the city. It neither disappoints, nor passes my expectation, but it is different from what I expected. I have seen so many places that I now begin to find [307] but little new. I don't observe such a number of beggars as I thought, for there are a good many, but less than in Malta. All the desire and eagerness for gaining money which is to be observed in those large capitals, where want, desire, and the allurement held out for possessing, by the quantity of objects, which flatter the taste and incite the passions on one side and poverty on the other, is also to be seen in Naples.

I found a fellow today with his hand in my pocket trying to steal something, but there happened only to be a kee {handkerchief} there. Bought a hat; only paid 2½ ducats for it.

[308] Naples: Thursday 23rd December

The weather this morning was very beautiful, like an October day. I walked out and went up Toledo Street. As I was going along, I stuck my handkerchief deep in my pocket so that no one should steal it. Seeing a good many persons enter a church, I also went in, and found that the inside had been decorated to make a *pompe funébre* (funeral) for the dead king.[114] Daylight was shut out in the interior, but it was lighted by a large number of chandeliers, and lamps. The ceiling was hung with long draperies, and in the center was built a kind of pyramid from all kinds of arms, swords, guns, pistols, axes, etc., and at the corners stood little cannons. Various [309] inscrip-

---

[114] Francesco I, King of the Two Sicilies, died December 18, 1830 and was succeeded by Ferdinand II.

tions were posted up around the room, with large torches on each side, and a soldier standing by them.

The thing was handsome, and after staying a while I left, and as I was walking down Toledo Street again, I thought I would see how safe my handkerchief was, and found it stolen. I could not help but laugh, although it was an excellent one, but I resolved to take care they stole no more from me.

Saw today Mr Fowls, for (from?) whom I had the letter of introduction.[115] He appears one of those good hearted persons, who is very ready to oblige. He also has openness of feeling and seems to have a good understanding. Dined at a restaurant, and found it good.

[310] A line or two out of a letter to Henrietta in answer to what she says about an affair with two married women etc: see her letter of 27th April 1830. I finish by saying:

"When I consider myself in the light of being destined to act in the world, it is not in relation to the society and individual circumstances and persons that surround me for the moment, but I compare myself to my result. When at the end of my life I have produced nothing, I am without result, then it shall be indifferent to me whether the name of Albert Brisbane be coupled with villain, scoundrel or devil. To be without result would be in my eyes to be worthless. The name becomes consequently a [311] worthless outside sign, which never reached what the interior thing wanted, consequently indifferent to it. With such a feeling, a man is more callous to such momentary and coincidental circumstances. They interfere no wise with his object. It is, however, true that I am too indifferent with regard to such things. I cannot apply to myself a virtuous code of morals. It seems to have no value in my eyes, inasmuch as it exerts no influence upon what I wish to attain.

I endeavour to put method in my acting, to suit the action to the thought, the thought to something farther. Put harmony between the mode of the art and the thought. When you execute a thing, do it up to

---

[115] This is confused. Earlier in Messina, Brisbane identified Mr Fowls as the Neapolitan consul general for the United States, who gave Brisbane a letter of introduction for a person in Naples. See above, Diary I: 246, December 9, 1830.

the thought. [312] One of my general rules is, "Act as you think, and think nobly." This is with regard to the mind, but with regard to that part of man which is animal, there are various indifferent particularities without rules and method.

Naples: Friday 24th December

Went this morning to one of the museums, and found it shut. Saw Mr Bautien.[116] He is to send me a drawing-master. I wish to take some lessons in outlining and perspective. Went afterwards upon the top of the hill, upon which is situated the castle St Elmo.[117] From it you have a most beautiful view of Naples and the surrounding country, the gulf, the shore, the distant country, [313] the city, with all its building, streets, the port, etc. the road to Rome, Salerno, and the great *campo* (plain), through which passes the great road to Rome. I have also been strolling about the streets looking at the city. I will later turn my observations into a written description.

Rogers paid me a visit.[118] Dined with him, and received by the way of Malta, from Constantinople, several letters which I feared were lost, one from J. Brisbane, 23 May, one from George and my mother together in the same sheet, 19 April, one also from Manesca, dated March 1829. When I had finished reading it, I said to myself, he has got the right view on his mind.

[314] Those from my father and George were of but little consequence. George's letter is evidently better than his last, with regard to the wording. It is written with more facility.[119] Four from H. {Four letters from Henrietta.}

Today is a distinguished one for the Neapolitans. It is a day in which they eat and stuff as much as possible. Fish and such things, however, compose their meals, but tomorrow they have free liberty, and the stuffing, I am told, is still greater. The doctors make a regular calculation upon the harvest they are to reap by those who stuff themselves sick. There were a great many people in the streets, a great quantity of provisions to be sold, and also

---

[116] Bautien is unidentified.

[117] The Castel Sant'Elmo is located west of the city.

[118] Rogers was probably the American consul.

[119] George Brisbane, Brisbane's younger brother, was eighteen in 1830. Later in life George became his brother's bitter enemy; the cause was apparently the division of their father's estate. In 1883 George assisted Brisbane's sometime mistress Lodoisca with her bigamy suit against his brother, and wrote a number of intemperate letters to Brisbane and his wife Redelia. See Introduction: 21, n. 50.

[315] a great deal of bustle, otherwise nothing particular. In the evening, squibs and crackers were heard popping in the streets, but I observed no other demonstration of their joy or reverence for the evening that gave birth to him, who created and saved the Catholic world.

I intended to go and hear midnight mass, but when twelve o'clock came, I felt too little desire, and the rushing of strong blasts by the window did not heighten it any. I remained home, and wrote till nearly three. I was engaged at various long letters. It however did no good to my eyes, they felt irritated after it. I have, of late, written too much by candlelight. I will do it less after tonight.

[316] *Naples: Saturday Christmas 25th December*

Today is the Merry Christmas. In America all go to church, all wish each other to be merry, and it is also the day in which mince and pumpkin pies are particularly sacrificed to the God-Belly. With the Neapolitans, they have treble mass to perform, they eat, as I am told, to excess, some squibs fired, and thus is Christ's birthday celebrated.

The present day has been as bad a one as could be. A strong south wind, quite a blow, accompanied more or less with rain, hindered me from putting foot out of doors till late. I have been writing, finished a long letter to Henrietta,[120] also one to my father, and one to Jordan.[121] [317] In my father's I request him to tell me the object of going to Amsterdam. Also I spoke about George, with regards to the wrong manner which was used with him, and various descriptions.

In the evening I went to the theater St Charles. I found the interior immense, rather too much. As for the voices, they must lose themselves in such a great space.[122] There are about six tiers of boxes. The interior is gilt from top to bottom, all the ornaments, all the fronts of boxes, so that you see nothing but masses of gilt wood. The place has one continuous appearance of gold work. [318] The fronts of the boxes are ornamented with carved woodwork and, as I said above, gilt. There is some few figures in

---

120 See Diary I: 298–99, December 20, 1830, n. 113.
121 Jordan is unidentified.
122 The Teatro San Carlo had just been rebuilt in neoclassical style in 1816. The interior furnishings in wood and stucco which Brisbane found so distasteful were designed to achieve acoustic perfection.

wood, also gilt and some bas-reliefs, all in bad taste however, and without beauty.

The ceiling is decorated with a large painting taken from the Grecian mythology. Over the scene in the middle, and on the lower part of what might be termed the architrave, which slants inwards towards the stage, is a large dial of a clock, which turns round, and out of clouds beneath it rises a figure representing time, pointing towards the hour with one hand, and holding a scythe in the other. On one side of him are several figures dancing, on the other the same number playing on instruments. The thing [319] strikes you, but the figures are without taste.

There was a considerable number of people in the house, but it was far from being full. The play was the siege of Corinth, and a ballet.[123] The principal actors appeared very good. The dresses and stage apparatus in excellent order, the scenery also good, but the architectural part false. There was not much applauding, but a good deal of talking among the spectators. The ballet was very well executed, the dresses and *mise en scène* (production) also very good. There must be a great expense attending this establishment. There was a fellow who hissed one of the *danceuses* (ballerinas). A large number began to applaud. As they stopped, he gave another hiss, immediately a large round of applause succeeded. As it died [320] away, forth came the hiss again. It came from but one person, but it set all the opposite party going again, and so on for several times. It was no doubt done to make fools of the applauding party. Came home about 11.

Naples: Sunday 26th December

The present day is better than yesterday, less wind, although still strong, but a good deal of rain. Commenced with lesson of perspective. I have a young man, who appears to understand his affair perfectly, and I shall no doubt soon understand the thing. Went afterwards on board the brig of war *Principe Carlo*, to see Mr Fowls. Went with him to different places, first to a Doctor's. He then [321] went afterwards to introduce me to some Prince, but found them out. I afterwards left him, as I did not wish to go to the theater. I returned home and studied out my lesson of perspective, etc.

---

[123] Giacomo Rossini (1792–1868) composed the opera *L'Assedio di Corinto*, which was first presented at the Paris Opera on October 9, 1826 in French as *Le Siège de Corinthe*.

The day has been passed without much effect, as all the rest. I have no method in what I do. This is on account of short residences, of a diversity of places, and subjects to attend to, so that I do about nothing. The weather also is bad, which hinders me from visiting spots and places and I thus also lose some time.

The Neapolitan vessels appear to me very well arranged. The part for the sailors is particularly comfortable. Their marina, however, is very small.

[322] *Naples: Monday 27th December*

The same strong south wind is blowing, but the day is better. Went out about twelve. A person called upon me in the morning who has already been once here, to inquire what merchandise he could carry to America to make money upon it. He is an Italian, who wishes to go. As he said, he had an idea of taking out gloves and some salable articles, but I don't see why he came to ask me about them. Perhaps he had some other object in view, but that did not strike me from his manner.

Had another lesson in perspective. I appear to understand the thing quickly. I intended in the evening to go to the theater, but a want of desire, or rather a [323] dislike of going there, as if I would only tire myself, or at least the fear of it, hindered me from it. It is quite an undertaking for me to go to the theater. I have to force myself to it. The fear of being *ennuyé* (bored) keeps me from going. It makes me rather pass an evening in my room.

Naples: Tuesday 28th December

The day is much better, and the weather is quite fine. Dined with Fowls on board the *Prince Charles*. Very good dinner. One of the lieutenants was with us. We were only three. I have not done much today, about the same as the other days. The public edifices, churches, fountains, and all such [324] things are built with but little taste, most all in the Italian style, burthened with ornaments, applied improperly and without beauty in form. Columns, arches, pilasters, every kind of construction heaped together, without any kind of discernment of taste, and correctness of feeling.

The dwelling houses are well built, calculated for a number of families, a little court to some; a large common entrance, or *porte cochère* and the general arrangement something like that of Paris. The city resembles something

Paris simplified, with less character, and poorer, there is not much wealth among the people.

There appears to be a general scantiness of means, consequently the general arrangement of things is on [325] an economical scale. A person can live cheap here, and can also amuse himself at a cheap rate, but from what I hear and see, there is not a great deal of society among the native inhabitants. They don't mix so much among each other. There are not so many parties and reunions. They keep more to themselves. A suspicious government perhaps may influence in a certain degree this circumspection among the people.

There seems to me less force, less character in the people, than I thought for. The people have the capability to carry on the common affairs of life. Their outside appearance is perfectly that of a people of undertaking and executing, but [326] place them in difficult situations, and I am persuaded there will be found but few capable of acting in them. The spirit of the people does not seem to produce individuals fit for acting in high spheres. The common daily life seems to go on well enough. The individuals are capable of furnishing to the mechanical part of it, and it steps on regularly like a machine. But if it is necessary to find men to act in higher spheres, who are capable of undertaking and executing broadly, you find they fail. There seems to be in the general appearance of things and persons, but little strength and force, and not much decidedness of character; you find a diversity of faces and [327] physiognomy.

There appears to be no particularly marked countenances, which might be said to form a national physiognomy. Darkish hair and eyes, brown skin and the general appearance tells you their country. I find handsome faces among the women. There is often in the features something clear and distinct, as well as handsome, but I don't say that beneath it also lies strong and fine feeling. A handsome nature and those various qualities, we are apt to apply to those faces which seem to have beauty and deep feeling in them. The cultivation of the mind in a woman seems to be the only means of opening romantic, enthusiastic, and such feelings. I should think that the general social state was against the production of handsome natures.

There [328] is not so much formal virtue; not so much price is set upon it. Poverty tends also to throw it into the market, and it is sold indifferently and not at high prices. Where there is not so much moral and intellectual cultivation among a people, these *galanteries*, love affairs, and intrigues dwindle down more into the satisfaction of animal feelings. Here there is not a high degree of intellectual cultivation, there is no direction given to the mind. It wants content and character. It is not, however, without activity, but it realizes itself in light and frippery ways, without method, and without aim, and object. Consequently its productions are in harmony with its manner [329] of acting. What is done seems not to be done with a solid foundation, a real feeling and a view of the aims and object of doing it.

As are the men, so are also the women, and I think that the Italian "love," in this part at least, has more of the pleasure piquant in it of intrigue, than deep feeling and enthusiasm. Its moving principle seems to be less an interior romance of the feelings, which demands some object to fill up that world of gay feelings and images, than in some cases the pleasure of intrigue, in others because it is easy to fall into it, and in many out of calculation, because it being more convenient, and interest leading them also to it.

[330] *Naples: Wednesday 29th December*

Went this morning to the Museo Barbonico.[124] I was not in there long. I passed hurriedly through one or two of the long rooms appropriate for statues. There is a great number, but few Grecian ones, however. A great many Roman statues and busts; many fine ones but also many things without merit. The place is very extensive and wants much study and attention.

Went afterwards to several churches, the architectural value of these places is nothing, their beauty is intended to consist in an overburthened and overcharged quantity of ornaments; gold leaf, different coloured marbles and gaudy decorations [331] are not spared. I find that the arts which flourish under the patronage of the Christian religion are very badly off; when that religion has called upon the arts to furnish her symbols, the objects she wished represented were too devoid of beauty. The beauty was not to be expressed by the perfection of natural forms; that with such a content, and such an aim, the arts could produce nothing freely. Scare-crow pictures, such as those of hell, and the like, and the expression of some moral feeling,

---

[124] Now the Museo Archeologico Nazionale.

by bodily contortions, and in such representations, where art becomes only a slave as it were, it is not likely for it to be free, and independent, having itself for aim, and [332] wishing to realize all the gay and beautiful images of the universe, which can enter within its circle, and receive the ideal forms and shapes of its beautifying interior.

Naples: Thursday 30th December

Left this morning about 11 to go to the top of Vesuvius; the weather was beautiful and could not have been more favourable. Mr Allan[125] offered me a seat in his carriage, and we were altogether five persons. The carriage goes to a little village, about three fourths of the way; the wagon road there ceasing, mules are procured to do the rest, and with them we proceeded as far as the bottom of the cone. On arriving at this latter place, numbers of persons flock about [333] us, and the noise, quarreling and yelling they made in offering their mules and inducing us to take them, was deafening. The sides of the mountain are cultivated on this side most of the way up, principally with the vine.

In comparison with Etna, everything is on a smaller scale. It is in miniature. You don't see those immense fields of lava, and on the sides of Etna their surface is roughened and broken with large shapeless heaps, and masses of the lava, throwing itself up and breaking in every form; but at Vesuvius, although the same irregularity is there, it is on a smaller scale. The broken and uneven surface is composed of small pieces like a molten crust, which had broken and [334] fallen to pieces in its course, producing irregular slabs and flakes, but not of a large size.

The soil grows upon this lava in quite a short space of time, in comparison with Etna. It is of a softer nature and sooner decays. The ascent is easy until you come to the foot of the large cone, which, as it is said, is 800 feet high. Its ascent is very difficult, or at least very fatiguing, as it is very steep, and its sides covered with sand, and small crumbled pieces of lava, thrown out a month or six weeks since. It required about three quarters of an hour to crawl up it. The sand gives no firm footing, so that at each step you slip about halfway as far down as you got up.

---

[125] Perhaps the same Mr Allen who ascended Etna with Brisbane. See above, Diary I: 218, December 3, 1830.

The top is of a circular form, said to be three miles round, but it does not seem to be [335] as much. The interior is hollow, in the shape of an inverted cone and is very deep, but within a month it has been nearly filled up with lava. In the center of the hollow rises up another cone, but quite small in comparison with the large exterior one. This again is hollow, running to a point at the bottom, and it is here that is situated the main vent; some weeks since, the top of this cone was much less elevated than it is now, but as the volcano has been throwing up sand and cinders, it has increased considerably its height and is now about upon a level with the sides of the outside one. Within two months the hollow of the great cone has been filled up three hundred feet, and the little cone in the middle [336] has increased its size in proportion.

After arriving at the top we walked around the edge of the outside cone, about one third of the distance, to find a place where we would descend into the hollow, or main crater, as it might be termed. The lava in this part is not far from the top, not more than thirty feet. In looking into this hollow, you see before you a large plain of lava, bounded by the sides of this hollow, and out of which rises the interior cone; upon this surface are also three lava vents, which throw up a good deal of smoke and cinders. The general appearance of the place is difficult to be described. Large quantities of sulphurous [337] smoke rise out of every part of this large crater. There are an innumerable quantity of little vents, so still volumes of vapour rise up and in many parts impede the view.

The surface of this field of lava is black, as it has nearly cooled, but there are innumerable fissures and cracks in it, through which you still see the lava, red-hot and burning away, as only at three or four feet from the top. You can walk upon the surface of the lava, although it is too hot in the parts where the fire is so near under it, to hold your hand upon it. In stepping over those fissures, the heat that rises out of them is very [338] disagreeable to withstand, and the sulphurous smoke almost strangles you.

In looking into the great crater, you see clouds of smoke rising from different parts of it, which, joining together above, seem as if the whole interior circle was one outlet for smoke. From the three little vents issue forth streams of fire, and the middle cone throws up little flakes of molten matter with a noise resembling the rushing of violent wind. One continual roar assails your ears, which resembles very much that of Niagara Falls.

I walked across the surface of the lava in the large crater, which was not difficult, to the bottom of the [339] middle cone, and commenced ascending it, although very difficult as it is, very steep, and its sides composed of small cinders and sand. In arriving at the top, you see at the bottom, in the interior, a hole, which I took to be twelve to fifteen feet broad, vomiting smoke and throwing out at short intervals showers of flakes of hot lava, or cinders, accompanied with a violent hissing roar, produced most probably by the rarefied air, rushing through this aperture.

We staid on the top till dark, in order to see the thing with better effect, and then [340] commenced descending to the place where the mules were left. As I was going down, I saw a lady before me, who appeared to find a good deal of difficulty, although she had a guide supporting her. Seeing this, I offered her my arm, which she accepted, and after some few words upon the difficulty of the descent, I asked her if she was not English. I thought perhaps she might be Irish or Scotch; and to my surprise she answered she was an American. I found she was the daughter of Charles Carroll and that her son, Mr Harper, was secretary or attaché of our legation at Paris.[126] I acknowledged my country-fellowship, and promised to call on her; [341] her daughter, son, and son's wife are also with her. Arrived at Naples about 9.

Naples: Friday 31st December

Today I went and subscribed to a reading room for a month, for which I gave a dollar, and today is the first time I have read the papers, foreign ones that is, since I left Malta, except some American ones in Messina. I have been today in one of my fits of excitement; the Revolution of Poland throwed me again into the world of enthusiasm.[127] I cursed

---

[126] Charles Carroll of Carrollton (1737–1832), retired U.S. senator from Maryland and the last surviving signer of the Declaration of Independence, was 93 in 1830. His daughter, Catherine Carroll Harper, widow of General Robert G. Harper, former U.S. Senator from Maryland, was close to 60 when Brisbane assisted her down Mt Vesuvius. Her three daughters had made a great splash (and excellent matches) in English society some years before; her son William Harper, American consul in Paris, was apparently not previously known to Brisbane.

[127] The tiny Kingdom of Poland, under Russian control, experienced a brief but unsuccessful revolt in 1830.

myself as an unlucky devil for not being in Europe during the acting of any of these great events. This is the beginning of the epoch of European freedom. The French e.g. {example} is now [342] realising itself fully in Europe.

The death of Benjamin Constant gave me great pain; I have shed a tear for him.[128] The causes he devoted himself to, related him, as it were intellectually, to those who desire ardently its triumph and universal promulgation. A man of clear views, a clear method of thinking, and the power of rendering them in a manner perfectly in harmony. I went to see in the evening the ladies I met on Mt Vesuvius. Mr Harper's wife pleases me the most. She is pretty, and has a clear quick mind.

Naples: Saturday 1st January

Went today to Pozzuoli, about six miles from Naples, a place of antique foundation, and where are some [343] remains of antiquity. They are however of no great account. Of the temple of Serapis, the foundation, several columns and some other small pieces are still remaining.[129] The architecture is Roman Corinthian. I took a boat, and went along the coast, stopping first to see Lake Lucrino, of which only a small proportion remains. The new mountain, as it is termed, which was thrown up by some eruption, destroyed the greater part of its basin.

Went afterwards to Lake Averna, or rather a pond surrounded by hills. There is nothing striking in its scenery although celebrated by the ancients, and the place where they sacrificed to the infernal deities.[130] The cavern of the Sybille is near it. It is a [344] large gallery cut in the rock, of which there are so many, at some distance after entering the main gallery.[131] A small narrow passage is next, leading to the bathing rooms of the Sybille, as they are termed. They are rooms cut in the rock for bathing, to which was a large entrance with a flight of steps, now however filled up. Visited

---

[128] Benjamin Henri de Bec de Constant (1752–1830), French political philosopher, was the companion of the novelist Mme Germain Necker de Staël (1766-1817).

[129] The market-place of ancient Pozzuoli was incorrectly identified as a temple of Serapis.

[130] Lake Avernus was a water-filled crater. The sulphurous fumes which emanated from it in antiquity caused it to be regarded as an entrance to the Underworld.

[131] The Sibyl's cave was hollowed out by the Greek settlers of Cumae in the sixth century BC. The famous Sibylline oracles were collected here.

afterwards divers warm baths, the water of which is naturally heated, said to be of Nero.

Went afterwards to see the spot where Virgil places the Elysian fields, and saw a part of the route taken by Aeneas.[132] These fields lay around the shores of an inland bay, separated from the sea by a very narrow ridge of land. This bay is not of much extent and is surrounded [345] by hills, which slope gradually down to the water's edge. Remains of subterranean graves are observed cut in the hills on both sides. It recalls however, but little to mind the Elysian fields, as existing in the imagination. The sides of these hills are covered in parts with little trees. There is not much plain to form a field, and there is nothing particularly bold or handsome in the general scenery. At the place where stood the ivory gate is a little church.

Along the coast opposite to Pozzuoli, where Baja is placed, are pointed out the spots, and some slight ruins of houses, called the Palaces of Caesar, Nero, etc. etc.; but they are without any interest of an architectural nature, as [346] are many other remains they show you, which is done to get money, and to which whatever names they choose are attached.[133]

Returned to Pozzuoli after about five hours' time, passing the remains of the bridge of Caligula, which consists of five or six supports that project out of the water. Met Mr Douglas at Pozzuoli, who accompanied me to the different places.[134] I paid, for two men and a boat, a ducat, about the same to the guide, and a Carolina for opening the gates of the grottos, baths, and such places. I returned to Naples about 5½ {5:30} o'clock and, as it rained very hard, did not go out, but made some perspective drawings.

[347] *Naples Sunday 2nd January*

Went to look in the morning for rooms nearer in the middle of the city, as I find the hotel where I am situated too far off. I found one opposite to the theater St Charles, which I bargained for, and took it at six Carolini per day, and am to go there tomorrow. I went afterwards and paid a visit to Mr Harper.

---

[132] Aeneas, the hero of Virgil's *Aeneid*, descended into the underworld by this route.

[133] The Roman baths at Baiae were surrounded by many sumptuous villas, now under water. The ruins of the baths were still visible when Brisbane visited, however. Perhaps these were the "slight ruins" he saw there.

[134] Mr Douglas is unidentified.

Afterwards studied, and wrote some, dined and went to the theater of St Carolino. They speak here the Neapolitan dialect, and play farces taken from such scenes as might be found among the people in the streets. They play with a kind of natural buffoonery, the piece entwined with the wit, and expressions of the persons it represents. They take [348] their scenes generally from the lower classes, and what you see at this little theater, you meet at every moment in the streets, as you walk along.

Naples Monday 3rd January

After my perspective lesson, I packed up my things, and paid my bill, and went to my new lodgings. The following are the prices I paid for the room, five Carolinas. It was a good one and not dear; for the breakfast of coffee and milk and butter four Carolinas, just twice too much; for a brazier of fire two Carolinas, about three times what it should be. I gave a dollar to him who brushed my clothes, a dollar to the *Cameriere*, (waiter) and half a dollar to the porter. I dined there five or six times for which they charged six Carolinas. [349] The bill amounted to 14 *Pezzis*, and 1 Carolina.

Called upon Rogers and took sixty dollars. Went afterwards to the reading room. I saw a paragraph stating that the Minister Humboldt was engaged in drawing up a constitution for Prussia. The thing is very probable, and must, in the end, take place. It would be wrested from the King by force, if the course he follows is not mild, and not giving holds to complaint. If the present King should die without giving it, and his son comes upon the throne, the people may get it by force, as they have not that respect for him as for the Father.[135]

Since writing the above I have read that the present King gives it, as he fears the future conduct of his son, in as [350] much as he is inclined to aristocratic views, and rather violent measures. I thought also that that would be one strong reason with the present King.

---

[135] Alexander von Humboldt (1769–1859), geographer and educational reformer, was Prussian Minister of Education in 1809–1810. Despite Brisbane's optimism, Humboldt's reforms were not implemented during the reign of the "present king" Frederick William III (r. 1797–1840). The revolutionary movements of 1848 would ultimately extract a constitution from his son, King Frederick William IV (r. 1840–1858). Brisbane uses the term "constitution" to describe a series of proposed political reforms rather than a governmental system.

Went in the evening to the theater *dii' Fiorentini*. This is a prose theater, where pieces more of a classic style are performed. They play here regular plays, and endeavour to act them well. I found the company of but little force, mere talkers. The acting, however, was as good as the piece, a flat thing, phrases of conversation stitched together, and recited by persons with different coats on from the spectators, and making a certain quantity of gestures and grins, which showed the thing was a play.

[351] *Naples Tuesday 4th January*

Went this morning to the Museo Barbonico. I was in several of the rooms, in order to have a view of what is to be observed, as I intend to go through the thing with a good deal of care. The weather is beautiful, a clear sky, a bright sun, and an agreeable atmosphere. I sit writing in my room with the windows open.

I have done but little today, the time in one manner and another slips away, and is without result. When a person has no method in employing his time, and he can do anything at any time, it often results that he postpones a great many things to that any time.

[352] I went in the evening to the *Theatro Nuovo*, where a kind of comic opera and such things are performed. This theater is inferior to that *Dii Fiorentini*. It is intended to be on a smaller scale; its pieces also are inferior. The acting was bad. The singing was not of much merit. The house was well filled, as it was a new play. There was no applauding, which I observe to be rarely the case at the theaters.

On returning home, stopped at the Caffé d'Italia to drink a glass of *acqua d'amaressa* (bitters) or lemonade, as is my custom, and after coming home, sat up till 2.0 o'clock working at a perspective drawing.

I often say to myself, "don't distract your attention with too many subjects" and repeat [353] Goethe's words in this particular, "*Wer bloß mit Zeichen wirkt u.s.w.*"[136]

---

[136] This fragment is from Goethe's *Wilhelm Meisters Lehrjahre*. See above: Diary I: 101, November 10, 1830, n. 41. The complete quotation is: "*Wer bloß mit Zeichen wirkt, ist ein Pedant, ein Heuchler oder ein Pfuscher*," translated as: "Whoever deals in omens is a pedant, a hypocrite, or a bungler." What this has to do with Brisbane's concern about his inability to concentrate is unclear.

Naples: Wednesday 5th January

The weather is as beautiful as it has been for the last three or four days. It is something extraordinary for me to see such weather at this time of the year.

Paid a visit to the American ladies. I find but little in them that interests me. It is singular that I find nobody nowadays with whom I can associate with pleasure. The beings I am thrown with seem to me indifferent, uninteresting, without price.

I went to take a walk in the public promenade, called the *villa reale* (royal garden). [354] It is a very long and tolerably broad strip of ground, planted with trees and bushes intersected with alleys, ornamented with fountains, statues, etc. which makes it a beautiful place. An Italian author says *"La Natura e l'arte sono concorse renarlo il piu delizioso del' mondo."*[137] He is speaking of it as a public walk. Although that may be exaggerated, some various times, still the place is handsome and agreeable. There are in it temples dedicated to Virgil and Tasso,[138] that of the latter in a round building with his bust in the middle. I stepped under it to look at it nearer, when a Swiss soldier, who was standing by, said I must take off my hat. I spoke to him in German, asking him why. He did not know, but inquired if it was not the King, lately dead.

End of Volume Four

---

[137] "Nature and art have united to make it the most delicious in the world."
[138] Virgil (70–19 BC) was the author of the *Aeneid*. Torquato Tasso (1544–1595) was an Italian Renaissance poet.

Table of Contents, Diary I

(Index Incomplete)

Inscription overleaf

"The real artist's feeling holds the thought (image) for when words fail. There stands the effect. The genuine scholar learns from the known, the higher and ungiven to develop, and this attains excellence."

Notes on last page

Mr Breed; Liverpool. Mr Eynard's two sons are with him.
Antonio Senderi Guida di Sicilia residente a Myrina all' albergo di Firenze.
Saverio Camino d'Antonio di Falerna
Circondario S. Hadriano Distretto di Nicastro

End of Diary I

ILLUSTRATIONS

1. Self-portrait by Brisbane, done at age 15 or 16

Photograph courtesy of the Department of Special Collections,
George Arendts Research Library, Syracuse University

2. Brisbane painted by his wife Adèle, done between ages 25-29
In private collection; used by permission of the family
Photographed by the authors

3. Brisbane at age 30, possibly painted in Paris

In private collection; used by permission of the family
Photographed by the authors

4. Brisbane in travel costume, of unknown date (perhaps in his 30s)

In private collection; used by permission of the family
Photographed by the authors

5. Photograph of Brisbane in old age (unsigned)
From a privately bound copy of
Albert Brisbane, A Mental Biography, Boston, Massachusetts, 1893
Used by permission of the owners

6. James Brisbane (*circa* 1822)
In private collection; used by permission of the family
Photographed by the authors

7. Mary Stevens Brisbane (*circa* 1822)
*In private collection; used by permission of the family
Photographed by the author*

8. Claude-Henri Rouvroy de Saint-Simon
Photocopy courtesy of the Bibliothèque Nationale de France, Paris

9. Charles Fourier
Original etching from a privately bound copy of
Albert Brisbane, A Mental Biography, Boston, Massachusetts, 1893,
used by permission of the owners
Photographed by the authors

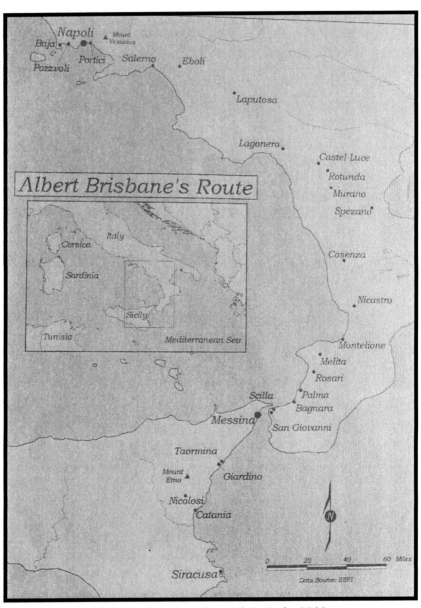

Albert Brisbane's Route

10. Map of Brisbane's travels in Italy, 1830

Prepared by J. Alvarez
Photographed by the authors

11. Johann Wolfgang Goethe (Diary I, October 27, 1830)
Original etching from a privately bound copy of
Albert Brisbane, A Mental Biography, Boston, Massachusetts, 1893,
used by permission of the owners
Photographed by the authors

12. "Ear of Dionysius" (Diary I, November 27, 1830)
Jakob Philipp Hackert, 1777 (Nordhoff and Reimer, 1994, cat. no. 725)
Photograph Courtesy of the British Museum, Division of Prints Service

13. Mount Etna, Sicily (Diary I, December 4, 1830)

Original etching from a privately bound copy of Albert Brisbane, A Mental Biography,
Boston, Massachusetts, 1893, used by permission of the owners
Photographed by the author

14. Naples (Diary I, December 20, 1830)

Original etching from a privately bound copy of Albert Brisbane, A Mental Biography,
Boston, Massachusetts, 1893, used by permission of the owners
Photographed by the authors

15. Victor Hugo
Original etching from a privately bound copy of
Albert Brisbane, A Mental Biography, Boston, Massachusetts, 1893,
used by permission of the owners
Photographed by the authors

16. The Italian Theater, Paris (Diary II, September 30, 1831)

Original etching from a privately bound copy of Albert Brisbane, A Mental Biography,
Boston, Massachusetts, 1893, used by permission of the owners
Photographed by the authors

17. The Tuileries and Carousel, Paris before 1871 (Diary II, October 8, 1831)
Original etching from a privately bound copy of Albert Brisbane, A Mental Biography, Boston, Massachusetts, 1893, used by permission of the owners
Photographed by the authors

18. Strasbourg Cathedral (Diary II, November 9, 1831)
Original etching from a privately bound copy of
Albert Brisbane, A Mental Biography, Boston, Massachusetts, 1893,
used by permission of the owners
Photographed by the authors

19. The Diligence from Strasbourg to Frankfort (Diary II, November 10, 1831)

Original etching from a privately bound copy of Albert Brisbane, A Mental Biography,
Boston, Massachusetts, 1893, used by permission of the owners
Photographed by the authors

20. Felix Mendelssohn-Bartholdy (Diary II, November 20, 1831)
Original etching from a privately bound copy of
Albert Brisbane, A Mental Biography, Boston, Massachusetts, 1893,
used by permission of the owners
Photographed by the authors

21. Rahel Levin Varnhagen von Ense (Diary II, January 3, 1832)
Etching by Wilhelm Hensel, Staatliche Museen Preussischer Kulturbesitz,
Kuptferstichkabinett, Berlin (West)
Photographed by Jörg P. Anders

22. Karl August Varnhagen von Ense (Diary II, January 3, 1832)
Etching by Wilhelm Hensel, Staatliche Museen Preussischer Kulturbesitz, Kuptferstichkabinett, Berlin (West)
Photographed by Jörg P. Anders

DIARY II

September 1831 to January 1832

Between diaries I and II there is an eight-month gap – January 1831 to September 1832 – which Brisbane probably described in two missing diaries, numbers five and six. During this period he traveled in Italy, first to Rome where he spent some time, and then to Florence. He eventually made his way back to Paris, quite indirectly through Switzerland, Holland and possibly England. In Holland he first encountered the works of Saint-Simon and pushed on to Paris to find his friend from Berlin, Jules Lechevalier, to introduce him to the society of the Saint-Simonians.[1]

1831: Paris, Monday 26th September – Friday 30th[2]

The weather since Monday has been very fine and the week has passed without much worthy of note. Greenough has been making my bust, which is a tolerable likeness, but it is exaggerated in the different features.[3]

I went Thursday evening to the *soirée* (evening social gathering) of the Saint-Simonians. I had a long conversation with Duveyrier {Charles, 1803–1866}, Enfantin {Barthelèmy-Prosper, 1796–1864} etc.[4] which produced a strong effect upon me, and one day or the other I will [2] no doubt end by joining them. They offer an unbounded circle of action to the activity of

---

[1] See Introduction: 3, 17–18.

[2] While the numbered pages of the second diary begin here, Brisbane wrote three pages overleaf, which are numbered A, B and C, and appear at the end of the text.

[3] This bust never appeared in the catalogue of Horatio Greenough's works. Possibly it was never finished, or was destroyed as a student or primitive study. Brisbane had originally met Greenough in Italy in 1831 where Greenough and Samuel Morse were studying art. Both young men moved on to Paris in 1831 where they renewed their acquaintance with Brisbane, and Greenough began working at sculpture as well as painting.

[4] See Introduction: 2, n. 4.

the individual; a new world spreads out before his {Saint-Simon's} efforts, and certainly there is a plenty to be done. Suffering humanity protests that if the present forms of society was {*sic*} to cease, she would not regret it, for it is not so perfect as to call forth her love and adoration. And were it {present society} to sink thus and to slide away and take up its residence in that eternity of passed forms, she {suffering humanity} would see it cease even without regrets.

In talking with Duveyrier, in order to wake new feel{ings} I took an interest [3] in their efforts and the doctrine. He said, "Supposing you were to hear that we had fallen thru, that the thing was broken up with, that we had all to disperse and to go away, what would be your feeling were you come, then, to take leave of me?" It struck me most forcibly: I felt at the moment that in such a case I would sacrifice my life to support their understanding. I felt it {the collapse of the Saint-Simonian movement} would in fact destroy a hope and an interest that had already taken hold of me, and which, {having} become immediately half of my existence, would be destroyed as soon as it was sufficiently defined to my eyes [4] and feelings.

A strong feeling draws me towards them and still there is a doubt, a general feeling of and then to change personality and modify your past feelings and interests, it is not the thing of a day.

There is something very mild and pleasing in Enfantin. I like him very well as I do many of the members and one great step is to feel yourself home again with them and possess no feeling of repulsion and dislike. Every one must begin at first {to} rebel against them and feel an instinctive opposition against their principles, and their ideas.

That with me is passed, for, did I condemn [5] their principles as not being comprehensive enough and for any other reason, nevertheless I would admire them for their undertaking and the efforts they make in a cause so general, so vast, and so exterior to all individual, interior[5] calculations of the individual. Besides, many of the young men who have rallied around the doctrine are of the first stamp. A superior society of young men could not be found in any nation at the present time.

---

[5] Brisbane repeatedly uses the term "exterior" to refer to a very broad ideal intellectual realm of greater possibility, reaching to the stars. He uses the complementary term "interior" to describe personal ideas, those not exposed to others' views.

[6] I went this evening {September 30th} to the *Opéra Français*[6] to see the *rentrée* (return) of Mlle Taglion.[7] She is without any doubt the first *danseur{se}* in the world, The opera was *Dieu et la Bayadère*. Before going in, I took a half a cup of coffee which predisposed me to listen with pleasure to the music as it excited me – and I enjoyed the dancing as well as the music very much. It excited me in the highest degree.

Just as I was writing the above, this morning, Saturday {October 1st} and going to continue a description of the *Opéra*, a poor woman came in to ask me to give her something, for she was [7] without bread to eat. When I reflected, I was amusing myself at the opera, while so many had not even a little bread to eat, I cursed the opera and despised myself that I found amusement there. How despicable is that feeling, where one congratulates himself that he has found an individual pleasure, that he has amused himself individually. I consequently shall not continue that description for a poor miserable feeling was at the bottom of it {selfishness}.

I went Monday {September 26} to see *Marion Delomée* {*Marion De Lorme*} at the {*Théâtre de*} *Porte-Sainte-Martin*. It is a fine piece; it is by Victor [8] Hugo[8] and you see in composing it he has given it the character of his own interior; that is, he has impressed upon the subjects his own feeling rather than them taking the subject as it was and dressing it up the best way he could as he found it. Mme Derval plays with deep feeling and passion; altho the circle of that feeling is not very broad, but she plays with force in it: the same may be said of Bocage.[9]

---

[6] The theater to which Brisbane is referring is the *Théâtre de l'Opera*. On September 30, 1831 there were performances of the ballet pantomime *Astolphe et Joconde* by P. Aumer, cited in Wicks, G. B., *Parisian Stage: Alphabetical Indexes of Plays and Authors*, 5 vols, Alabama (1953), part II: 5, and the ballet *Le Dieu et la Bayadère* by Eugene Scribe, cited in Wicks (1953) part II: 24.

[7] Marie Taglion or Taglioni (1804–1850?) was one of the best known ballerinas of the nineteenth century. She is credited with developing dancing on point as the principal ballet form.

[8] Victor Hugo (1802–1885), French author, wrote this tragedy in 1828. He became friendly with Brisbane, probably as a result of their mutual interest in Fourier's ideas. According to a letter (November 16, 1929) from Brisbane's son, Arthur, to his daughter, Sarah, Brisbane named one of his sons Hugo in honor of their friendship. (Brisbane papers, private collection)

[9] Mme Derval and Pierre-François Bocage (1791–1862) were actors in Paris.

Paris: Saturday to Tuesday October 14

Saturday I did nothing to remark. I was at home in the evening, [9] and the day slipped away imperceptibly: leaving nothing behind it except some errands I had performed, some plans I had been at, etc. There is always in the course of the day some place to which you must go, some visit, or something to see; and one or two such things performed and the morning is lost.

Sunday I went in the morning to hear the *predicatoire*[10] of the Saint-Simonians. Two persons spoke.[11] After the first had finished, a young man, quite young, perhaps 20, rose and addressed the audience – his hair was very light, his face pale, there was something hesitating in his manner, [10] and {he} spoke almost with a tone of a woman. There was a friendliness and the feeling of youth about him which touched the audience; he spoke with a simple eloquence and he was four or five times interrupted with strong applause – to speak with freedom and the simple and feeling eloquence of a young heart produces, so often, more effect than deep reasoning of an old mind, even where combined with a brilliant eloquence.

I went afterwards to the funeral of William Cooper,[12] nephew of Cooper. He died of a consumption. The minister made a prayer over [11] the grave, and I, consequently, this morning have heard the prayer of a religion which is now passing away after having lived its immense life, and of one which is endeavoring to take birth in this world. (For the *predication* of the young Saint-Simonian was a prayer to those who heard him, to pair with the Saint-Simonians in their doctrine to ameliorate the conditions of the most numerous and poorest class of humanity.) The prayer of the minister over the grave struck stalely and flatly on my ears, notwithstanding its strong words and messages, and the other struck me deeply because it was in [12] harmony with what I felt and with the present state of the world. It gave something to the mind to do in it, whereas the other was a more indi-

---

[10] A public declamation of Saint-Simonian doctrine, which the members called sermons. Brisbane usually uses the Saint-Simonians' own terminology; below he refers to these presentations as *predications*.

[11] According to *Le Globe* of Monday October 3, 1831, Jean Reynaud (1806–1863), a principal Saint-Simonian lecturer, spoke first, followed by Moïse Retouret.

[12] William Yardly Cooper. He was the son of William Cooper, brother of James Fenimore Cooper (1789–1851). The William Cooper family had been traveling in Europe when the son contracted tuberculosis.

vidual rhapsody on artificial feeling discordant with the natural feelings of a man as he is at the present time.

In the evening I was at the Saint-Simonians. Their religious feeling is to work with a feeling of unity and deep interest as a system of ideas which they animate with life; because its effect will be good upon the condition of man and their interest in it takes the form of faith because the feeling which animates them is good, for the object before them is to ameliorate the condition of mankind.

[13] Monday {October 3rd} – I went in the evening to the {*Théâtre de l'*}*Odeon*. I did not like the interior of the theater; it is large but arranged with bad taste; gaudy and without purity of design: and it had neither a very clean appearance. *The Mare with the Jour Miastre* {unidentified} and *Catherine the 2nd*[13] {was played}. Mlle George (Marguerite-Joséphine, 1781-1867) played Catherine. She played gloriously. It was a very fine piece of acting. You could see the gorgeous Empress before you, half woman-half heroine. Ambition in her head and a woman's feeling in the heart. I would pronounce her to be the first actress in France. [14] There is no woman on the English boards whom I saw that could be compared to her.

Paris: Tuesday 4th October

I went this morning to see Mr Rives, our minister.[14] He is no doubt a man of a pure, active, positive mind. His whole interest really seems to lie in the election in America, and the rise and fall of the popularity of the leading men. As politics no doubt have been half the affair of his life, it is a kind of business for him, as a trade is for the generality of people.

He gave me a ticket [15] to go to the Chamber of Deputies.[15] I went in the part reserved for the corps diplomatiques and I sat next to the Dey of Algiers,[16] who was also there to see the proceedings of the

---

[13] The play was written by Simon Lockroy and Auguste Arnould, cited in Wicks, part III: 44.

[14] William Cabell Rives (1795–1868). Originally a Jeffersonian who served in the House of Representatives from 1823–1829, he became a Democrat under Andrew Jackson, who rewarded him with the Ambassadorship to France. It is not surprising that he was so attentive to the United States elections (though transatlantic news did not travel quickly). Upon his return to the US he was elected to the Senate.

[15] See Introduction: 10–11, nn. 27, 29.

[16] This person was more likely a representative of the Dey. Algiers had recently become a dependent territory of France, after Charles X (r. 1824–1830) had sent troops in to

house. Salverte[17] made a speech against the hereditary peerage; he spoke well and with force, but he reasoned althru{ough} with *pensée* (thought), that is, there did not seem to be any deep sentiment of progress at the bottom which seemed to push him on instinctively. For that feeling of progress sees movement and progress in every change. If they think in destroying hereditary peerage,[18] they will [16] found this {French} throne on a firmer basis, by so completely surrounding it by democratic institutions, they are, I think, much mistaken; and Salverte, perhaps is a man who very conscientiously thinks so from reasoning.

Royer Collard made also a speech;[19] it was not very long. He spoke with force; he was at the point of view of something absolute. He wanted to find some absolute form of government which should be seated upon the unchangeable foundation of absolute reason – he wanted that absolute reason, [17] which is superior both to the king and nation, should reside in the government of the people: his speech was that of a philosopher *qui était au point de vue de la loi – son absolue connue grand principe qui devait régir la forme des gouvernements et qui était superieur au Roi et à la souverainéte nationale.*[20] Human nature does not want the absolute; *et particulièrement la pensée absolue,* (and particularly the absolute idea) because there is a feeling of progress in humanity and as soon as you wish to apply

occupy Algeria in June of 1830, in retaliation for the notorious flyswatter episode of 1827 when the Dey had swatted the French ambassador.

[17] Ann-Joseph Eusèbe Salverte (1771–1839) was deputy from Paris. He was proposed as Minister of Finance in a cabinet under Odilon Barrot (1791–1873) that was suggested in the Chamber as an opposition government, but which was never appointed.

[18] The issue of creating an hereditary peerage in France had just been raised by the newly appointed first minister, Casimir Périer (1777–1832), as a test of his authority with the king. Debate on this measure was used by several independent deputies to indicate whether they supported the king (leaving peer selection unchanged), or supported Minister Périer (favoring a change in the appointment of peers). As a result, the arguments often turned on quite narrow definitions and arcane ideas as the deputies spun out their points. See Mellen: 114.

[19] Pierre-Paul Royer-Collard (1763–1845) was an important intellectual and political figure in France, a member of the liberal group led by Guizot and others who had opposed Charles X in July, 1830. See Introduction: 11, n. 29, and also Brisbane's later discussion of the French liberal group, Diary II: 125, November 21–22, 1831, n. 80.

[20] "... whose point of view was that the law was absolute, like a great principle which could determine the form of governments and which was superior to the king and the sovereignty of the nation."

something absolute to it, it revolts. Man [18] can feel deeper and discover by his feelings a greater progress than he can discover by calculation and thought.

Paris: Wednesday October 5th

I spent a part of the morning at the Louvre in examining the paintings. I have at present a great love for the painting of the earliest masters, both of the German and Italian school, but I have a greater liking even for the old German masters. It seems to me I find a deeper sentiment [19] in their paintings. You see in the old Italian masters the foundation of grace and beauty: it ripened quickly and exhausted itself also in a short age; whereas the old German school seems never to have entirely developed itself; the technical part seems never to have completely expressed the sentiment. It strikes me, to resume, that there is a deeper and profounder sentiment in the paintings of the old German masters than in those of the Italian schools. I enjoy as much one of those old pictures as the fine ones of the most flourishing epoch.

[20] I went in the evening to see *La Muette de Portici* at the *Théâtre de l'Opera*. It was not well played. There was a coldness in the actors and in the audience; I think it is much superiorly performed in Berlin.[21] It produced scarcely any effect upon me.

Paris: Thursday – Sunday October 6–9th

On October 8th I wrote a long letter to my father. In it, I undertook to give him some idea of the actual political state of France. To do this I went up to the first revolution. I made some observations upon Mirabeau, Robespierre,[22] and said, with regard to Napoleon, that he had absorbed the revolution, [21] but that, in time, it had not lost itself; it took, then, another direction.

---

[21] Brisbane describes discussing this opera with friends in Berlin during his first winter there 1829–1830. (*MB*: 93)

[22] Honoré, Comte de Mirabeaux (1749–1791), was a political theorist who had spent time in England observing their constitutional system. Despite his title, he came to the Assembly of the Estates General as a representative of the Third Estate. He became an important figure in the National Assembly of 1789 advising on the constitution and helping to persuade Louis XVI to recognize it. Maximillian Robespierre (1758–1794) was one of the leaders of the radical "mountain" faction that subsequently pushed for

In the evening I was at the *Digne Preparatoire* (solemn preparation) of the Saint-Simonians. In fact, it is a private conference where only those persons are admitted who are known to be favorable towards the doctrine. The professions of faith are here read, which is necessary before entering into the Saint-Simonian family.[23] It is intended to be a familiar meeting as far as possible, although a good deal of restraint exists and questions and difficulties are presented and discussed.

The 7th I was in the house a good deal of the day reading and writing. I was to go and introduce Duveyrier to Cooper {James Fenimore}, but he does not come at the time agreed upon; in the [22] evening I was at home.

I spent the 6th almost as the 7th.

I went this morning, Sunday, to see a review of a part of the National Guard.[24] There were 30,000 perhaps, and at least the square of the Carousel was full.[25] They did not make much show on account of being so compactly brought up {being so closely packed together}. I saw the King {Louis-Philippe}. He took off his hat and bowed often. He appears smiling and affable. I could not see his face very well, but his general appearance was common, nothing imposing about it. The company as he passed along cried, "*vive le roi*" (long live the king), but without enthusiasm, and some did not. The spectators remained indifferent. The whole view was flat and without animation.

[23] In the evening I went to the *soirée* of the Saint-Simonians.[26] This is arranged in order {that} those persons who wish to see the Saint-Simonians

---

the king's execution and then led in creating and enforcing the policies of the "terror" that mobilized France to face civil war and attack from Europe.

[23] Brisbane refers to a ritual of commitment required of those applying for full membership in the Saint-Simonian society. Regular members of the society often reconfirmed their membership at these rituals.

[24] The National Guard was a domestic militia. Since commissions could be bought, uniforms were relatively expensive, and there was no required or long-term service in the ranks, the National Guard drew primarily from the bourgeois and petit-bourgeois and served as much as a police force as an army. Membership, especially for the petit-bourgeois, had become a mark of social status by the late 1820s when Brisbane was in Paris.

[25] The Carousel was the arch at the eastern end of the Tuilleries garden and was, in 1831, an entry to the royal residence of the Louvre. The surrounding wall and much of the building at that end of the Louvre were destroyed during the Paris Commune battle in May 1871; only the Carousel stands today.

[26] To accommodate the increasing numbers of people who had become interested in the Doctrine, a Saint-Simonian headquarters was established, the Salle Taitbout, on the

{illegible} and become better acquainted with the family, can do it. Those persons who feel full well disposed towards the Doctrine, and who naturally feel an inclination to become members of it, are by this means offered the occasion. It is doubtlessly to draw many young persons to them, for I observe that an exchange with the members produces more effect than to read coldly their ideas at a distance.

[24] In going in, you would suppose you were entering a fashionable circle. It has all the appearance of a fashionable *soirée*. Some look rather more genteel than others, but there are many remarkably handsome faces among the women and the men hold {model or dress themselves} in the fashionable young view. There is a great deal of conversation and less restraint and there are often discussions among different sets of persons. I feel a call with Enfantin and with Bazard. They are both superior men; Bazard perhaps has the most piercing view and the freest thinking mind. I feel, myself, [25] and acknowledge, that their ideas contain more, are deeper, fuller of life, and a vast deal more important than the ideas of Shilling or Hegel.[27]

Pure systematizing, without having humanity constantly before you and your system, is good for nothing. In themselves they {systems} are of little value, they must be connected with man and the world and their value {of the systems} is only their relation to them {man and the world} and the life they {man and the world} have in them.[28]

---

street of that name, where members of the Saint-Simonian "family" were "at home" several days a week for conversation. Here were held both public events, such as this *soirée*, and private events, such as the marriage Brisbane describes below. (Diary II: 30, October 11, 1831) The Sunday night *soirée* featured music and dancing and became so popular that admission had to be restricted to invited guests. See Carlisle: 127.

[27] Friedrich Wilhelm Schelling (1775–1854) was a German philosopher and leader of the Romantic school. He did not gain widespread recognition until after the death of Hegel.

[28] Brisbane insisted that any schemes or theories for helping humanity had to include practical systems that could be applied in existing society. He returned to this issue repeatedly in his correspondence with Manesca (Diary II: 41–46, October 13, 1831) and in his expressed irritation with the triviality of Berlin society (Diary II: 122–27, November 21–22, 1831). Brisbane's concern with the practical was central to his decision to become involved with Fourier (*MB*: 172–73, 177–80, Guarneri: 30) and emerges sharply in his later explications of Fourier's ideas. This approach was basic to Brisbane's thinking, a result of his rural American upbringing in Batavia and reinforced by those around him in Paris. It should be noted that Laurent's sermon at the Saint-Simonians' on that Sunday, October 9, 1831 (see *Le Globe*, October 10, 1831) complained at length of the sterility of all political groups and the need to rally workers by promoting a practical Saint-Simonian workshop program. It was also that at this point, towards

[26] *Paris: Monday 10th October*

I went this morning to see Lechevalier {Jules, 1800–1850} and had a talk with him on the {Saint-Simonian} Doctrine – I wished to understand their ideas with regard to a future life and I see they are nearly those of the German Philosophers. One of the aims of the physical existence of the individual is the intellectual results he leaves behind him and his influence upon society. *L'homme se meurt en vivant; et vit en mort* (man dies in living and lives in dying); that is, his {man's} physical existence {is} subjugated to his intellectual existence; the condition of that result is the condition [27] of his exhausting his physical existence (dying). But his intellectual result being the condition of his physical existence, he lives the most when he has developed that {his intellect} the most, and that is his death. He lives the most as he approaches death and that same force which makes him die makes him produce his intellectual result and thus in dying or by dying he lives.

The Hegelians say, for example, that ideas Plato [29] put in the world are Plato's; those ideas exist [28] in the world, and he is eternal in those ideas. Lechevalier, speaking in the spirit of the Doctrine, says Christ deposed his individuality in the world and is existing in all individuals, more or less. It is not only His {Christ's} ideas, but it is particularly His life He puts here, and we are living of His life; His life is living in us. His life is our action as our action verifies His life; His immortality is life and action itself, which in their turn perpetuate that immortality.

I have of late got out of this habit of speculation [29] and abstract thinking. My habit of mind at the present moment is rather commonplace: speculation upon politics. This spirit of peoples, which has been so vivid in me for a long time past, is much weakened. Speculation upon the interior and the individual are much less in my mind.

I was in the evening at the *Enseignement des Artistes* (Artists' Instruction),[30] and I went, after it was over, to see the ballet of *La Belle au Bois*

---

the middle of October, that an ideological division was beginning to develop between the two high priests, Bazard and Enfantin, over how much emphasis should be placed on the development of a model Saint-Simonian community of workers, versus further clarification of the Saint-Simonian philosophy.

[29] Ancient Greek philosopher (429–347 BC).

[30] A presentation or discussion led by Saint-Simonian artists.

(*Sleeping Beauty*). Mlle Taglioni [30] danced in it, but her part was very short. However she was supremely graceful, as customary.

Paris: Tuesday 11th October

I went at 1 o'clock to the Chamber of Deputies and remained till half after five. The discussion was without interest. Various persons who had made amendments developed them. These were propositions tending to constitute a peerage by election or by the nominations of the king.[31] They were more listened to and all repeated. This shows the Chamber does not feel itself a constitutional power [31] and it does not like to broach new or branching questions. I think the thing will end by conferring on the king this power of electing the members of the peerage.

In the evening at the Salle Taitbout a Saint-Simonian marriage took place; it is the first one.[32] The ceremony was extremely simple but there was some feeling in it and on that account possessed more virtue than the worn out ceremony of the Catholic church. There was more feeling, more meaning, [32] and more solemnity in this marriage in the new family, than in the one of the exterior world; it struck me so. There was feeling in it, and that which sustains a thing with feeling and sentiment is holy and right; for its only value is its feeling and sentiment.

All the members of the family were present and the house was crowded. Bazard and Enfantin entered last, and were seated as usual; a stand was placed near Enfantin covered with scarlet velvet, [33] {and} a book which contained the *formule* (form, model) of the rites. Bazard addressed the audience. He spoke upon the subject, saying it was the first ceremony, that it of course would be simple in its form. And he congratulated the family upon seeing another progress taking place; and although it was not exterior and did not produce a strong exterior effort, that nevertheless it was a progress and it was to be rejoiced in; the bride and bridegroom were seated opposite to their fathers. Enfantin said to them this *formule*, which united them, to which they assented. They kissed their fathers.

---

[31] This was a continuation of the debate Brisbane had heard earlier. Diary II: 14–16, October 4, 1831.

[32] *Le Globe*, October 15, 1831, announced that the first Saint-Simonian wedding had been celebrated October 11, 1831. There are no official Saint-Simonian accounts of this ceremony, so Brisbane's description is particularly interesting.

{The following Brisbane inserted as a footnote at the bottom of page 33 of the diary.} The whole was extremely simple, Mme Bazard[33] addressed them feelingly, and a few words from Mr Bazard ended it.

[34] *Paris: Wednesday 12th October*

I received today a letter from Henrietta.[34] She makes a candid but singular confession to me. She says:

> . . . If you come to Berlin to study here, as I thought you intended, I will certainly be very glad to see you. You will find a sincere friend in me who will, as she did before, take the greatest interest in everything that concerns you – in one word, a true friend, but . . . you must not expect anything else. I can neither feel nor listen to any affection, that is not friendship. You must not [35] speak of love to me, and you must never ask, nor expect, any explanation upon this subject – etc., etc.
>
> But let me now, again and again, tell you my friendship is quite the same as it was. Don't think the word cold. It contains more sweetness than does love itself.
>
> Our destinies lie too wide asunder from each other. It would be madness to revive in you a feeling I cannot partake."

This letter certainly struck [38][35] me singularly. I read it with a curious wonder: for an instant a gleam of disappointment passed thru me; but it is already a long time since that love I felt for her has been fading away in my mind, and it seems not strong enough in me in order her declaration should produce a strong effect upon me. The cause of her determination remains an enigma to me. There is a curious kind of mystery in it to me – what can be the reason? I imagine a thousand things – it produced a strange effect upon me for a [39] moment as I said a feeling of disappointment passed thru me.

---

[33] Claire Jouhert Bazard was the wife of the "high priest" Bazard, and her ideas on the role of women were influential. Enfantin's designation of her as high priestess in the Saint-Simonian church troubled her husband. The issue of women's participation in the Saint-Simonian religion, as well as Claire's possible affair with Enfantin, were factors in the break-up of Saint-Simonianism in early November 1831.

[34] Henrietta Solmar introduced Brisbane to Rahel Levin Varnhagen von Ense in Berlin. See Introduction: 13, especially n. 35.

[35] Pp. 36–37 are left blank. Brisbane notes on them that they were skipped.

I then read on with curiosity and surprise a kind of laugh – I laughed without wishing it or without reason: the muscles seemed to draw my mouth involuntary with a laugh and I laughed and gasped; but not freely. It was more the effort: however one way or the other there was very little feeling about it. I certainly do not love her with passion; that has passed and her avowal produces but a slight impression upon me.[36]

[40] *Paris: Thursday October 13th*

I answered today the letter I received yesterday from Henrietta. The answer was rather figurative, somewhat worked up and a little metaphysical. However the main {thing} I said was to ask the reason of her determination. I asked that under a dozen *formes*.[37]

I spent the afternoon in the museum examining the paintings. A museum is a fatiguing thing. You see a wall with an immense diversity of ideas, incongruous, unharmonious and contradicting, [41] plastered upon it. It fatigues the mind to run over such a diversity of ideas and subjects.

I received in the afternoon a very long letter from Manesca. I had sent him the source of the works of the Saint-Simonians and I wanted his opinion upon them. I see by his letter he is a complete Saint-Simonian thoroughly, and deeply and by long reflection. He has only refound himself, so to say, in finding them. He has felt as they feel, but they have added thoughts to their feelings, and found a system for it, their [42] *formules* by which they can realize it and apply it to society. Manesca has not undertaken that, and

[36] Brisbane is puzzled and hurt at Henrietta's rejection. From the intensity of his nervous reaction it is clear he has developed very strong feelings for her, no matter by what name he calls them. However, on reviewing other diary entries, it appears that the root of his upset, as much at Henrietta's words, was also his inability to live up to his own grandly naive ideas about the simplicity of passion and the insignificance of commitment to all but great thoughts – ideas he elaborated upon in both diaries. From entries in Diary I it is clear Brisbane had developed a strong but impersonal sexual appetite. In an earlier letter to Henrietta (Diary I: 311–12, December 23, 1830) he had responded to her criticism of his numerous amours with a rather cold-blooded explication of the unimportance of sexual fidelity and morality compared to the philosophical contribution he was destined to make. He repeats this sentiment elsewhere in connection with his feelings about his future wife Adèle. Diary II: 231, January 22–29, 1832. In later entries in Diary II: 211, January 8–15, 1832, he further justified his amorous adventures with a mechanistic explanation of passion as an ordinary "portion of us; we satisfy them as we would move an arm or walk." Brisbane's expectations of himself and others underscore his youth.

[37] See Diary I: 62, October 29, 1830, n. 28.

without that, the feeling is nothing. It affects no one but he who feels it and it only makes him unhappy for he feels something should be done to ameliorate the condition of mankind and he sees no remedy.

He assures us the Saint-Simonian doctrines would be received and applauded in America. In that case I would not hesitate a moment. I should know what I had to do. I should at length [43] have an object before my eyes; I should find something to which I could dedicate life, activity, and body. His letter gave me the greatest pleasure and excited me in the highest degree. Could a commencement once be made in America, or could some individuals be found who were disposed for any such thing, I should like to go and head it.

Manesca . . . {Bottom part of the page is torn out and 3–4 lines are missing.}

[44] . . . called *The Right of Property*. He must be no doubt more or less in the circle of the philosophy of the eighteenth century. It is easy to change such minds and give them the right direction. I should like to enter into correspondence with that man, and if he could be changed, it would already perhaps be a good deal gained.[38]

I was in the evening at the *soirée* {bottom part of the page is torn out, the other side of the tear indicated above} [45] entire S{aint}-S{imonian} feeling. It {perhaps a letter from Manesca to the Saint-Simonians} pleased them also very much and they intend to answer it, and they will send him *The Globe*, all their publications.

This letter has raised me up. It has done more than a month's study. It has opened the prospect of doing something there, and I would not give a farthing for my belief without action with it; and was a field opened there? Did I think I would find the soil to work upon {if} I am a Saint-Simonian? [46] For there is nothing offered now, to the activity of the individual, half as immense. It is immense, the circle of action offered you and the effect you may produce. The strongest minds are at present often engaged in trifling

---

[38] The author of this work, *The Right of Property*, was presumably a contemporary of Brisbane, since he imagines having a correspondence with him. The debate on hereditary peerage that Brisbane had attended the previous week (October 4, 1831) in the Chamber of Deputies discussed property rights: whether a peerage was property and therefore could not be arbitrarily taken away. This work may have been mentioned in the earlier debate.

meager discussion which seem too trifling for babies' work, in comparison with the field the Saint-Simonians open.

The idea of being able to do something in America has given me an impulse. It has raised me [47] up and has left but a narrow space between me and the Saint-Simonians, but it is still a difficult one to get over. I am near them, but to enter within them will still require a very decided effort.

Paris: Friday 14th to Sunday 16th October

The letter I received yesterday has excited me very much. It has given a life and movement to me, and I feel as if I had found some decided object to which I could turn my attention. It has given a vigor and movement to me, and I feel as [48] if I could dash ahead and bring up any object without turning circles or being dislocated by exterior objects. I went and introduced Duveyrier to {James Fenimore} Cooper. They had a long talk. Cooper talked with his accustomed force and conviction or orthodoxy, but Duveyrier may feel as strong on his side, and in that subject, at least, produced a certain effect upon him. I thought Cooper seemed rather struck with some of his {Duveyrier's} views and reasoning, and he formed some rather strong objections [49] to ideas which he {Duveyrier} seemed to be the surest and most convinced of.[39]

The 15th: I was writing during the day. In the evening I went to the theater *Les gymnases* {*Théâtre de Gymnase Dramatique*}. I saw Leontain Fay, Jenny Vertpri and Jenny Colore. *The Marriage of Reason* was the play.[40] I disliked it without intending to be so. It is a deep critique of the present order of things.

[50] I went this morning, Sunday, to the *predication* (preaching). Parts of it were very fair. Barrault (Emile, 1799–1869) spoke.

I went in the evening to the *soirée* at the rue Mousigny. There is a feeling that pushes me to swear and join these people as an anchor to which you can fasten the activity of your life, and when I get near them, there is something arises which throws me off again. Various little particularities

---

[39] In a letter of December 1831 Cooper declined to join the Saint-Simonian religion. See Introduction: 20, n. 45.

[40] Written by J. Coralli, cited in Wicks, part II: 49. The three performers to whom Brisbane refers are unidentified.

took place, which revolt me, self love or vanity is wounded and mangled there. That spurs me the most. I left tonight despairing, hating and wishing to hold everything in contempt.

I wrote the following pages while laboring under that fashion. [51] Feeling is what I want, is what I have need of. I would wish to feel deeply, profoundly, and let its sound be melancholy sad, anything {rather} than none at all. I am still in that battle with myself, that longing for the truth. Character and depth of feeling I have; that suspecting and thinking I have, that doubting of myself. Almost or quite convincing myself {that} those around me are very superior, and every thing I may see in them that shows force or character, I seize it. I compare myself to it and find [52] myself inferior to it. And thus, when I have doubted myself and convinced myself of a need of character and feeling in me, then I curse myself and feel as if I could shout out the damned brain that holds no more than it does. When a man doubts of himself, that is the most cursed feeling: and it has nearly led me to consider myself an entirely inferior individual.

I think I have in myself every thing that is bad, and but little that is good. I often leave the [53] Saint-Simonians with repugnance and revolt in feeling against them. I see there some of the most powerful members. I don't think I possess such a devotedness, and could do what they have done. I consider myself incapable of reaching the point they have, and feel I could not act with that force and character in it. I hate the thing. I would avoid it, and have nothing to do with it, and then I wish to feel independent of it, and I seem to thank fate interiorly that I am living in a world where [54] I am independent and can do as I like and what I like, and nothing if I like; that is, take no part in anything, and if I feel incapable, stand aloof and not compromise myself. To various individuals, independence and personality are a terrible thing. To submit and consent to let yourself be classed, to humble your self love and let your capacity be ranked at a low rate, it requires a terrible effort. If you feel perfectly independent, you feel you can remain nothing, and if you are [55] nothing, there is the feeling, at least, in it that you may become everything.

The question with me is, "Have I the stuff in me to join the Saint-Simonians with heart and soul? Have I such a character, that I could disregard every consideration of a family or exterior nature, and stand up and put forth with force and firmness, a set of opinions or principles which the world would look at as ridiculous?" That is the question with me; have I that stuff in me? It is no consequence whether the [56] Saint-Simonians' doctrines are true or not. Have I in me character that would enable me to stand up in the face of the world, and sustain there my opinions and convictions although they might appear to them ridiculous? That is the question, and I fear I have not. I am afraid I would feel the work to be supported by some more powerful character. I would not act spontaneously by myself, but would require to see someone go before me to work up and follow the path.[41]

[57] *Paris: Monday to Friday 17th – 21st October*

The emotions which the letter of Manesca produced upon me have somewhat passed again. I feel myself still in revolt, and not in harmony with the hierarchy and the leaders of it. I am not yet identified enough with the cause to love its disciples and consent to submit and obey. When I accept it and am willing to dedicate [58] my efforts and activity to it, I shall consider then myself the equal of the Saint-Simonians and consider them engaged in the work I love, and which I embrace. The relationship which will then exist between us will be different from what it is now. For I, of course, now must look upon them as persons whose relationship to me is to convert me, to make me abandon, so to say, the social opinions and life I had, to enter into theirs. And there [59] must always be some force, consequently some repugnance and some regrets in the change and the passage to it.

My former opinions and preceding labors could hold but little value in the eyes of the Doctrine, and it is difficult thus to sacrifice the preceding voices and ideas a person has gathered and identified with himself. They become a part of himself. They are mixed for his self-love, his vanity, his consideration for himself, etc. It cost me a great effort to get rid of the ideas I had taken from Helvétius, and sacrifice them to those of Hegel.

[60] Another thing: have I in me the force to work exclusively for the propagation of those ideas? Dedicate all my efforts and activity to them? Can I love mankind so much as to sacrifice all my individual liberties,

---

[41] After having declared his enthusiasm to lead an American, practical, Saint-Simonian program in reaction to Manesca's letter (Diary II: 42–43, October 13, 1831), it is interesting to see Brisbane discuss his insecurity about his leadership abilities.

desires, tastes, etc. in laboring for them? That is, to sacrifice all those with labor, to support and propagate the Doctrine? So, for example, if I wish to make a voyage to execute any project, that I could sacrifice them {the project} and labor with application and perseverance for the [61] Doctrine, and dedicate to it my time, likings, and activity. At the present moment I would not. Should I join with them, I might break with them if they should confine me too much, and if for any reason I might take a dislike in some particulars to them. I cannot stand up against *ennui* (boredom) and dislike, and their doctrine is not near strong enough in me to bear down every other feeling, and make me stand up against dislike and labor.

I think it will come.

[62] *Monday and Tuesday {October 17-18}*

I was writing long letters to Manesca and Williams.[42] I spoke to Williams about the Doctrine and I sent him some of the principal works. I gave him also a history of my story with Adèle.[43] He knew half of it in Florence. I gave him the result.

In writing to Manesca, I wrote very favorably of the doctrine and said [63] if I could make a commencement and get some persons around me, I think it would decide me to enter into the Doctrine and dedicate myself to it.

Wednesday evening, I was at an evening party given by Mr Rives. There were mostly Americans, a plain party, no dancing, cards. It broke up 11½ {11:30}.

Friday it rained violently. A young German, Mr Bronst or Barosst,[44] whom I saw last night at the Saint-Simonians, came to see me. We had a

---

[42] An American friend whom Brisbane probably met in Italy.

[43] Adèle LeBrun would become Brisbane's first wife. He had met her in Rome, where he stayed for two or three months on his way from Sicily and southern Italy before returning to Paris in the summer of 1831. Brisbane married her in 1833 and brought her back to his family in Batavia, where they had a son, Charles, and a daughter. However the marriage broke up in 1838 and she returned to Italy with Charles, got a papal dispensation and remarried an Italian, Count della Rocca. It is interesting to note the difference of tone in his discussions of Adèle and Henrietta. Whatever his intentions might have been towards Adèle, whom he had met more recently, he was still very emotionally involved with Henrietta. It may be that his passion cooled towards Henrietta when he met Adèle. For a chronicle of this relationship see Introduction, 13: n. 35.

[44] Brisbane does not clearly identify this person. The following Sunday (Diary II: 73, October 23, 1831) he refers to him as Arnst.

long [64] talk upon the opinions and doctrine of Herr Krause,[45] a German who seems to have conceived a new principle or felt a new feeling for humanity. He appears in many points to coincide with Saint-Simon. Hereditary wealth is destroyed in principle, and this young man, who is his disciple, says he has even worked out more the details of the scientific as well as the part relating to the fine arts.

It is to be remarked, and perhaps the remark has deep [65] meaning, that in England, France and Germany, three men have risen up with new principles for society, and feeling a new life for mankind. Owen's[46] principles, the weakest, appears founded upon utility. Krause appears philosophical and scientific, to be able to bring it down to *formules* which he can apply to society of men and give them an organization, so that they will set forth and labor in the spirit of the new conception. [66] He did not conceive, I think, an enthusiasm and ardor for a feeling embodied in definite and concrete *formules*, as "*à chacun selon sa capacité, à caque [chaque] capacité selon*

---

[45] Karl Christian Friedrich Krause (1782–1832) was a German philosopher, a student of Hegel and Fichte. In the summer of 1832, after Brisbane had become involved with Fourierist doctrine but was still in touch with the Saint-Simonians, he traveled to Munich to study with Krause. On August 12, 1832, Brisbane wrote to Karl Varnhagen von Ense (Pickett, Letters: 22), "He is a man very superior for the direction he has taken . . . his immediate aim is not the amelioration of the condition of the poor and suffering classes, rather, he wants to enter into the interior of man and change it entirely. You see that this is the opposite of Fourier . . . I believe Krause has risen above all the prejudices that there are in our civilization. . . . The more I have spoken with him the more I am convinced that he has gone to the bottom of things. . . . He speaks against Saint-Simonianism but I pardon him because I see that from his point of view he has reason." Krause's sudden death a month after this letter was written may be one reason why Brisbane did not stay in Munich. It is clear that Brisbane was not yet a thorough disciple of any social theory, but was enthralled with many different ideas for the improvement of society. The version of Fourierist theory which Brisbane presented in his later American writings (see Introduction: 25, n. 60, for an extended bibliography) can be perhaps more clearly understood when viewed as a composite of the various ideas that took his attention in Europe.

[46] Robert Owen (1771–1858) was a Scots mill owner and reformer who established a model factory community in New Lanark, Scotland. Later Owen established a model American community in New Harmony, Indiana. Brisbane was impressed with Owen's ideas for the organization of American labor, and had read a great deal about him, according to his son Arthur Brisbane (Brisbane papers, private collection), and visited New Harmony. Here Brisbane faults Owen's theories because they are based on utility. Yet, a week earlier (Diary II: 41–42, October 13, 1831) he praised the Saint-Simonian formulas as a means by which the system could be applied to society.

ses oeuvres. Il faut travailler à l'amélioration de la condition de la classe la plus nombreuse et la plus pauvre."[47]

These principles are so general, he can with difficulty work for them no further than to present them to the conception of others. But to be active, a definite feeling must be in the heart, and that must be created by definite *formules*, which can [67] be presented to the feeling, as well as the intelligence of everyone. And when that feeling becomes an interest in the heart, {it} excites an enthusiasm and ardor there. Enthusiasm and interest communicated to different persons, and producing an intimate conviction and bond between them, and giving their activity a same direction, indicating {to} them a general and common object or religion.

Saint-Simon, it strikes me, [68] has particularly felt the social, industrial, and religious organization. Life, love, and sympathy are the highest principles. The moral first manifestation of them all in society is the highest science, love and sympathy in the heart, animated with life and action springing out of it. Our enthusiasm, thru the moral, giving a common object and some direction to it, is religion.

Saint-Simon was life. He felt deeply the progress [69] humanity was to render. His sympathy and feeling revealed to him that new progress and perfectionment {perfection}; it did not come first to him thru his mind or thought. It was the ardor of his sympathies, the life that was in him which made him practice the new principle. Krause, I think, must have come to it more thru the mind. It was not an overflow of life and sympathy which impelled him on, but it was the breadth of his thoughts which put the conception in his mind.

[70] The nature of the French character is more calculated, I think, to produce the real feeling and conception of a new progress. Matter there {in France} holds a certain result, and is more or less beautified. The material life is carried, then, in France to a higher point than anywhere else. The cleanliness of body, of person and dress, the taste{ful}ness and elegance of dress, and the nice and careful arrangement of exterior things shows that the material part is not neglected. Matter holds a more important place

---

[47] From each according to his ability, from each ability according to the tasks. (I give my translation for this phrase which is more literal, "Each according to his capacity, each capacity according to its works." Manuel: 629) We must work for the easing of the conditions of the most numerous and poorest class.

in France than in any other country, and it is beautified, worked out, and seems to be worthy of attention [71] of the mind. The spiritual holds also an important place.

They are theoretical and general in their views and systems. There is a good deal of theory and generalization of principles, but realization is mixed with it. When an idea is felt and believed, the first thing to do is to realize it, so that the material and spiritual, theory and realization, sympathy and action, are found in the French nature. And it is out of that nature, most probably, that a new feeling, guided by intelligence and [72] animated with life, would arise. The social life, the spirit of society, and society also, are carried to a high degree of perfection and development, and this new conception and feeling, rising up out of a society so polished and to such a degree formulated and defined, must also necessarily be social in its nature, and social arrangement must be one of the principle objects and direction it takes.

[73] *Paris: Saturday, Sunday 22nd {to} 23rd October*

I was in the evening to the Italian Opera[48] to hear the *Barbiere*.[49] I did not enjoy myself much. I was fatigued and I did not feel the music. I saw Arnst[50] in the morning. He gave me more of the ideas of Krause, upon his doctrine. He is a very intelligent, active and good young man. He possesses intelligence and feeling.

Sunday I went to the {illegible} of the Saint-Simonians to hear their *predication* and in the [74] evening I was at the *soirée*, but I cannot say I amused myself much there. I know many of the persons very intimately and I don't yet sympathize with them enough. I know scarcely any of the ladies, and thinking I would be leaving Paris before long,[51] I delayed forming any particular acquaintance with some of them. The place consequently is rather

---

[48] This is the Italian Theatre. See Illustration 16.

[49] The opera *Il Barbiere di Siviglia* was composed in 1815 by Giacomo Rossini (1792–1868) and was based on the play, *Le Barbier de Seville* by Pierre Augustin Caron de Beaumarchais (1732–1799).

[50] The same young German whose name Brisbane recalled as either Bronst or Barosst after meeting him at the Saint-Simonians earlier that week. See Diary II: 63, October 17–18, 1831.

[51] This is Brisbane's first mention of his intent to leave Paris. He gives no explanation for it here, but later in Berlin (Diary II: 152, 154–55, December 7–14, 1831), he expresses his discomfort at the growing divisions among the Saint-Simonians. His difficulty making

empty for me. I don't find there close, deep interests and [75] sympathies so necessary to create pleasure and interest.[52]

Paris: from the 24th Monday to Monday 31st October

I shall now leave Paris in two or three days. I received a letter yesterday {October 23} from Henrietta, and she seems to think there is a danger from the cholera.[53]

On Saturday I was at a ceremony of the Saint-Simonians. They received a large number of children [76] in the family. The ceremony consisted simply in kissing them. The room was very handsome and it had a great deal of meaning in it. A marriage afterwards took place. It was Bazard's daughter who married M. Lenoir or Lenore.[54]

I wrote a long letter to my father, some of it upon the French revolution, and something about the Saint-Simonians. I sent also a *resumé* of the doctrine to S. W. Stenais (unidentified). I wrote to Manesca concerning the interview [77] with the Minister of Public Instruction.[55] I saw the Minister Wednesday. He seemed to care but very little about the plan of principled instruction I was to show to him, and had it been true, he would, no doubt, have paid as little attention to it, as if he knew it was false. With such men there is but little to do. Besides, I think he is a man of very ordinary talents and entirely incapable of organizing a general system of primary instruction.

---

a total commitment to the Saint-Simonian cause (Diary II: 57–61, October 17, 1831) may have played a role.

[52] In his first diary Brisbane had revealed a taste for unencumbered sexual activity with only a fleeting interest in his partners (ironically, a sensibility that emerged just as he had been struck by the degradation of women in Turkish society, and concluded that such degradation blocked the advance of civilization). Now in the second diary, his earlier references to the handsome and fashionable Saint-Simonians, the lack of restraint in conversation (Diary II: 24, October 9, 1831) and his current comments that he had delayed forming any particular acquaintance among the ladies because he knew he was leaving, suggests that he would have been busy making such acquaintances with expectations of success and intimacy were he staying.

[53] There was an outbreak of cholera in Berlin in the summer and fall of 1831 during which Hegel, among others, had died.

[54] The man who married Bazard's daughter was St Cléron, an editor for *Le Globe*.

[55] Marthe-Camille-Bachesson, Comte de Montalivet (1801–1880) was Minister of Public Instruction in Perier's cabinet from March 13, 1831 to October 11, 1832. See Diary II: 15, October 4, 1831.

[78] Before leaving I have been buying various things, some books, lithographs and some little presents for some of my acquaintances there {Berlin}.

I would rather spend my winter in Berlin than Paris. I detest the rainy weather and the muddy streets of the latter city during the winter months, and I prefer also the social life of the Germans to that of the French. Besides, I am afraid that if I do not spend this winter in Germany, I shall not spend another one there, and I consider it very important for me to know the [79] German language well. It must serve me in America if I am to act there.

Paris, up to Friday 4th November

It is twelve at night. Tomorrow I leave. The thing is without a feeling in my heart; I am indifferent. It is as much without impression upon me, as if I were going to breakfast. I have just bid Greenough good-by; he was in bed. He raised his arm and said, as we were talking, "Brisbane, I have sworn by the God to do something in this world."

[80] There was feeling there. I think he will do as much as the epoch allows. A man cannot get beyond the circle of his century, no matter what he is; he must work within it. Greenough has great natural force and a superior mind. I think he will do something in the arts, if anybody can, at the present epoch, and that I doubt strongly.

[81] *EXIT Paris: Saturday 5th to Tuesday 8th November*

I left Paris the 5th at 7 in the *Messageries Royales* (Royal Coach Services) for Strasbourg,[56] paid for my place in the interior, only 25 francs,[57] for the conductor 8 more. That is less than half the common price or amount of competition.

I paid not much attention to the country as I passed along. The weather was rainy and I had already passed over the same road once before.

---

[56] Traveling from France to Prussia's capital, Berlin, in 1831 was a trip of many days. The route Brisbane took brought him first to Strasbourg in France's eastern Department of Alsace. From there the coaches followed the Rhine River north to the cities of Speyer, Worms and Mainz, and then to Frankfurt. From Frankfurt, Brisbane traveled on to Berlin in Prussia.

[57] This was equivalent to about $12 at the time. While a substantial sum in 1831, clearly it was reasonable for stagecoach travel.

I read the first day a brochure, very [82] lately published by Chateaubri-
and,[58] relating to a *progrès* (motion) for the banishment of Charles X and his
family. It is very violent against the path the government of Louis-Philippe
has taken. He lashes it with the whip of disapproval and disdain. The book
is well written and it pleased me.

The second day I was reading *l'explanation de la Doctrine*, first year.[59]
The criticism of that book upon the actual social order is sublime and it
shows what an immense deal might be done and what an immense deal
[83] there is to do. There is no doubt the actual social system tends to orga-
nize hatred and destruction in society instead of love and confidence. And,
excepting the scientific progress and the accumulation of industrial facts,
there is in almost every country in Europe a moral retrogradation. France is
strong intellectually, for she is carrying out, developing and attacking, the
result of a system of social ideas.

Prussia, or that part of Germany, is strong because there is a great
breadth of interior intellectual life in the nature of [84] that people; they
have also a destiny in the world. England has accumulated a great many
industrial facts, but she is rotten to the heart. All the rest of Europe is waiting for some new renovating principle. It is waiting to begin living a new
life. Was Saint-Simon the man destined to throw into the present epoch the
fundamental feeling of that new life, and the idea with it, that was to grow
up with it and guide its development? I am not intimately, body and soul,
convinced of it, as the real Saint-Simonians would be. It has not yet entered
[85] into my feelings and become hope, interest and object there; that I
think will come when I am called upon to act.

The country remains very much the same after leaving Paris until you
come into the part about Strasbourg called Alsace, as you approach the
Rhine. The country changes, and at a considerable distance from Strasbourg, it takes the character of the country upon the borders of the Rhine.

---

[58] François René, Vicomte de Chateaubriand (1768–1848), was a conservative monarchist
and brilliant man of letters who wrote that the power of God and king were best suited
to manage human affairs; therefore the people should not meddle with these powers.
He had been a strong supporter of Louis XVIII (1814–1824) and an even stronger supporter of Charles X (1824–1830).

[59] *Doctrine Saint-Simonienne, Exposition Première Année*, 1829, attributed to Barrault,
Bazard, Carnot, Duveyrier, Enfantin, Fournel, and Rodrigues, Paris, 1830.

A very striking difference is to be observed between the real [86] French population and the Alsatians. I consider the French cloth as decidedly very superior. The Alsatians are Germans or very near it, but they are also inferior, much inferior to the Germanic {as opposed to French/Alsatian} Germans' order. They are degenerated because it would appear they speak the German barbarously, altho it is the popular language. The style of building in Alsace, the manner of living, etc, are nearly Germanic or have at least a great deal of it in them, but inferior also in this respect to Germany. The population of this part appears much [87] less intelligent, slower, not as developed and not as hardy at understanding and perceiving as the French population.

I was but very little fatigued by traveling the three nights; I could have gone on so for a long while together.

Strasbourg: Wednesday 9th November

The first general impression the view of the cathedral[60] made upon me was that of wonder and astonishment mixed with delight. I pronounced it to be the most [88] wonderful building ever erected by the hands of man, and such remains my opinion. The pyramids of Egypt are mere material force by the side of it; they are raw matter. The temples of Greece are matter carried to its highest point, that is, perfect beauty of form. Form is the expression of matter; perfect beauty of form is consequently its highest expression.

But in this marvelous building matter seems to have changed its nature; it seems no more the expression of itself. As I stood contemplating it, [89] there seemed about it a deep spiritual mystery. It seemed so complicated, such thousands of forms, such endless and unceasing variety that, as the mind looked upon it, it discovered there a world of ideas, a world of sentiments. As the eye followed those immeasurable and multiplied forms after passing over the life of the savior piously sculptured, and the whole hierarchy of holy personages with the eternal father at the head, and rested upon

---

[60] The Cathedral of Strasbourg was built over a four-hundred-year period. Work began on the crypt in 1015; the nave was completed in 1275 and the construction of the elaborate west façade, which so impressed Brisbane, was designed by Erwin of Steinbach and completed in 1318. A north tower, 465 feet high, was added in 1435. Being the tallest point for many miles (until twentieth century construction) this tower dominated the countryside and added to the cathedral's overwhelming impression.

those grotesque animals as if every sentiment should be placed [90] there, then passed to those darting and piercing forms rising one above another with their light, open and fragile ornaments, as if they were given there to spread out and catch the air, to help the whole to rise more quietly, easily to its destination the skies. There seemed in them a mystery, a deep meaning, the mind pursued with eagerness, as if it was conscious; it was contemplating the symbol of man and the world.

It is a marvelous building, and who would dare say in standing before it, there was not a deep and powerful source [91] of inspiration in Catholicism; if in its immense bosom there was imagination enough to give the life and form to such a stupendous piece of art, and at the same time pious force enough to throw such an immense symbol of its feeling half immeasurable, a thousand feet into the air, what must have been that Catholicism, how poor, meager, and starved is Protestantism by the side of it.[61] That cathedral seemed to me almost a living being. It seemed to have soul and mind, as [92] though it might arise and take action, as if the animating spirit had passed over it. I felt as if I could kneel in homage before the spirit of the wonderful building and, as to the Christian, a strange mystery, something incomprehensible spread over the unseeable spirit place in heaven beyond his view, he is worshiping, so {it} seemed to me, the spirit of this edifice.

There is, as I observe, a great deal of poverty and want in Strasbourg. [93] I see the streets filled with poor people and a great portion of the population bears the appearance of poverty and want. There is but little prepossessing in the city, and everything seems done meagerly and scantily.

While I was inside of the church listening to the deep sounds of the organ and the chanting of the priests, and reflecting how weak, how totally devoid of strength, was that once powerful Catholicism, a woman seated upon a stone step before an altar with a child in her arms beckoned to me and made a sign to give something to [94] the child. I gave it two sous {half a penny}. The woman seemed to thank me with an extraordinary degree of earnestness. After examining something at the end of the church I returned, and in doing so passed near her. She again began thanking me, and I thought to

---

[61] It is interesting to note the contrast here between Brisbane's reflection on the power of Catholic inspiration and his immediately following distress at its failures. (Diary II: 95–96, November 9, 1831)

ask her if she was so very poor; I could divine no other reason for this show of thankfulness. She said she had eaten nothing that day. "Look" said she, and she took the child and laid bare its legs; "Look." They were but skin and bone, and on one [95] was a large sore just healing up. A priest passed by with a pale face and deep wrinkle between his eyebrows. The organ pealed forth its powerful notes. The chanting of the priests filled the echoing roof with reverberating sounds. I passed on. "Catholicism," I said, "Are you so dead, your head is so weak that it cannot raise itself to help one poor being? And man, is all social feeling torn out of your heart? Is social love banished from it? You have need of a new life and a new feeling to fill [96] your heart." If Saint-Simon had not felt the first great principles of that new life and sentiment someone must hasten and do it for us. 12 o'clock at night.

Frankfurt: Thursday 10th to Friday 11th November

I left Strasbourg upon the French side at 6 o'clock, in the diligence[62] for Frankfurt, slept over night at Speyer and arrived at 8 o'clock in the evening the next day in Frankfurt.

The road {from Strasbourg to Frankfurt} passes constantly thru' a plain. From the {Rhine} river, several miles into the interior, spreads out a broad [97] strip of land, which is perfectly level and very fruitful and highly cultivated. The population is entirely German; the manner of living and the style of building are also German. The population, however, is but little developed, but little life in them and not as intelligent by far as in some parts of Germany. They resemble rather more the Swiss population. All the villages you meet on the road appear inhabited by peasants. At least you don't find any prominent individuals, men [98] of talent and force in them, which is a characteristic of the United States.

I observed scarcely any Gothic buildings. At a town before coming to Worms, is a church in the Byzantine order; very old and there are some Gothic parts to it. I expected to find more Gothic remains along these shores of the Rhine, for it was upon the river that architecture took its rise. When I arrived in Mainz, I found the diligence left Frankfurt {for Berlin} at

---

[62] These were large coaches that traveled between principal points on generally established routes and schedules along which there were relay stations and inns. These coach systems often had government support because they carried mail and documents.

6 o'clock instead of 10, as they had assured me in Strasbourg, [99] and that I should not get there in time for it. It does not leave again till Monday, so that I lose three days by it. I cursed the lying scoundrels in Strasbourg for having thus told me a lie, perhaps to induce me to go in their diligence. In leaving Mainz I forgot my cloak, a piece of stupidity, and I have not got it yet. I have arranged my affairs in this little voyage rather more like an ass than a being with human brains in his head.

[100] I was in the *coupé* {passenger compartment} of the carriage from Strasbourg to Mainz, and in it with me was a young Englishman who had lived a long while in Prussia and who is established as a merchant in Odessa. I never got on so well with an Englishman as in this case. The reason, no doubt, was that he had been so long from his country that he had not imbibed the artificial (for it cannot be natural) spirit which to me is so disagreeable and appears [101] so brutal.[63] He had an intelligent mind and a conscientious manner of thinking.

I talked to him during the two days {of the trip between Strasbourg and Mainz} of the doctrine of Saint-Simon. I endeavored to lay it open to him and make him understand it. I refuted, or at least reasoned down, all the objections he presented and made a very strong impression on his mind. He said he would read the books of the doctrine and make himself acquainted with it. I gave him [102] the *Exposition* of 1828 {1829} and *l'Enseignement Central (Principal Teachings)*.[64] In finding reasons to make him understand clearly different points, I explained a good many things clearlier {more clearly} than I knew them before for myself. I spoke to him with a certain degree of faith, and I am sure, were I to find myself with individuals opposed to the Doctrine, that I would uphold {it} with heart and soul

---

[63] Brisbane's reference to the British as disagreeable and brutal is interesting and would support his later recollection of England as a "spiritual iceberg . . . Every man striving and struggling for wealth . . . cold commercial life . . . everywhere material calculation and practical preoccupation." (*MB*: 156) This comment, indicating earlier time spent in England, raises a question about the chronology of his travels, especially to England and then Ireland where he was horrified by the poverty which he attributed to the commercial intent of absentee English landlords. (*MB*: 155–70) See Introduction: 16–18 for a discussion of possible travel schedules.

[64] The first title presumably was the book Brisbane had been reading earlier on the trip, *Doctrine saint-simonienne, Exposition Première Année*, 1829. The second is one of several pamphlets published by the Saint-Simonians. Copies can be found in *Oeuvres de Saint-Simon et d'Enfantine*.

as that only would be necessary to my accepting, without reservation, the principles of the doctrine. But when I was with the Saint-Simonians at Paris, [103] that feeling of opposition, which I suppose must be in my nature, kept me opposed to them and repulsed me. I could not join with them. I sympathized with the doctrine, but when I came to the individuals, something repulsed me, I could not become one with them. I suppose it was my feeling of individualness, and self-will, independence that was at the bottom.

I paid in Strasbourg 3 francs for dinner 3 francs for two nights lodging.

[104] *Frankfurt: Saturday – Monday, 12–14th November*

I have nothing to do in this place. The time spent here is completely lost Monday evening I leave at 6 o'clock and until then the hours will hang like enemies upon my hands. Mme Schlegel,[65] whom I knew in Vienna, is here. I went in the afternoon to see her. I saw something of German life again at her house, and I felt a pleasure [105] in seeing again the manner of living, which I found so friendly and genial to me. She introduced me to her son Veit,[66] a painter who has a great deal of talent, taste and purity in his style. I visited the gallery of painting. They have some very fine things of the old German school, and a good many landscapes etc.

I left my cloak in Mainz Friday, and I went down today, 14th to get it, as the *kutschefur* {coachman} waited to send it to me. When I returned I went to see a piece [106] by Meerbach, one of his finest things. It represents two young girls sitting together; one represents the Germany, the other Italy. I consider it the first modern thing I have seen, and I hold it worthy of the first masters of the Italian school.

Left Frankfurt in the afternoon 6 o'clock in the diligence for Berlin. I shall be there Thursday 4 o'clock, it costs about 80 francs.[67]

---

[65] Dorothea Mendelssohn Schlegel (1763–1839) was the widow of Karl Wilhelm Friedrich von Schlegel, a German poet and scholar and younger brother of the poet August Wilhelm von Schlegel. Schlegel had accompanied Mme de Staël on some of her German travels and is credited with introducing her to German Romanticism, which she introduced to French and English writing circles.

[66] Philip Veit, a well-known contemporary artist, was Dorothy Mendelssohn Schlegel's son by her first marriage to Simon Veit.

[67] This was a distance of about three hundred miles and took several days. Brisbane made the trip to Berlin at a more leisurely pace in 1829, stopping to visit various places of interest, among them Weimar, where he called on the elderly Goethe. (*MB*: 80)

[107] *Tuesday – Thursday 15–17th [November] Arrived in Berlin*

I arrived this afternoon, Thursday, 4½ [4:30 p.m.] in Berlin. I felt a great pleasure in approaching again this city, and the idea of seeing my friends gave me a great deal of joy. As I entered the Potsdamenstrasse Pforte (Potsdam Street Gate), I looked with interest and pleasure at every thing around me. The houses, every material object seemed to have a value. [108] There was a deep feeling of pleasure in seeing Berlin again. As soon as I arrived and went to a Hotel, I wrote to Henrietta {Solmar} saying I would call around in half an hour. As soon as I had changed clothes, I went. As I rung at the door, as I thought I would see her in a moment, I felt an agitation of the heart, it seemed too large for the breast. There was a tumult in the bosom. I entered and stood before her. She looked not changed; she looked precisely the same. I felt a deep and real [109] pleasure in seeing her, but without passion,[68] without that longing which a passion for a particular thing gives the feelings. It was that of esteem, that of friendship.

She rose and advanced towards me. I took her in my arms and kissed her several times, (but she did not kiss me, that is, she did not return it as I gave it). After a few moments we sat down and began talking, and it seemed in half an hour as if I had only left her yesterday.

[110] I went afterwards to visit Mme Beer,[69] who lost lately her only son; she seemed completely crushed by his death. It seemed to have torn out her existence and left her never-the-less alive.

Berlin: Friday November 18

I went this morning to see Gans.[70] It gave me the greatest pleasure to see him again. He looks well. He spoke of Hegel's death [1831] as of a great loss. However, [111] it does not strike me as being of much importance.[71] I had a long talk with him about my travels, political subjects, etc.

---

[68] Brisbane's rather brash behavior here seems a continuation and confirmation of his earlier naivety. He is still emotionally involved with Henrietta and he still cannot understand how he might appear to her. See above: Diary II: 39, October 12, 1831, n. 36, and below: Diary II: 211, January 8–15, 1832, for his definition of passion.

[69] She was the sister-in-law of the famous composer Giacomo Meyerbeer (1791–1863).

[70] Edouard Gans (1798–1839) was a follower of Hegel who had tutored Brisbane the previous winter when he was taking Hegel's lectures at the University in Berlin.

[71] This is an odd comment for one who had spent so much time and effort with Hegel's

I have been running about a great deal, looking for lodgings, paying various visits, etc. I feel a great pleasure in being in Berlin again, and seeing my friends again, and leading once more the German social life. In the evening I was at Mlle Solmar's.[72] Gans was there.

{Pages 112 and 113 are left blank}

[114] *Berlin: Saturday 19th, Sunday 20th November*

Today, the 19th, I came into the new lodgings I have rented under the Linden.[73] I pay 50 thalers for three months.

I have spent these two days in getting things arranged paying visits, etc.

I have seen nearly all my friends,[74] Mr Mendelssohn, Robert, Ebers {Paul}, Nerst, Steinbach, Mrs Richter, etc.[75] They [115] fatigue me all with questions about my journey, etc. I have but very little of the vanity of many travelers; I talk but little about what I have seen.

I dined at Mlle. Solmar's and was at Mr Nerst's in the evening. Tomorrow I will begin at the university. I shall be again to work with science, but I feel one good thought in the social sciences is worth all the speculations of staid, still, abstract science.

[116] *Berlin: Monday 21st and Tuesday 22nd November*

I have but very little time for writing and the first days of my stay in Berlin will be but scantily written down. I heard this morning at the university,

---

lectures. (Diary I: 53, October 25, 1830, and *MB*: 88–89) Possibly Brisbane means that Hegel had finished his work and his death would not diminish its significance.

[72] The use of the more formal Miss Solmar, instead of Henrietta, shows the change in their relationship. Brisbane may have been brought to book for his earlier philandering. In any case, he never again refers to her as Henrietta in the rest of the diary.

[73] Probably Brisbane refers to Unter den Linden, a fashionable part of Berlin.

[74] See Introduction: 12, especially n. 33, for a description of Brisbane's first winter in Berlin, when he had been introduced to Rahel Levin Varnhagen von Ense and her circle. It was here, among Rahel's many intellectual, artistic and business friends, that Brisbane made his principal German acquaintances.

[75] Mr Mendelssohn may be Joseph Mendelssohn, banker and uncle of the composer Felix Mendelssohn-Bartholdy, whom Brisbane knew in Berlin the year before and encountered in Rome. There were several notable Mendelssohn households in Berlin, and Brisbane does not distinguish between branches of the family. The person named Robert may refer to Rahel's brother or one of her nephews. In 1814 Rahel Levin's brother Ludwig, a well-known writer and journalist, had adopted the pen name Robert, as had her other brother Markus (d. 1826). Several relatives surnamed Robert were part of Rahel's circle. Several people with the surnames of Nerst, Ebers and Richter

Gans and Michelet. The former pleases me very much; besides the subject, there is character in the manner of expressing his ideas, and that gives it interest Michelet is flat and stale, and altho the ideas may be well [117] worked out, they remain without life and interest.

Monday I dined with the Ebers. In the evening I was at a party at Mlle Solmar's. Tuesday I dined at Henry Beer's.[76] In the evening I was at a new opera with the Ebers called *Margaret of Anjou*, by Meyerbeer.[77] It seemed to me there was a want of unity, of character in it; it had no general and strong character and it seemed also like a compilation.

[118] I feel a reaction of general nature operating and taking place in my mind and feelings. It began some time since to take place with {my} ideas. It has now attacked both {my opinion of} countries and persons. No doubt the Saint-Simonianism is the main and most powerful reason.[78]

When I left Berlin after passing the first winter here, philosophy seemed to me the highest study, the most noble science. Abstract contemplations, building systems with the thought, seemed the highest function of the faculties of the mind. Philosophy now appears to me a [119] thing dead, without life, in which the thought and faculties of the mind become the mere playthings of themselves. The mind having nothing to do, and not having received a new impulse, turns upon itself and commences systematizing and speculating and then forces the world within {into} the system it amuses itself in building up, a labor about as noble as that of the boy who having nothing to do, sucks his thumbs.[79]

There is a reaction with regard to philosophy; with it I have a kind of contempt for metaphysical [120] systematizers. They do nothing; they are without life. They die and leave no family, only a few persons who think like they, without anything common in feeling and social life.

---

appeared in Rahel's correspondence of the late 1820s, (as published in *Gessamelte Werke*). From Brisbane's limited references, it is not possible to identify them further.

[76] Husband of Mme Beer mentioned above; brother of the composer Meyerbeer.

[77] Giacomo Meyerbeer, *né* Jakob Meyer Beer, wrote *Margherita D'Anjou* in 1820 when he was under the influence of Rossini. It was not his most original work.

[78] Drawn in the diary just underneath this sentence (as if to emphasize its importance to Brisbane) is a continuous series of several descending zigzags.

[79] It seems that by the winter of 1831–1832 Brisbane had gotten himself into an ideological contradiction. He had become so enthralled with Saint-Simonianism's universal answer to all the world's woes, that he could no longer accept philosophy as offering an answer. However he found the requirements for becoming a Saint-Simonian too onerous.

I loved Germany and very much, it was becoming my land of predilection. I began to place it before every other. Or least it began to appear to me as if I would prefer it to any other to live in. The German people afterwards began appearing to me as if they were not the ones who [121] would join ardently in giving humanity its futurity. I considered them still as an honest, upright, conscientious, good natured and good feeling people, but humanity and the progress of the world did not seem, to me, to interest them and become an object, among others, of their activity. This lessened my love for them. I liked Berlin very much and wished to return there again. I remembered with pleasure the agreeable winter I had spent there. There was a longing to [122] return and I did it. The first moment was full of memories and pleasure. I saw again the social circle I had been introduced to, and the first moment seemed to be a renewal or continuation of the last one spent formerly there. I soon perceived, however, I had changed interests, that I loved something different from what I loved before: my mind had taken another direction and with that change in myself, things, persons and interests about me seemed also to have changed their nature and taken another direction and another value. The direction of the [123] society I had been accustomed to, and whose nature pleased me, seemed to me now valueless. The amusements of that society, and what seemed to them full of gaiety and life, seemed to me now pale and flat and the amusements [of] child's play; valueless, without aim and object, mere amusement for gaiety without a thought beyond it.

I feel now that a reaction has taken place within me with regards to {German} society. It has much less value in my eyes; [124] a portion of its attraction and pleasure has gone. It seems a circle, without an outlet, and I want to find some outlet which I can see thru' and see some destination, some aim and object beyond it, towards which it converges its activity and efforts. Their society, thus, has lost a great deal of its interest to me; and this could not take place without a reaction in the same proportion taking place with regard to the individuals who composed it. Those who are the most advanced, I see them with interests in their minds {but} which [125] are there without much life, which are more or less circumscribed and containing but little futurity. Gans, who formerly seemed to be a leader to me, a man out of whom a new direction and new ideas were to flow, appears now a man animated with the ideas of another system, that of the liberals of France,[80] who does not live in his own life and creates out of himself, and who at the furthest feels only a revolution in favor of the middle class and cannot get beyond it, altho' revolution has already been [126] accomplished by the people in whom he feels.

I liked Mlle Solmar very much. She seemed to me to possess a feeling mind and a great fund of good nature, besides an acute understanding and a great deal of general knowledge. I saw her constantly, she interested me, and there was a certain degree of love between us. A change has taken place, there also. We seem now to be ungenial to each other. I think I have even become disagreeable to her, and I must confess also that I began to dislike her turn of mind and character.

I find the society I know, and consequently [127] the individuals, without aim and object; no direction, which leads to something beyond the present moment. They amuse themselves in their own circle, enjoy themselves and laugh at her {Henrietta Solmar's} wit and when it is done they have laughed and amused themselves and the most that is left is the wrinkle of the smile upon their mouths.

I begin to feel sick of Europe. It seems to me an old and debauched being, possessing no more that feeling of youth which marches conscientiously, purely towards an object when it [128] feels and thinks it. My feelings turn again towards America, the young land of realization and the people of practical and social progress.

Berlin: Wednesday 23rd to Tuesday 29th November

I dined today, 23rd, with the Ebers paid a visit to Mr Nerst, Mr Beer, and was afterwards at Mlle Solmar's. The 24th I was at Mme de Beugnelin's, Mme. Caspar[81] and afterwards at Mlle. Solmar's.

---

[80] This was not a positive evaluation. In describing Gans as a supporter of liberals, Brisbane was most likely referring to such men as Guizot and Royer-Collard, men who had helped drive the revolution of July 1830 and had assumed power and political office under the new king, but who, Brisbane commented earlier (Diary II: 15–18, October 4, 1831) did not favor political changes that were sufficiently far-reaching. Later (Diary II: 195–200, January 4, 1832), Brisbane emphasizes how insignificant he considered all political change to be relative to the changes Saint-Simonian ideas could achieve.

[81] Fanny Robert, the daughter of Rahel's younger brother Markus, was the wife of Johann Ludwig Caspar (1796–1864).

I find this visiting is very hollow, without aim and object [129] and without product and result. I think I shall give it up and remain home a good part of the evening and study. The 25th I went in the evening to hear the opera of *Fidelio*.[82] It seemed to me to contain some deep, rich and expressive music. I was afterwards at a party at Mme Caspar's.[83]

During the few days past I have read more, but mostly the Saint-Simonians works. I have not yet begun with the study of the works upon [130] Juris Prudence of the German authors.

I find but little sympathy or feeling in the circle of acquaintances I know, for the Saint-Simonian Doctrine; not for the doctrine alone but for the thing itself {the idea of creating a solution to human suffering}. I find a great deal of egotism. They are wrapt up in themselves, not materially but spiritually. There are two kinds of egotism: the material egotism of the English, but you find among the easy classes of the Germans a spiritual ego-tism. That is, [131] they have a circle of enjoyment; a cultivation of musi-cal, literary and other tastes may enter in it. It is an enjoyment of a more spiritual nature, but they don't like to be disturbed in it, and don't like to leave it. They remain in their circle of enjoyment. The sufferings of human-ity don't reach them, and they don't like to be troubled with the thoughts of them, for it would disturb the equilibrium and balance of their minds and break in upon their habits, which give them their pleasures [132] and amusements.

Egotism everywhere, and in every thing, appears the predominant char-acteristic of society. Every one is in himself and no one is in humanity; no feeling for the large and suffering multitude, in the universal interests and welfare of the large human family. They see only their own narrow, cir-cumscribed and individual interests and those who enjoy, do it so, entirely without thinking of those who suffer. They are so completely absorbed in themselves [133] that they don't appear even to suspect there is anything different and out of themselves, and when suffering comes and spreads out its hand, it is even pushed away with impatience as if it begged without right and without need.

But humanity will have a happier and better futurity, for a germ of feel-ing for the suffering multitude has been thrown into the world and it will

---

[82] *Fidelio* was written by Ludwig van Beethoven (1770–1827) in 1806.

spread itself it, will grow into mankind. At [134] present there is no God, no Providence in the world, and the larger portion of society, plunged in ignorance and poverty, are unseen, unheard of. They wander without aid and counsel, forgotten, without hope in their souls. And that harmony, which God seems to have placed in the universe, is not in the least reflected in the social world of man. Everything is war, every hatred; that antagonism replaces harmony, and instead of [135] a foresight of love, we find blind hazard, coupled often with a blind and brutal force.

Call {for}, then, with every feeling the reign of providence upon the earth. And could I see mankind happy, and justice and love reigning upon the earth, then I would see in the world the harmony of God, and in that feeling there would be both religion and worship. With these, [136] there shall be no religion in the mind, no worship in the heart. Or if I cannot see God in the world and among men, I care much less about seeing Him any where else and {it} is indifferent to me whether He exists or not.

The happiness, riches and good things of the earth are spread by blind hazard; a chosen few who have an overflow and surfeit of everything. While the greater mass suffer, even that overflow is used to [137] the detriment of the greater and suffering portion. Is there any justice, any foresight, any harmony in such an order of things? Is any God or Providence to be there in the social world? Nowhere. They who are atheists have a foundation to maintain their belief upon.

There is harmony in exterior nature, there is a God there. But I see none in human societies, religious with regard to the exterior will, and atheistical [138] in regard to the social world.

Berlin: *Wednesday 30th to Wednesday 7th December*

I saw today, Tuesday, a circular from a printed letter from the Saint-Simonians, by which it appears that Bazard is no more chief of the Industry in the hierarchy; Rodrigues (Oldine, 1794–1850) takes his place.[83]

---

[83] *Le Globe* November 28, 1831 (VII, no. 332) offered a lengthy description of the assembly of Sunday, November 27 at which Enfantin announced Rodrigues' appointment as Director of Industry. The issue also contained the new director's statement of purpose. Several long-simmering differences among the Saint-Simonians had exploded by the end of November, especially concerning the role of women in the priestly hierarchy, and disagreement concerning the application of the Doctrine versus its continued

The religious question and the organization of the hierarchy is no doubt [139] at the bottom of the affair. Enfantin is placed as supreme chief. I think it must be that the members of the doctrine wished to take a greater religious development, placing the moral chief higher than the industrial chief, and something more of the kind, which perhaps did not match the views and feeling of some of the more positive members of the Doctrine. It says Bazard has returned to consider, *et dans ce moment il s'abstiens* (and in that moment he withdraws). [140] The whole affair made a disagreeable impression upon me, as it must, I think, upon everyone. It seems to break in upon the harmony of the Doctrine and create parties within it; and parties suppose different views and feelings. That produces a bad effect, for there should be but one feeling and that directed towards an exterior object.

I said to myself, I think it is very probable this incident will tend to define more clearly the organization [141] of the hierarchy and perhaps establish in it some more principles; for it must, of course, have still a great many practical imperfections.

Bazard, I think, was much less penetrated with the religious sentiment than Enfantin and many others. I think he must have been opposed to a greater development in that [religious] part. We will see what will be the result of it. I think it will give [142] more practical purpose and add more principles to the hierarchical organization of the doctrine; nevertheless the sensation it leaves upon me is disagreeable, rather disturbing particularly with regard to the governmental and hierarchical part.

Is not the cause of suffering humanity immense enough to absorb them, their interest and attention without quarreling about [143] minor interests within themselves?

I see by later papers {*Le Globe*, December 5, 1831} that the quarrel is already serious and that there is but little prospect of reconciliation between those who have gone out. Those who have remained {are} Bazard, Reynaud, Fournel, Maurize, Linoin, P. Cazeaux, Barnet, Carnot, etc.[84] Personal feelings or personal passions [144] seem to be mixed with it, and when they

---

elaboration. Bazard had finally withdrawn as high priest and this provoked further defections, among them Lechevalier. See Carlisle: 166–70, *passim.*

[84] Henri Fournel (1799–1876), Hippolyte Carnot (1801–1888). Armond Maurize, Linoin, Euryle Cazeaux and Barnet are not further identified.

come, there is but little hope of reconciliation. Jean Reynaud has protested. He speaks against what they are doing with violence; there is individualism and bitterness in his protestation. They, the other side, point out this individualism or personality, and not with that good feeling which would draw love and good feeling between them. [145] It must be that questions of organization of systems, ideas, and of minor mechanical parts of the hierarchy, fill their minds and are their interests. Where is the general feeling? The amelioration of the suffering part of mankind?

It seems here but feeble in its influence over them, for it does not dominate personal considerations, and they quarrel for personal opinions [146] and views. That is rather miserable. The purest motivation should animate such an undertaking. It should be founded upon the deepest love, pity and enthusiastic devotion for the suffering portion of humanity. Out of such a foundation a pure social system might arise, but if personality and individuality with their ideals and views are to work there, who can answer for a hierarchy [147] that came out of it? And that they hurry to constitute their hierarchy seems to me entirely anticipated. There is time for that, and time should be the construction of it. The whole affair together enrages me. I felt it stupid. They appear to me to be all quarreling about personal views and consideration.

We will see. Mankind has need of all those who will [148] make sacrifices for him, anyway.

During the last week I have been at one or two dinner parties and at several *soirées*; today I dined at Mendelssohn's, in the evening I was at Robert's. Society lacks here a certain interest. People seem to come together only to be together and to laugh and talk among themselves. There is no object exterior to that. It seems as if there was need of a question of general interest being thrown among them, to [149] give a direction and a value and interest to their social diversions.

Berlin: Wednesday 7th to Wednesday 14th December

The past week I have been reading Aristotle's *Politics* with Liebenow, my German teacher. I have read the *Iliad* of Homer. I have attended Gans' lectures upon philosophy of law etc. Gans does not like the S(aint-)S(imonian)'s. He finds it all monstrous, [150] and that sentiment which occupies so important a part in their doctrine appears to him very foolish and simple and nothing manly about it. He does not comprehend them, or rather he takes no interest in their life and interest, and that is one of the main conditions, that a certain interest should be felt in their undertaking. And in that aspect, it may be said, philosophers are as much behindhand [151] as any other set of people, for they are likely to take as little interest in it as the generality of persons.

I have written this week ten letters and received one that was from Adèle {LeBrun}. It is very short. She says she has received my letter of the 25th September, and will answer it at length from Florence. It appears that she must be returning there.

One of the letters I wrote was to Bazard, the other to Duveyrier. I requested of them [152] both, some explanation with regard to the late schism which has taken place in the family. Here are some passages:

(To Duveyrier)
Parmi tous les hommes, parmi touts les parties parmi toutes les categories, je reconnais que c'est en vous qu'il réside le plus de vie, le plus d'enthusiasme; la plus de dévoument. Je reconnais que votre but est plus grand, plus humain, et plus saint que touts les autres qui existent aujourd'hui dans la pensée des hommes. Je reconnais que votre conception dépasse infini{ment} . . . {the rest of page 153–154 is torn and continues on top of p. 154–155} . . . *à voir une providence, un Dieu dans le monde et il y aura alors une société réligieuse. Aussi, en verité tout que les choses comme elles sont un peut monter à voir un Dieu centre part dans l'universe, mais vis-à-vis de la société, il faut rester athée.*[85]

(To Bazard)
. . . *néanmoins, malgré en considerations puissantes qui m'entrainent au tout de force envers vous, je finis à l'idée de la fondation d'une*

---

[85] "Among all the men, all the parties, all the categories {within the Saint-Simonian movement}, I recognize that within you exists the greatest life, enthusiasm and devotion. I recognize that your objective is more grand, more human, more sacred than those that exist today in the ideas of other men. I recognize that your concept infinitely surpasses . . . {missing part of page} . . . to see a providence, a God in the world and there could thus be a society that was religious. Also, in truth all of these kinds of things {which

pouvoir [156] *nouveau, quelques bons et quelques saints que soient les sentiments et les intentions de ceux qui veulent l'élever. Pour moi le Saint-Simoneonisme doit être {illegible} des elements; et le temps doit bâtir, corriger et arranger la construction de la hiérarchie et des pouvoirs.*[86]

[157] *Berlin: Wednesday 14th to Wednesday 21st {December}*

I have passed this last week with regard to studies about as the former {week}. With my German master I am reading Schiller and Goethe,[87] and I am still at work with Aristotle. There is no sentiment of futurity in Aristotle; he takes the present, dissects it, examines with a keen perception the organization of the present and the nature of all its different parts, [158] in short, its whole mechanism, but remains rigorously within that present; he is consequently in the highest degree positive. There is a good deal of resemblance between him and Hegel's manner of speculating.

I had a long conversation with Bonneren {unidentified} upon the Saint-Simonians, France etc. Not withstanding, he does not seem much to like the French, he thinks they are *kind-beutels* (childish, sieve-minded, forget easily). Notwithstanding [159] the profound studies he has made of the German philosophy, he does not comprehend the part France is playing in the European civilization. Neither does he seem to possess that spirit of progress, that desire of change and amelioration which seems common and inherent at the present day in the French blood. Michelet, for example, comprehends nothing of Saint-Simonian's and but very little of the European movement of which France is [160] the animating principle, the life and authority. All the philosophy he has learned does not make him *dépasse* one step (take one step beyond) the circle of the system he has accepted.

---

presumably Brisbane had mentioned on the torn page} incline us a little to see a God centered universe, but concerning society it is necessary to remain atheistic."

[86] ". . . Nevertheless, despite powerful considerations which pull me with all their force towards you, I end up with the idea of the founding of a new power, sometimes good, sometimes sacred, that would be the sentiments and intentions of those who wish to rise. For me, Saint-Simonianism ought to be . . . of the elements, and time ought to build, correct, and arrange the construction of its hierarchy and its powers."

[87] The two great German Romantics, whose works Brisbane discusses at some length in his first diary. See Diary I: 56–57, October 27, 1830, n. 26.

If he was a shopkeeper, I think his opinions upon things exterior to his system would be about as lucid and as good as they are now. He has a dry, uninventive mind; he has been able to comprehend Hegel. He is profuse; he has accustomed [161] his mind to generalities, to theories, to abstract voices of thinkers, and to systems, which classes them in an abstract and difficult-to-be-conceived manner; and with all that, he is a child. He does not feel what is going on in the world, not the value of the movement of the present civilization. He has swallowed the ideas of his master, repeats them by heart and without regard to circumstance and moment, without any futurity superior to the present; and if [162] he should deduct {restrict} severely his principles, it yet would be the end and aim of the existence of the universe.

Berlin: December 1831 up to Sunday 25th and to Sunday 1st of the year [1832]

I received on the 23rd a letter from my father, dated New York, 11th November. It is a long time since I have received any letters from home and the reception of the present gave me the greatest pleasure. It contained nothing particular except the decided opinion my father [163] expresses, that George {Albert's younger brother, b. 1812} will be nothing. I consider George has a good deal of character at the bottom of his nature, but he wants someone who can give him a direction. That is wanting, and I am afraid he will not find it himself.

Christmas eve is a celebrated evening here: it is a family festival where presents are reciprocally made on all sides and where children particularly receive a good many things. Servants [164] also receive a present, common-ly of money, that day. In the evening I was at the Ebers', and von Schinkel,[88] Gans and some other persons were there. I carried some bonbons with me. I gave to Miss Ebers a pair of English scissors. I received a little writing desk and a worked tuft to make slippers of. The evening was passed away agree-ably, and ended with a handsome supper.

[165] I wrote on the 28th a long letter to my father. I gave him some account of the studies I had been pursuing and the aim I propose in trav-eling in Europe, which was to comprehend and understand it, to inform myself of what was going there in science and politics.

---

[88] Karl Friedrich von Schinkel (1781–1841) painter and architect.

I will note down here some of my opinion, judgements, and ideas upon various matters to see [166] later what changes I may make in my view of things, also, what progress in my judgement and knowledge of subjects, and finally, to see if any prejudices of an individual nature may arise with time to alter them.

Upon Architecture: Schinkel

Architecture seems to me to be that brand of the fine arts, at the present time, which offers the last degree of inspiration to the [167] artists, and the least chance of success in pleasing the taste and feeling of society. And for this reason, when a building is to be erected it must be the original of something. We must respect the object to which it is dedicated. And the deeper our love and veneration for that object, the greater is the inspiration of the artists, and the greater is the effect his work produces upon the world around him.

[168] This explains the reason why Religion only can produce an order of architecture, and that only when it exercises a full sway over the minds of men. The same feeling animates the artist and society about him. There is harmony there. With a higher fancy and a higher imagination, he finds forms and symbols for the devotion and love which his belief imbues in him. And [169] out of his hands arises a monument whose forms and symbols express his feelings and beliefs, and whose general forms also {are} the expression of the highest feeling of that religion, of its nature and of the source of his inspiration, {and} contain all his devotions, his whole faith. And society around him finds in it, its religion, the power that guides them. And with one voice, harmoniously, they acclaim to the great work, the symbol of earth [170] and heaven, their present life, their future hope, of the highest power, which they love and adore. No dissident voices are then to be found, no differences of tastes, but all find in it the expression of their highest love, their deepest devotion. They are absorbed in the soul of the building.

Tho inspired, {the} architect must be in intimate communion with his building; the more intimate is his interior with the object for which he is building it, the deeper and truer [171] will be his inspiration. And when his object is his whole devotion, and faith as religion may be the entire content both of mind and heart, there arise such stupendous creations as the Strasbourg Cathedral. The whole Catholic belief, its faith, its very nature, its hierarchy even, are incrusted and made to form into those godly edifices. The general forms of the building, as well as every particular one, [172] is a strife to reach upwards. No crosslines come to hinder that essay, window above portal window, tower above tower, and those half columns stretching to any length, and upon which masses of the same can be piled again into the infinite. The whole is a strife to reach the heavens and it is only the feebleness of man which {illegible} and cannot help it further in its course.

The nature of the Christian religion, which rises from the earth to the [173] heavens, where is placed its God and the hierarchy in those general forms, {is} repeated in the smaller details. The portal spreads and becomes the whole building: there is a regular succession and harmony in the forms, and all starting from one point, but classed and repeated hierarchically and in harmony with the first form. The most important part of the building as it is, {is} its entry. Thus the [174] towers and general forms are the original point carried out and expanded hierarchically. The beliefs are found everywhere in the sculptures and symbolic ornaments.

At the present day, as the religious inspiration has left the earth, there are no objects left which man adores enough to produce any real inspiration. Consequently, there is not the least made of an original architecture in the present day [175] forms. And principles of every past architecture are combined together in some monstrous production, without meaning, faith, or harmony, and are erected which express nothing, and are the simple creating of the individual, often {a} discarded fancy of the architect attached to no general belief and feeling of the world about him, consequently without effort and producing neither admiration nor dislike upon [176] the society, for which he erected them.

Schinkel is a man of genius. He has done all a man could do in his epoch. He has gone back to the Greeks and initiated himself completely in their esthetic feelings and their taste. He has translated their forms into his world climate. This theater, his museum[89] are beautiful, their purity and simplicity of forms strikes the connoisseur. [177] And I see they produce

---

[89] The *Schauspeilhaus* and the *Altes* Museum, built between 1819 and 1821.

but little effect upon the mass of society, and no two opinions upon them are the same there. Consequently, I consider these creations {are} *au dehors* (beyond) the spirit of the people. {These creations} possessing, consequently, the proportion value which an individual mind full of fancy and genius possesses, with regard to the mind of society.

These productions, consequently, are without a [178] deep nature and real worth. It shows Greece is comprehended by the Germans, and it is a monument to that power of the people to enter into the conception of many different nations. That simplicity of form and proportion of the Greek architecture, that simplicity of expression does not agree with the complicated and deeper civilization of our epoch. It {Greek architecture} is no expression of our society. {It} is, to be sure, in it, but it is only in [179] a corner, a moment of it, so that I would nearly say it was out of it.

Henrietta S.: When I was here two winters ago I had a liking, an affection, at moments a love for her. My esteem perhaps was greater than my love. Our intimacy was close and there was a considerable degree of affection between us, but more on her side than mine. This winter, however, there is a complete change, and on both [180] sides. With regard to myself, I must confess I retain more of that love, more of that affection. And altho I esteem and like her natural character, and to a high degree; nevertheless, as she is, as habit, education and circumstances have made her, I cannot even say I like her. Her character is disagreeable to me. I find it in the highest degree egoistical, incapable of supporting anything which is contrary to her manner of feeling and thinking, rather pettish and impatient, now and then a drop of spitefulness. But I acknowledge these [181] are not natural qualities. And in her character, never having married, living always according to her wish and fancy, she has got so accustomed to herself, so to say, that she hears with impatience what is against it. Hence arises this egotism of character and feeling. To me, very disagreeable little objects and wishes and petty habits form her instance.

There are now and then moments when her natural character shines forth, then I love and admire her. They pass a moment afterwards, [182] then I dislike her as she is, and she is disagreeable to me.[90]

---

[90] Compare Brisbane's feelings here to his earlier hopes and disillusion with Henrietta. See above, Diary II: 34–38, October 12, 1831 and 108–09, November 17, 1831.

I was last night, the 31st, the last evening of the year, at Gans'. He had a little party of gentlemen. I like such parties because everything is spoken of, even the common run of trivial society subjects.[91]

It is a custom here to give a party or be in society the last evening {of} the year. They remain together [183] till past midnight, and as midnight strikes and they enter into the New Year, they congratulate each other, wishing reciprocally a happy year, success, good health, etc. Schultz, Bach {unidentified} etc. were there. The company drank each other's health and then nearest friends kissed each other and shaking hands exchanged wishes and hopes. It is an agreeable festival. There is a great deal of sociability, good feeling, [184] and an interchange of hopes and sentiments which forms an important feature in the social life. These festivals have a great value, they are the maintainers of the social life. They bring individuals nearer together, and their hopes, wishes and sentiments produce a real social feeling, which is such an important part in life and constitutes so much of its happiness. A strong feeling came over me as we rose and drank each other's health. [185] The necessity of the feeling of union and interchange of sentiments to constitute social happiness, the hope that it could one day be so {for} man. A doubt crossed my mind whether we would be all among the living on this next anniversary. We separated late.

[186] *Berlin: Sunday 1st of January 1832 to Sunday 8th*

Today is the first one of a new year of that space of time which forms the links of the human life, the first one of a new link. And how many are {there} who drag those links thru in suffering and misery. The past year is gone, what has man done, and what have I done? The individual {is} the symbol of the whole; thought and [187] action, action in thought, but thought not independent.

Conceptions springing out of nature and necessity; wishes and calculations, out of conceptions; thus follow action and effort, satisfaction {and} disappointment. Then the result: Life, thought, action; and man and new dreams. There arises from the earth the mysterious being, history, which is the accumulated life of men's life and {is} later place{d} among the high-

---

[91] Brisbane's observation here is interesting in light of his earlier dislike for the triviality of Berlin society. See above, Diary II: 121–28, November 21–22, 1831 and 148, November 30–December 7, 1831.

est attributes of God. It is a [188] sheet of three leaves, and upon them is written thoughts, desires, realization, and at the bottom of each one stands subscribed, hope, hope.

It is the first day of a new birth; the last one has had its hopes and efforts. The recollection of my friends pass thru my mind. I wish them success and prosperity, doubly to the family. Success, success enthusiastically to the Saint-Simonians; to you also, [189] Adèle, peace and contentment, intellectual satisfaction; my wishes for your prosperity follow you. Your recollection {my recollection of you} is with me, and dear to me.

Greenough. {Horatio, the sculptor} hope and success.

Williams, {American friend in Paris} the present as it is, but more content, more in your present circle, more strongly vivified. The recollection of the rest of my friends come{s} in masses; prosperity to them. I unite myself for a moment in their [190] desires and hopes; peace and success.

But above all in mankind, to those masses of existences with wishes, wants and hopes, unity and harmony if possible; peace, peace, love and exchange of sentiments and providence upon earth. Associate and live as brothers; away with war, hatred, and envy, of oppression, of misery. Why {do} men reciprocally impose upon each other. They know not the law of humanity and [191] the nature of God. His nature has for its armaments the opposed qualities which now govern men and they will change as they know Him.

I visited all my friends, as is the custom here, and in the evening I was at Mendelssohn in the *Leipziger st*{rasse}.

The weather here is very fine. Three or four days had been very cold, but perfectly clear and the rest of the time, mild and clear.

[192] Humanity, will you have a better futurity? The S{ain}t-Simonianists must be realized, it must, and young men who have saddled the undertaking upon your {their} backs, success, courage; you will have the thanks of humanity.

The damned, the infernal injustice of this world shall not last for ever. This world of mud, of vile dirt, shall disappear, where eight beings in ten suffer morally and physically, where the artists cannot breath, or find the least shred of inspiration, where the fairest among women are [193] whores and live by the traffic of the body. Away with it; futurity shall write its history with letters of shame.

4th January

It is to be remarked how few subjects of general conversation society has now; little individual interests, city news and little topics of such a nature. I have often been at large society, and this evening, for example, at Mendelssohn and son where a word falling about the Saint-Simonians would give an entirely new direction to the conversation and rouse up and occupy the attention of everyone.

[194] *Politics*

The first thing I knew of the Saint-Simonians was by one of their works, which I bought in Holland.[92] I began to read it, and when I came to Paris {in the summer of 1831} I saw Lechevalier and the rest of the Saint-Simonians and began to understand their doctrine.

The first thing which struck me in it was the immense social change they wished to operate, and the immensity of the action for which the individual could work there. The object was so universal that all the other smaller aims and undertakings of the world around [195] me seemed insignificant and lost in the comparison.

My interest had been with the liberal party and in the later realization of the Republic.[93] I thought it would take place and I had confidence in its success. The {Saint-Simonian} doctrine commenced by weakening my interest in the politics of the liberals. Their object seemed small and insignificant by the side of that of the S{aint}-S{imonian}'s, but I did not

---

[92] The date of the trip to Holland is not clear. See Introduction: 17–18, for extended discussion of the chronology of Brisbane's travels and his first encounters with St-Simonian writings.

[93] In an earlier discussion (Diary II: 125, November 22, 1831), Brisbane had spoken of his disapointment with the narrowness of he Liberal party empowered in France in 1830. However, from his statement it is clear that at some earlier point he, too, had been influenced by this group. Brisbane would have brought an interest in republicanism with him from America, but he rapidly became exposed to French republican ideas as well. The *salon* of the elderly General Lafayette had become a gathering place for liberals and Saint-Simonians. See Spitzer, A.: *The French Generation of 1820*, Princeton, New Jersey, 1987. Brisbane attended a reception at Lafayette's in 1828, shortly after first arriving in Paris. (*MB*: 66) He probably continued to attend as his Paris contacts expanded to include the Saint-Simonians and Americans such as Greenough, who, in the fall of 1831, was sculpting a bust of the general and had become a regular visitor at Lafayette's "Tuesdays." See Greenough, Frances B., ed.: *Letters of Horatio Greenough*, New York, 1970 and Wright: *Letters of Horatio Greenough to Samuel Morse*.

give up my old interest without an effort. In destroying that interest of my mind, it seemed to destroy [196] interests of life and it plunged me into a kind of melancholy, sad indifference. I took interest in nothing. I did not give myself the trouble of reading the newspapers, or following the political debates. The customs of existence seemed cut out and seemed to make a blank of it.

This was of course a detestable state of feeling, and it excited in me a hatred against the S{aint}-S{imonian}'s,[94] and it broke off in a great measure that friendship between Lechevalier and myself. I left [197] for England some days after, and traveling there, and other objects, distracted my attention and set me in my common tone again. I there read their {Saint-Simonian} works and my interest began gradually to pass from the liberalism to Saint-Simonianism. At the present moment that change is complete, but it cost an effort, and for a time I felt myself in strong contradiction and opposition with the doctrine and revolted, so to say, against it.

[198] Liberalism has consequently lost the greater part of its charm and interest for me. My interest is no more there nor in the republic. The immense results, the immense development contained in germ in the S{aint}-S{imonians} for the world is my interest. It is much more immense and much more living. The Europeans seem to think the world is in Europe, but look at immense Asia, which is waiting for a renovator. What [199] treasures its immense soil must contain.

The history of man so far has been the history of boys fighting and waging war for play things. They have cast aside the interest they had in those toys, and now each nation will develop specifically and fully its nationality; and when the European nations have accomplished that work, then they will go and [200] renovate the old world. I like the liberals but their objects seem rather small, and it is in the objects of their efforts that I take but little interest. A Republic in France has also lost its charms for me, but I think

---

[94] Brisbane recounts this early episode of internal conflict generated in him by Saint-Simonian ideas. See Introduction: 16-18 for a discussion of possible chronologies for Brisbane's encounters with French ideas. The scope of Saint-Simonian ideals appeared so vast as to trivialize all his previous philosophical and political speculations. The possibility that all his earnest philosophical study might be in vain apparently frustrated and enraged the twenty-two-year-old Brisbane. Brisbane describes below, Diary II: 205–15, January 8–15, 1832, his resentment at the fact that his individual personality was insignificant in the Saint-Simonian context.

it will come, however, and from that to S{aint}-S{imonianism} there is but one step. An immense piece is playing on the theater of the world. I wish to live [201] long enough to see a part of the first act, to be able to judge how the piece will go.

With regard to the English politics, I take not the slightest interest in it. Their reform bill[95] interests me as little as a protocol. I wish for England a complete and thorough revolution. The abuses to be destroyed are immense; the remedy must be violent. The thing, unfortunately, [202] is so. The nation must undertake the cure, or it must die. A G{eneral} E{lection} in my present opinion is necessary in England; and if it is necessary, let it come. Were I an Englishman I would wish the same. Sometime I even think in my deep hatred against the aristocracy and priests, that I would even undertake the part of Robespierre.[96]

For politics is also [203] without much interest for me, at least party politics, which is completely so, {for} there is no discussion of principles there. It is only a strife between individuals. In that I certainly shall never take part.

I was Saturday evening at Mme Nerst's. A large party was there; it was given on account of Mlle Solmar's birthday. I had entirely forgotten it until late, which was a fault, for it is customary [204] to pay a visit to the person and offer your congratulations.

Tuesday I was at Mme de Varnhagen's *spontini* (unplanned, informal gathering) and some others were there. M. de V{arnhagen} appears to comprehend the Saint-Simonianism and thinks it must realize itself in the world.

Berlin: Sunday 8th to Sunday 15th January 1832

This present moment in my life is a time of incertitude with regard to what I shall undertake or do: I see no road marked out [205] before me; or among the various roads which I shall pursue, towards what object shall I turn

---

[95] Since 1830, a movement for electoral reform had been building in the House of Commons that would redistribute electoral boroughs. A reform measure had been rejected by the House of Lords in 1831. The reform act finally was passed in March of 1832 when William IV (1830–1837) threatened to "pack" the House of Lords with many new appointments.

[96] Maximillian Robespierre (1758–1794) had been a leader of the radical republican phase of the French Revolution.

my activity and efforts? What shall I undertake? These are questions surrounded with a dusky vapor, in which only confused forms and wishes and
desires are seen, but nothing {is} seen clearly which fastens the sight and
call{s} upon me to follow. Various images of undertakings, [206] various
objects flash before me; but none fasten imperiously my attention. Perhaps
I don't know them intimately enough to feel them thoroughly and become
identic {identified} with them; or perhaps is there an interior indifference
in me which couldn't feel those objects deeply enough for them to have
complete mastery over me, and make me devote myself to them? That is my
feelings, my [207] driving principle. The very flesh or material existence, so
to say, is not one and identic{al} enough with my ideas and thoughts to act
for those ideas, so that action and ideas become one: the realization of the
principle; the idea strong enough to drag the act with it.

In one word I don't feel strong enough.

The above is one side of my present state. Another is doubt of the difference {different} [208] ways open before me, but a much keener piercing
doubt, the doubt of myself. I have reasoned myself down to a weak and
inefficient nature and mind; used all comparisons, carrying them out and
applying them with the severest consequence. I have gone thru with this
process, suffering the harass and piercingness of this infernal scorpion {of
self-doubt}, casting self criticism and sweat under it, until at times I endeav-
or [209] to repress it with force and by violent efforts, but it comes back like
the image of a diseased mind, for it is within itself. When will it leave me?
Could I look forward and not backward within myself and consider myself
only in relation to the object I wished to realize, see myself only in my aim,
perhaps it would leave me.

I have read all the works of the Saint-Simonians. I understand [210]
their doctrine and the immense social change it would produce. I have
faith in the history. Consequently, if it realizes itself, humanity must make
a progress. Nevertheless, I don't feel ready to dedicate myself in action to
its cause. I remain undecided, and other objects, other interests {are} in my
mind at the same time before it, and I don't know whether I ever shall dedicate myself entirely *avec corps & l'aime* (with body and soul) [211] to it.

Passions are a part of us. They form a portion of us; we satisfy them
as we would move an arm or walk. Education stamps you with a certain

shame, but at the bottom, the satisfaction is as natural as the use of our limbs.

It is against the free nature of the thought to make itself the slave of the thoughts of the others, [212] and it is for that reason that we rarely find a large number of persons who consent to accept, for example, point for point, a difficult system of philosophy created by a single head.

My present manner of feeling with regard to the Saint-Simonians:

During my stay in Paris I was intimate with many of the Saint-Simonians, and all in general. I saw [213] them constantly and studied their doctrine. It is true, during all the time I was in Paris I felt myself in a kind of contradiction or in opposition to them; not however with the doctrine. It was only with the individuals, and this was owing to various shades of feeling. The first was I seemed to lose my individuality among them; their enthusiasm and efforts seemed to leave everything behind, and I felt myself lost among them. It is an [214] inequitable feeling, a feeling coupled more or less with the sentiment of opposition and contradiction, when you see your personality without value, eclipsed, and its activity producing no effect. As I could not join them and make their object completely my own, so as to appear working independently, (because I loved it) for an immense objective object, I would feel {felt} in contradiction to them, that is, {put aside} [215] by men whose doctrine I accepted, but in whose activity I would not take part.

Various other reasons concerned to place me in contradiction with them.

However, as soon as I left Paris, that disappeared. When I was alone, the doctrine seemed to belong to me as if it was attached. I seized it and defended it. The former feeling of opposition eased and I accepted it as an immense undertaking, [216] and I seemed to receive more force by belonging to it.[97]

Berlin: Sunday 15th to Sunday 22nd January 1832

This morning, 15th, after two lessons in the morning, one in literature, the other in philosophy, I went to dine at Mendelssohn's (Joseph).[98] I paid

---

[97] It is interesting that Brisbane feels most in sympathy with Saint-Simonianism when he is not in the presence of the Saint-Simonians themselves. This whole process of resistance and surrender sounds like a religious conversion.

[98] Joseph Mendelssohn was the father of Felix Mendelssohn-Bartholdy. This is the first time Brisbane designates a particular Mendelssohn family, but in all probability many

a visit to Ebers, another to Beer's and went afterwards to Miss Solmar's where I had been invited. There was a party there, and I will give a little description [217] of the manner of passing the evening.

As I came in, I found Mme Nerst and Mrs Richter occupying the sofa before which stands a tolerably large round table, and the rest of the company was sitting about it: Miss Solmar, Mrs Caspar, Hr. Schall, Mrs Meyer, myself, Miss Richter, Hr. Wilderbruch, Baron Martens, Mr Caspar, Baron Lauer.[99] Upon the table stood the tea things and first, tea was taken. A bowl of punch was afterwards [218] to be made. This, however, is not a custom and was only owing to a bet which had taken place between Miss Solmar and Baron Lauer and Martens. The conversation rolled firstly upon various little topics. I was talking with Mrs Richter, who looks very handsome, but she is beginning to show a little the effect twenty-five or six years produced on a fair face. When I was here before she did {not?} look more than twenty.

The general conversation turned upon various little [219] things more spoken of; something about the theater with some remarks and some laughing. At length came a fertile subject, which has been a fertile subject of tittletat for the whole city.

As there are no political subjects, no subjects of our exterior and general matters which interest the people here, they are forced in their social circles, as well as alone, to have recourse to little matters of the day and locale, having in general [220] a certain individual interest, recommended by a personal acquaintance of the matter in question. Such subjects occupy the attention, consequently the conversation is generally light and frivolous, and seems also without aim and object, further than merely to talk, mixing remarks and jests with it, a laugh and a great [221] deal of good nature.

Society here seems to have here no further object, consequently, than to come together, to laugh, talk, all with a great deal of good nature. Drinking tea, playing cards; that is {for} the old people, however, {and} not in most circles; and often another side room is allotted for that. And often afterwards {there is} supper, which, however, is only {the} case when a large

of his previous visits with the Mendelssohns had been at this home. See above: Diary II: 114, November 19-20, 1831, n. 75.

[99] Identified in this party from Rahel's writings are: Fanny Robert Caspar, Rahel's niece; Karl Schall (1780–1833); Marianne Meyer; and Johann Ludwig Caspar (1796–1864), Fanny's husband.

company has been particularly invited beforehand, consequently in more ceremonious cases, and then to break up and go away. There is the object within itself, and nothing beyond it, and this is done [222] over and over again and so often repeated; and nothing seems to come out of it, farther than keeping their nature in a good humor and continuing it as a tradition, handing it down from family to family. But I hope, in the end, it will become productive and have a result. I believe it also, and I prophesize the German character or nature and their social existence, their manner of associating together, will have a great result. It will not remain [223] barren or die, but a world with a great result and great things in it will arise out of it; the germ or seed is there. It will produce a tree, which will bear all the fruits of the intellectual world, perhaps also great undertakings, and executed, animated with the genius of science.

To return {to the topic being discussed around the punch bowl}, Graff (Count) Reder went lately to Hamburg in the hopes of marrying a rich heiress. There, however, he was refused. This has given [224] occasion to an immense deal of talk; a caricature was made upon the subject, and some jests found their way in some of the papers. This subject came upon the carpet and it filled the {illegible} and the mouths of everyone. This subject was discussed, {illegible}, etc. It shows the vacancy of the mind and the want of higher subjects to engage the attention, where such trifles become objects of attention.

They have made the punch. A long discussion took place concerning the [225] number of lemons, and a vote was taken whether it should be made with water or tea. The punch was made in the side room, in the meantime we were standing about in both rooms and little conversations were going on. When the punch was made, it was placed upon the table and we took our seats around. We first supped and then came the punch. It was drunk slowly out {everyone slowly sipped his punch} and accompanied [226] with abundance of talking laughing, etc. The merits and demerits of the punch were discussed. Everyone was pressed to drink double what he did.

At length a song was proposed, and it was decided Br. Martens should lead and the rest would follow the air; he commenced and everyone joined in. It produced a very fine effect, and it struck me that what a thoughtful and sublime effect it must [227] produce, when a large choir, for example in one of those immense Gothic cathedrals, united their voices together in one chant, in one belief, and a melodious harmony thus wafted among the high arches, a sign of adoration to a being in whom all men believed.

Miss Richter sang also a song, then afterwards Schall {sang} one or two, but in a curious manner, which was the only interest in it. Mrs Caspar imitated one or two actresses and after 12 o'clock, after a good deal of [228] such amusement, we separated.

During the present week I have been twice at Mme de Varnhagen. She as well as M. de V accept the S{aint}-S{imonian} doctrine or a great part of it. She wrote me a letter the other day upon the subject, with a great deal of warmth to which I answered in the same feeling.

I was at a party at Mrs Steinbach Friday. These parties were rather tiresome but they have a great value; it is one of the moments of our civilization, which separates it from the Turkish and oriental in general.[100]

[229] *Love and hope*

Love, humanity and hope, armed with those two sentiments you are strong. As the world is at the present moment there is an immense necessity that humanity should be loved that those who love should be animated with hope.

Berlin: Sunday 22nd to Sunday 29th January

I received the 24th two letters from Adèle {LeBrun}. One was of two leaves and a half and contained some [230] of her writings or compositions which I had upon another occasion begged her to send to me. She has a remarkable style of writing and {I} must study her manner of thinking more closely to completely understand it. The other letter which was in answer to mine of the 20th November was as full of feeling and affection as the first she wrote to me. I don't comprehend her; I would have to see her again to understand her and know her mind. There must be a depth and richest {richness} of feeling in her interior, her letters are beautifully written and

---

[100] Brisbane here refers to the Turkish Muslim custom of not mixing the sexes at social or ceremonial occasions. In his earlier diary and in his autobiography, (*MB*: 115–19) he argues that keeping women separate meant that men would always be harsh and intemperate in their dealings with each other, and that the calm and patient influence of women should apply in all aspects of society.

with the [231] greatest depth and purity of sentiment.[101] However, was she still far superior to what she is, I could not think of any nearer connection. I must remain alone, independent, without feeling or care of a personal nature. I answered her letter at eight.

Opinion upon Hegel's philosophy

When I came to Berlin and from the time before, the high opinion which I had of philosophy as the highest science had considerably diminished – I saw all those systems of philosophy produced [232] no social effect, realized nothing in society, nor tended to better the condition of mankind. Besides, the philosophers themselves even don't comprehend the wants of mankind and society. They don't know what the social and political object of the world is; they don't love humanity. You find but few conceptions in their systems for the amelioration of the condition of the suffering part of mankind.

They stand cold and indifferent before the sufferings of society and lastly, they don't comprehend what [233] constitutes the real nobleness and dignity of mankind. I think you would ask them in vain for a social doctrine by which the classes would be elevated and ennobled. They don't know what constitutes the dignity of mankind and the great political movements are often not as well understood and felt by them as by persons in circumscribed paths of life. The German philosophers don't comprehend (there are some exceptions, Hegel is not one) the political movements [234] of France and if they comprehend it, they don't feel it and take interest in it.

These considerations which are true depreciate them and their systems very much in any opinion. It was even going to an extreme and I was getting a complete despising for them. However, the study I am now making of Hegel has brought me back again and made me see there is a deep and important meaning in those philosophical works. They are a great sign; however, I consider they produce but [235] little effect in pushing society and mankind ahead. Their speculations are cold, without life and apply not to society. I do not consider them now as the highest science, the highest

---

[101] Earlier, when he was enthralled with Henrietta Solmar, Brisbane's mention of Adèle was very brief. See above Diary II: 62, October 17, 1831. Now that Henrietta has apparently rejected him, he shows greater interest in Adèle, though he still clings to his ideal of the unencumbered idealist and reformer.

science is the social science. The S{ain}t Simonianism opened my eyes and made me see clearly the value of a great many things, among others, of philosophy of political parties. It showed me also the aim of society and offered me the highest object which can be given, the activity and effort of the individual.

[236] One of the marked features of the German philosophy and also of the German literature is the high station they assign to the thought and the mind in general. The mind is the most wonderful object in nature and stands far above it – the thought can comprehend God, the effort of the universe was to come to a consciousness of itself. It produced the thought which turns back and contemplates, comprehends the different orders or degrees of the universe as they arise one above another in their [237] effort to reach to itself. Goethe is the sublime egotist who sacrifices the world to his interior himself. Even his own passions, wants, and etc. are all suborned and made instruments in ennobling, in wishing that interior; he wishes the greatest contact for it. He considers the universe in it and thus lives within the world he has thus created within himself and he looks out of it upon the exterior world, dressing us in the ring of his own feelings, thoughts.

A being who had thus [238] studied, whose whole existence was a work of construction of his own interior, it is no wonder he should have produced such a world of beings and many of his characters are the purer{est} and most {illegible} the feelings can conceive. The heart of woman was particularly his field; the princess in *Tasso*[102] is a model for eternity.

I am thinking at present of arranging what I have [239] upon Hegel's philosophy and publishing it in French. However, I feel it would be rather dangerous or at best it would sustain a great loss to be thus transplanted singly and alone in a foreign language. To comprehend the entire value of the German philosophy you must see and study it in Germany. One system thus taken alone seems broken from the whole and cast down in the world. In Germany one system has arose {arisen} out of another and another followed it in the succession of time. And all the systems, the philosophy itself,

---

[102] Goethe's *Torquato Tasso*, written in 1790, concerned the sixteenth century Italian nobleman Torquato Tasso, whose feelings for the two daughters of his protector ultimately drove him insane.

rose out of the genius of Germany. And it did not rise alone and unattuned with arts and other sciences.

Theology, literature, jurisprudence, history etc. rose with it and each new [240] philosophical conception arrived to be a new departure, every thing followed. The charte{r} of knowledge further still rolled open and a brighter field {was} given to surrounding sciences. German philosophy has risen up with German literature and other sciences around her; as she has grown they have grown. She borrow{s} their poetry and their scientific *recherches* {research}. They are fundamental ideas and each step forward was a conception given by her {philosophy}. And it is thus the German scientific world has arisen here miraculously and opportuniously {opportunely} from out of the genius character and feeling of that wonderful people.[103]

---

[103] In this last discussion of Hegel's philosophy, Brisbane seems torn in two directions, starting with a fairly sharp criticism of the weaknesses of German philosophy and ending with a completely contradictory conclusion about the "genius character" of the wonderful German people.

Index[104]

---

[104] In Diary I this section was named Table of Contents.

Preceding the actual title page of Diary II are three unnumbered folio pages: A, B and C.

Folio page [A]

Left fascia has some drawing and glued onto the bottom of the page is a news clipping: "*Society for Ethical Culture – Lecture* by Mr Louis H. Ehrich at Chickering Hall at 11:15 A.M. 'A Temple Not Built Within' all interested are invited."

Right fascia has the upper right hand corner of the page torn out so the words at the top left of the page are not complete.

Commis . . .

commenu . . .

Philosophical lesso[ns]

Paid Liebenow[105] 6½ *Thaler*

5 do[106]

Paid up to the 7th 5 do 24 Jan.

2½ do

5 do 18 feb.

5 do 12 feb.

7 lessons not given 3 do 22 minutes

---

[105] Brisbane's tutor in Berlin.
[106] Possible abbreviation for German ditto – *desgleichen*.

Herr Reichenow[107]: Kanonics St 10.17 rep.

Commenced with Liebenow to take 3 lesson per week the 7th Feb.

Commenced with Reichenow to take double lessons the 9th Feb. Commenced with Reichenow to take from 1 to 4 the 15th March. Left off the 2nd April.

Schideler: 23 Jan. 30 *thalers*

Feb. 30 *thalers*

Folio page [B]

Left fascia: To Liebenow, Rosenthaler Strasse, No. 56

Right fascia: Paris & Berlin

September To January 1831-32

Folio page [C]

Left fascia blank

Right fascia page numbering begins

End of Diary II

---

[107] Another of Brisbane's tutors in Berlin. Apparently he was also engaged to work with a servant of Brisbane's, Théodore. There were troubles with Reichenow later, when Brisbane sent him funds to pay Théodore which were never delivered. Pickett, *Letters*: 27, letter from Paris, January 3, 1833.

APPENDIX I

James Brisbane, Esq. Obituary

From the Spirit of the Times, *Batavia, New York, Tuesday June 3rd, 1851, page 1.*

Death of James Brisbane, Esq.

We have to announce the death of JAMES BRISBANE, Esq., which took place at his residence in this Village, on Thursday last, the 29th ult., at the age of 74 years, 7 months and 17 days.

He was emphatically the oldest inhabitant of Batavia, and at the time of his demise had resided longer on the "Holland Purchase" than any man living. His Funeral was attended on Sunday last, and a large concourse of people testified their respect for his memory by following his remains to the grave.

In the language of the Buffalo Courier, the life of Mr. Brisbane has been an eventful one, and part of the details connected with it may not be uninteresting to our readers, to many of whom his countenance was familiar, while his peculiarities have become part of the history of the "Holland Purchase."

Mr. Brisbane resided in Philadelphia, his native place, we believe, until the year 1798, when he embarked from that city, with stores for the supply of the large body of men then engaged in the survey of the "Purchase." He remained at the little village of Stafford, Genesee county, six miles east of Batavia, until the 2nd of January, 1800, when, in company with Joseph Ellicott and others, he returned, for a short time to Philadelphia. In the year 1802 he opened the first stock of goods ever offered for sale in the village of Batavia, which were brought from New York, via Albany, the Mohawk,

Lewiston and Buffalo. In the same year the Post Office was established in this village and Mr. B. was appointed Post Master, upon the recommendation of Mr. Ellicott. The name of the Post Office was "Genesee Court House". The duties of this post could not have been too onerous, as, at that time, a mail was only received fortnightly, at this remote frontier settlement, being transported, sometimes upon horseback, sometimes on foot. In 1806, Mr. Brisbane resigned the office of Post Master, and left Batavia for New York, where he remained a short time engaged in the Book business. In the year 1808, however, he returned, and resumed his former Mercantile occupation upon the spot where he had opened his first establishment.

Mr. Brisbane continued his mercantile pursuits for many years but finally abandoned them for more lucrative employment. His intimate relations with the Holland Land Company and their agents enabled him to take advantage of various fortunate circumstances connected with the disposal of their property, and in this way he became the proprietor of large tracts of real estate. His quick discernment and just discrimination enabled him to select such property as he could foresee would become highly remunerative, and he purchased largely, and at low prices, of the most valuable lands upon the Company's domain. In this way he laid the foundation of a colossal fortune.

In his private character, Mr. Brisbane carried peculiarity to the verge of eccentricity. In his manner to strangers, he was cold, even repulsive, but in his intercourse with friends, was affable, polite, and entertaining. Possessed of a most retentive memory he was referred to decide any disputed point, and was rarely at fault. His early life had been so full of incident that an interview with him was at all times highly interesting, and his daily associates recur, with feelings of gratification, to hours spent at his social board, where the time glided imperceptibly away under the influence of his genial and pleasant conversation. Full of anecdote, an agreeable *raconteur* and a wonderful observer, he never failed to interest his hearers. In his charities he was equally peculiar as in the other acts of his life. He often gave liberally where he acknowledged the justice of the claim, but generally with secrecy. The enjoyment of great wealth is supposed to render necessary great liberality, but rarely do rich men, however they may labor to justify the expectation of "much from them to whom much is given", receive the credit due them, and especially is this the case, when their good deeds are only known to themselves and to the parties benefited.

Mr. Brisbane had been through life singularly free from sickness of any kind, and on the day but one before his decease, was attending to his usual avocations. When informed that the malady, an inflammatory affection of the viscera, was likely to terminate his life, he expressed himself ready to go, and, in the same spirit of entire resignation, met the destroyer. He leaves two children only, Albert, well known as an enthusiastic advocate of the social principles originated by Fourier, and George, who are the sole heirs to his vast estate.

◈

APPENDIX II
"Letter on Adèle" by Albert Brisbane

A one page manuscript in the collection of the Illinois Historical Survey, University of Illinois, Champaign-Urbana.

The letter has no salutation and is dated December 13. On the back, in pencil, is added "1848", and "Letter on Adèle ... beautiful", in the handwriting of Albert's widow Redelia. The letter concerns Albert Brisbane's first wife Adèle LeBrun, from whom he separated in 1836, and who subsequently returned to Europe and married Count Agosto della Rocca. Brisbane visited her in Italy in 1848, where they experienced a happy reunion from which her husband discreetly absented himself. Apparently it was after this meeting that he wrote the following:

I have seen Adèle again: I have just left her. Oh, I have seen her again with that same pleasure, that deep sweet delight. What a joy; what a sweet exchange of purest sympathy. How deep is the bond. She is the sister of my soul. Inexpressible feeling: mysterious sympathy that cannot be explained; it is there; felt like the {illegible} of the sun, but cannot be explained. How true and deep is the affection I feel for her. Oh I would have taken her in my arms and told her in tones {illegible} the company of the gods, that I had a love for her pure and infinite as heaven. My soul would have whispered to her soul in the pure spirit language all the heavenly truths of divine affection. Oh, how great is the sympathy, how great the tenderness, how great the affection which I bear her. Pure mind, noble spirit, my soul, my being is wedded to yours for all eternity. My God, my God, what a world is this: what dreadful is the {illegible words} of the mortal world. What barriers between us. What a natural affection, and yet it must be treated as unnatural.

The affection for her is a spiritual and universal affection, deep, intense, real, but is not a material, limited affection i.e. I do not feel as if I wanted to be united to her materially – as if I wanted material love; I want the infinite affection of the soul, I want to love her soul – and infinitely, with all joy, all {illegible}, all infinity, all celestial delights. I want her as a heavenly companion, an angel from God, bearing the stamp of his goodness and truth: a heavenly soul being on earth, and carrying my soul through its evolution to the great centre of its home {*sic*}.

What effect has time on the feelings? None. I have not seen her now for 12 years, yet on beholding her again, my soul linked itself with her soul as intuitively as it had ever done; my heart was twined with hers and she was as near, as dear, as if no time had passed. The sympathy of the soul is ever fresh, is ever new. Time does not {illegible} on it to change its form and nature, as it changes the forms of material things.

Oh how I could have taken her in my arms and offered to her all the friendship, all the affection, all the sympathy that I {illegible} her; and told her that she was a bird of paradise that brought light to me from his celestial home, and filled my soul with its rays.

{No signature}

APPENDIX III
Speech to the Icarian Society

Inspired by revolutionary developments in Paris in the winter of 1848, Brisbane sailed to Europe and arrived in Paris in time to witness the violent workers' revolt in June 1848. He then traveled in Europe and returned to Paris for the anniversary of the uprising, to give the following speech, which led to his deportation by the French authorities as a "dangerous radical."

From the Démocratie Pacifique, Paris, (editor V. Considérant), February 25, 1849.[1]

BANQUET of the HALL of FRATERNITY

25 February 1849

ANNIVERSARY of the REVOLUTION of February 1848

Our friend Brisbane, the American Socialist, has aroused great interest and ardent sympathies in speaking of the attitudes regarding France that he has just found in Germany and Italy who offer homage to France, the hope and support of the suffering peoples.

From the Démocratie Pacifique, February 27, 1849.[1]

Citizen BRISBANE, the American socialist:

Citizens, I came to Europe to observe this great movement which began in France. I have visited Belgium, England, and Germany, and I can say what these countries think. And first let me state that the United States salutes, in the republic of France, a well-loved sister who will one day save the world. In other countries of Europe, wherever there is an idea

---
[1] Translation by Sarah Brisbane Mellen.

of progress, all eyes are turned to her {France}, as towards a mother and a liberator. (*Applause*)

But between the two nations of Germany and France there is a more intimate link. Germany has, in fact, upset the corrupting altars of a selfish world, as France upset the thrones. To-day the sentiments and principles of Democracy are penetrating all Europe; one finds them even in the most isolated villages of Austria; and on all sides people turn towards France as towards the sun of Humanity!

But all nations are not so advanced: therefore the ideas of {17}93 – the democracy of '93 – are forerunners everywhere of the social ideas spread by you at the glorious February epoch. Democracy is everywhere in Germany, and she has flung herself with ardor into the Movement because she feels that in this way she will arrive at a better social state. Those who think thus, depend upon it, are 99% of the population. But socialism, which is the real revolution, is dominant in the Rhenish provinces, in Bavaria, in fact in all Northern Germany, and these countries are even more advanced than France, for there the peasantry is socialistic, and this is the result of its suffering under feudal privilege. That revolution of the south is only at {the level of} Democracy, but the wise sentiment {which} dominates there will soon understand social ideas. This moment is not far off, and soon all Germany will be socialist.

Italy is already republican, but she is only republican. France, united with Germany, will lead her victoriously into the Movement, for France has prestige everywhere, and everyone knows it is she that has suffered most for Humanity.

Thus, what Napoleon could not do with a million men – conquer Europe – France would do today with less than a hundred thousand soldiers; for she would no longer be serving the cause of one man, but that of an idea; therefore she need only inscribe this idea on her banner, and I am quite confident that there will not even be need for the hundred thousand; she will find allies everywhere. That is to say, one needs no longer fear barbarian invasion, for the heart of Europe is with noble France.

I have therefore mounted the rostrum only to speak these simple words and to tell you that you now have as your only enemies – ignorance and evil passions. But since France is able to say to the foreigners: "I have been the martyr and the liberator of Humanity" the masses will believe her. And they know so well that it is to her they turn constantly, that in thinking of her they say to themselves: "If she succeeds, we are saved; {but} if she falls, we are lost for centuries." (*Applause*) Fortunately, I see about me men who will work unceasingly to enfranchise the Universe. (*Hear! Hear!*) Therefore, let France fulfill her task, let her go forward boldly, and she will deserve God's benediction! Let her go forward holding in one hand the olive-branch – symbol of peace – and in the other the blade of vengeance! And if the aristocracy should rise to exploit again and to oppose progress, let her crush it with the vengeance of God. But if she accomplishes her mission with only the help of love, oh! She shall be blessed, for she will have filled the glorious role destined for her by Providence. By her sufferings, by her miseries, by the blood of her political scaffolds, she has been martyred for all nations; they offer her this homage – they have hope in her; and I am here to tell her so. (*Applause*)

BIBLIOGRAPHY

Appleby, J. O.: *Capitalism and the New Social Order: Republicanism of the 1790's*, New York, New York, 1984.

_____: *Inheriting the Revolution*, Cambridge, Massachusetts, 2000.

Arendt, H.: *Rahel Varnhagen: the Life of a Jewish Woman*, trans. R. and C. Winston, Baltimore, Maryland, 1997.

Beard, J. F., ed. *Letters and Journals of James Fenimore Cooper*, Cambridge Massachusetts, 1960.

Barrault E., et al.: *Doctrine Saint-Simonienne, Exposition première année*, Paris, 1829.

Berry, B.: *Americans' Utopian Experiments: Communal Havens from Long-Wave Crises*, Hanover, New Hampshire, 1992.

Beecher, J.: *Charles Fourier: The Visionary and His World*, Berkeley, California, 1986.

Bertier de Sauvigny, G.: *The Bourbon Restoration*, Philadelphia, Pennsylvania, 1966.

Bestor, A.: "Albert Brisbane, Propagandist for Socialism in the 1840's," *New York History*, 28, 1947: 125–58.

_____: *Backwoods Utopias*, Philadelphia, Pennsylvania, 1950.

Brisbane, A.: *Association; or, A Concise Exposition of the Practical Part of Fourier's Social Science*, New York, New York, 1843.

_____: *A Concise Exposition of the Doctrine of Association*, New York, New York, 1844.

_____: *General Introduction to Social Science*, New York, New York, 1876.

Brisbane, R.: *Albert Brisbane, A Mental Biography*, Boston, Massachusetts, 1893.

_____: *The Social Destiny of Man; or Association and Reorganization of Industry*, Philadelphia, Pennsylvania, 1840.

_____: *Theory of the Function of the Human Passions, Followed by an Outline View of the Fundamental Principles of Fourier's Theories of Social Science*, New York, New York, 1856.

_____: *Treatise on the Function of the Human Passions; An Outline of Fourier's System*, New York, New York, 1857.

Brock, W. H.: "Phalanx on a Hill: Responses to Fourierism in the Transcendentalist Circle," Ph.D. Thesis, Loyola University, Chicago, Illinois, 1996.

Brumfield, A. (Stallsmith): "Agriculture and Rural Settlement in Ottoman Crete, 1669-1898: A Modern Site Survey" in Baram, U. and Carroll, L. eds.: *A Historical Archaeology of the Ottoman Empire; Breaking New Ground*, New York, New York, 2000.

Carlisle, R.: *The Proffered Crown*, Ithaca, New York, 1987.

Chazanof, W.: *Joseph Ellicott and the Holland Land Company: the Opening of Western New York*, Syracuse, New York, 1970.

Cross, W. R.: *The Burned-Over District: The Social and Intellectual History of Enthusiastic Religion in Western New York, 1800–1850*, Ithaca, New York, 1950.

Darwin, C.: *Expression of Emotion in Man and Animals*, London, 1872.

Delano, S. F.: *The Harbinger and New England Transcendentalism*, Rutherford, New Jersey, 1983.

Fellman, M.: *The Unbounded Frame: Freedom and Community in Nineteenth Century American Utopianism*, Westport, Connecticut, 1973.

Fogarty, R.: *Dictionary of American Communal and Utopian History*, Westport, Connecticut, 1980.

Fourier, C.: *Oeuvres Complètes de Charles Fourier*, 12 vols., Paris, 1966-68.

_____: *Social Destiny of Man; or, Theory of the Four Movements*, tr. Clapp, H. and Brisbane, A., New York, New York, 1856.

_____: *Social Science; the Theory of Universal Unity by Charles Fourier*, A. Brisbane, ed., New York, New York, 1877.

Greenough, F. B., ed.: *Letters of Horatio Greenough*, New York, 1970.

Guarneri, C.: *The Utopian Alternative: Fourierism in Nineteenth-Century America*, Ithaca, New York, 1991.

Kephart, W.: *Extraordinary Groups: An Examination of Unconventional Life-Styles*, 3rd ed., New York, New York, 1987.

Lavater, G.: *L'art de connaître les hommes par la physionomie*, Paris, 1820.

Levy, P.: *The Enlightenment, an Interpretation*, New York, 1966.

Lewald, F.: *Meine Lebensgeshichte – The Education of Fanny Lewald*, tr. Lewis, Hanna B., Albany, New York, 1992.

McDougal, H. C.: *Recollections 1844–1909*, Kansas City, Missouri, 1910.

Malraux, C.: *Rahel, ma grande soeur: un salon littéraire à Berlin au temps du romanticisme*, Paris, 1980.

Manuel, F. and F.: *Utopian Thought in the Western World*, Cambridge, Massachusetts, 1979.

Matthews, J.: *Toward a New Society: American Thought and Culture 1800–1830*, Boston, Massachusetts, 1991.

McNeal, R. A.: *Nicholas Biddle in Greece; the Journals and Letters of 1806*, University Park, Pennsylvania, 1993.

Mellen, A.: "Adolphe Thiers: the Making of a Conservative Liberal," PhD. Thesis, New York University, New York, New York, 1991.

Mendelssohn-Bartholdy, F.: *1862: Letters from Italy and Switzerland*, tr. Wallace, A., London, 1991.

O'Leary, A.: *Delineation of Character as Determined by the Teachings of Phrenoloogy, Physiology and Physiognomy*, Boston, Massachusetts, 1860.

Pellarin, C.: *Life of Charles Fourier*, 2nd ed., (tr. F. G. Shaw), New York, 1948

Pettitt, R.: "Albert Brisbane, Apostle of Fourierism in the United States 1834–1890," Ph.D. Thesis, Oxford, Ohio, 1982.

Pickett, T.: *The Unreasonable Democrat, K. A. Varnhagen von Ense*, Bonn, 1985.

Pickett, T. and F. de Rocher, eds: *Letters of the American Socialist Albert Brisbane to K. A. Varnhagen von Ense*, Heidelberg, 1986.

Pitzer, D. ed.: *America's Communal Utopias*, Chapel Hill, North Carolina, 1997.

Riasanovsky, N.V.: *The Teaching of Charles Fourier*, Berkeley, California, 1969.

Saint-Simon, Claude Henri Rouvroy de: *Oeuvres de Saint-Simon et d'Enfantin, Publiées par les membres du conseil institué par Enfantin pour l'exécution de ses dernières volontés*, 47 vols., Paris, 1865–1878.

Spitzer, A.: *The French Generation of 1820*, Princeton, New Jersey, 1987.

Stockwell, F.: *Encyclopedia of American Communities*, Jefferson, North Carolina, 1998.

Tewarson, H.: *Rahel Levin Varnhagen: the Life and Work of a German Jewish Intellectual*, Lincoln, Nebraska, 1998.

Varnhagen von Ense, K. A.: *Denwürdigkeiten des Lebens*, Karlsruhe, 1845.

Varnhagen von Ense, R. L.: *Gesammelte Werke*, 10 vols., ed. Feilchenfeldt, K., Schweikert, U. and Steiner, R., eds, Munich, 1983.

Wicks, C. B.: *The Parisian Stage: alphabetical indexes of plays and authors*, 5 vols., Alabama, 1950–1979.

Williams, C. L. T.: *Joseph Ellicott and Stories of the Holland Purchase*, Batavia, New York, 1936.

Wright N., ed.: *Letters of Horatio Greenough to Samuel Morse*, Madison, Wisconsin, 1972.

Unpublished

Albert Brisbane, letter to Michel Chevalier, April 24, 1832. MS 7601, *Fonds Enfantin, Bibliothèque de l'Arsenal*.

Michel Chevalier, letter to Albert Brisbane, May 24, 1832. MS 7646, Archives IV, *Fonds Enfantin, Bibliothèque Nationale*.

Fonds Fourier et Considérant (Victor), Archives Sociétaires, 10AS, inventoried by Edith Thomas, 1991. Archives Nationales, Paris. A selection from this collection – 28 dossier 9 – is available at the Western Historical Manuscripts Collection, Ellis Library, University of Missouri, Columbia Missouri.

Albert Brisbane, letter to William Seward, July 19, 1838. Seward Archives, Princeton University, Princeton, New Jersey.

INDEX